Working wi
and
the Children Act

A Practical Guide for the Helping Professions

MARTIN HERBERT

Head of the Clinical Child Psychology Specialty
Child Health Directorate
Plymouth Health Authority

 Published by The British Psychological Society

For Viv
Who, more than once in a while,
deciphered and typed my
manuscripts

BLACKBURN COLLEGE
LIBRARY
Acc.No. B.C. 47142
Class No. 362.7026 HER
Date. 13.9.94

First published in 1993 by BPS Books (The British Psychological Society),
St Andrews House, 48 Princess Road East, Leicester LE1 7DR.

Copyright © Martin Herbert, 1993

All rights reserved. No part of this publication may be reproduced or
transmitted, in any form or by any means, without permission.

This book is sold subject to the condition that it shall not, by way of trade
or otherwise, be lent, resold, hired out, or otherwise circulated without
the publisher's prior consent in any form of binding or cover other than
that in which it is published and without a similar condition including this
condition imposed on the subsequent purchaser.

A catalogue record for this book is available from the British Library.

ISBN 1 85433 093 4 paperback

Typeset by Litho Link Ltd, Welshpool, Powys, Wales
Printed in Great Britain

Whilst every effort has been made to ensure the accuracy of the contents of
this publication, the publishers and authors expressly disclaim responsibility
in law for negligence or any other cause of action whatsoever.

Contents

Lists of figures and tables

Preface

This book is written for the helping professions: those who work with families – parents, adolescents and children. It is about children in need, and its particular focus is those aspects of helping that are psychological and social in what they have to offer. This means that the book is largely concerned with individual difficulties, and with the personal relationships and interactions that take place within families and the problems to which they commonly give rise – not only for their members, but also for the community in which they reside.

The Children Act 1989* came into being after the publication of my book, *Working with Children and their Families (1988)*. It introduced radical changes in the legislative base of child care and has resulted in the most comprehensive changes in local authority care work for several decades. The legislation has considerable implications for child care policies, practices and resources of social work and health service agencies. This necessitated a revised edition of the book in order to explore the implications of the legislation for family practice, be it in the social, health or educational services. As it happened, in the course of revising and updating this book, rethinking ideas and issues in the light of the Act, I discovered that what I had was essentially a new practice guide. Certainly, the changed focus of the book demanded a new title: *Working with Children and the Children Act*. To work with children almost always presupposes working with parents and, indeed, families. While the concerns of 'needy' children – in the *general* sense of being emotionally disturbed (sometimes referred to as 'damaged' or 'frozen' children) – are dealt with, particular attention is now given to 'children in need', in the terms of the Act (for example, children who are disabled).

The Act makes a strong commitment to client participation and provides for a better framework of accountability than earlier legislation. My emphasis in the text on the 'collaborative model' of work with clients is crucial in this respect. The emphasis on objective assessment, planning and evaluation is a vital part of such collaboration and accountability.

There are *three key principles* which underpin the Children Act:

1. An emphasis on the paramountcy of *the child's welfare*.
The Act extends the 'welfare principle' by outlining duties to consider the child's religious persuasion, racial origin and cultural background.

---

* The whole Act applies to England and Wales. Part X which relates to nurseries and child minders and other provisions listed in s.108(11), applies to Scotland. The Adoption (Scotland) Act is amended by s.88(2) and Schedule 10, Part II. The provisions listed in s.108(12) apply to Northern Ireland.

Living and working, as we do, in a multi-ethnic society, it is of critical importance that caseworkers should be sensitive, not only to the norms, sensibilities and sensitivities of people from different cultures but also to the stressful life experiences they endure in a sadly racist society. Racism extends, far too often, into service delivery.

It is not only in matters of race, nationality and creed where prejudice has its corrosive influence; it affects women and female children in many subtle and unsubtle ways. In many senses of the word, they are 'disabled' in our society – demeaned in the same way that those of our clients to whom we attach the label 'disabled' are patronized and robbed of their self-fulfilment. The book deals with these important issues and contains suggestions for further reading on ethnic and cultural matters.

The text provides a means of assessing, an exposition on, and checklists of, disability (physical and psychological), children's needs and influences which facilitate – or detract from – their welfare. A knowledge of normal child development is a *sine qua non* of good practice. There is a section indicating the kind of information that is important, and a guide to further reading.

2.   An assertion that local authorities should promote the *upbringing of children by their families.*
This book focuses on systemic (that is, family-orientated) assessment and interventions designed to help parents/caregivers to be more responsive, effective, self-reliant and confident in the care and management of their children. Parent training is a major theme. There is an emphasis on the father's role as well as that of the mother.

3.   The Act redefines the notion of parental rights to introduce the concept of *'parental responsibility'.*
The book addresses itself to the issue of parents' duties, rights and authority which constitute this responsibility; also criteria for judging whether the child's needs are met adequately in the discharge of their duties. To this end, it contains information, checklists, assessment proforma and interview guides.

Part 1 of this book introduces the subject of assessment, especially (but not exclusively) in the light of the Act. This involves looking at a multiplicity of family problems – the difficulties typically presented by parents and children. The reader is provided with a framework for assessing the specificity (the 'what', 'where', 'when' and 'whether') of family difficulties, and for estimating the response to children's needs (that is, methods to assess parental responsiveness). Special attention is paid to the means of communicating with, and listening with understanding to parents. The importance of inter-agency communication is stressed. Key information about normal development in children is also provided. There are references to books and articles which will supplement the knowledge base for family work. Communicating with children in order to find out their views or to elicit reliable evidence, particularly with regard to sexual abuse, is a particular concern in work with children, and is therefore given appropriate space, together with guidelines and techniques.

Part 2 is about planning and implementing a programme of work or a therapeutic intervention. This raises the *why* question (the issue of causation) and the *how* question ('How do I best help my clients?'). Several broad approaches and specific methods and techniques are described. They include giving advice, counselling, communication and parent training, play and family therapy, psychodynamic and behavioural work and finally skills training for better social relationships and effective problem-solving.

The requirements of the Act are detailed throughout the text and in several Appendices, and their implications for educational, social and health workers are explored. The reader is introduced to the ASPIRE model of Assessment, Planning, Implementation and Rigorous Evaluation (Sutton and Herbert, 1992) as it applies to a wide variety of problems, ranging from fears and phobias to defiance and delinquency in children/adolescents, and from poor parenting skills to emotional, physical or sexual abuse by adults.

This book should help the practitioner to analyse and decide on choices, and to initiate actions which stimulate change in families that are 'stuck' in self-defeating, unproductive and growth-inhibiting patterns of living. Facts are helpful; and facts about child rearing (although this is *not* a book about child care) and family relationships will be provided. But facts on their own are not enough. I hope to provide the kind of facts (based upon many studies) and a way of thinking about family problems (the so-called problem-solving approach) that will enhance your child protection role and lead to *practical strategies* for helping parents and children to help themselves.

A word of caution about the use of the checklists and rating scales in the book, is necessary. They are provided as aids to the description, recording and on-going monitoring, of client attitudes and behaviours. They are *not* diagnostic tests, nor are they standardized ('normative') instruments. They help you to be systematic, detailed and objective in your assessments and monitoring of change in individual clients. They provide you with information and clues to suggest a further investigation or, perhaps, a referral to a specialist where there is a particular concern about an issue that lies outside your experience or expertise.

As this is a practical guide or workbook, I have tried to keep the text itself relatively uncluttered by citations. The sources for theories, facts and findings are listed in the References and Further Reading sections.

PART I

Assessment

Your starting point after a referral and the allocation of the work, is an assessment interview to establish what is going wrong in the life of the family, and what, if anything, needs to be done. This is also the starting point for this guide. I will be recommending a systematic movement through a sequence of assessment stages, each marked by a question:

What?   What is the problem? What is going wrong? What changes are desirable?

Why?   Why is there a problem?

How?   How can I help?

In all of this, there runs the somewhat awkward question – *who* is my client? Among the professionals involved in child care and protection, the social worker with statutory duties and powers has a particular responsibility for the protection and promotion of the child's physical, emotional and intellectual development and also the prevention of abuse in individual cases. For much of the time you will be working with child *and* parents within families – often called in by the parents themselves for guidance over a 'difficult' child. Occasionally you may find yourself 'split' by divided loyalties, conflicting stories, unclear professional–personal boundaries, and areas of moral ambiguity. You may be required to make decisions based on uncertain predictions. In all of this you can call on the following:

- Yourself: your knowledge, skills, experience and professional values.
- Others: moral and technical support from your team is vital, as is consultation within and between agencies.
- Evidence: the better informed you are, the more factual and comprehensive the data you collect for decision-making, the more effective will be any intervention.

All of this presupposes a painstaking assessment, progressing (possibly) to an intervention, and a careful evaluation of its progress.

The chapters that follow provide the information you need to move from step to step in working with the family.

It is necessary early on to establish client–practitioner responsibilities. Who is the key worker who coordinates work with the family and holds things together? Are you, for example, the sole professional person involved, working directly with one person or the whole family, or are you part of a team where a social worker, psychiatrist, psychologist or community psychiatric nurse takes primary responsibility for the well-being of a particular individual or family? It is advisable to establish the boundaries of one's responsibilities.

1 *Assessment of children in need*

Some Implications of the Children Act

There are, as was said in the Preface, three key principles which underpin the Children Act:

1. An emphasis on the paramountcy of the child's welfare. It is put this way:

When a court determines any question with respect to the upbringing of a child or the administration of a child's property or the application of any income arising from it, the child's welfare shall be the court's paramount consideration. [s.1(1)]

(A welfare checklist is provided on page 4 of this book.)

2. The Act rests on the belief that children are generally best looked after within the family with both parents playing a full part and without resort to legal proceedings. *An Introduction to the Children Act 1989: A New Framework for the Care and Upbringing of Children* (Her Majesty's Stationery Office) asserts:

▶ the new concept of parental responsibility;
▶ the ability of unmarried fathers to share that responsibility by agreement with the mother;
▶ the local authorities' duty to give support for children and their families;
▶ the local authorities' duty to return a child looked after by them to his/her family unless this is against his/her interests;
▶ the local authorities' duty to ensure contact with his/her parents whenever possible for a child looked after by them away from home.

3. The Act uses the phrase 'parental responsibility' to sum up the collection of duties, rights and authority which a parent has in respect of his or her child. That choice of words emphasizes that the duty to care for the child and to raise him or her to *moral, physical and emotional health* is the fundamental task of parenthood and the only justification for the authority it confers. The practitioner has to bear this in mind, as the overriding purpose of the legislation is to promote and safeguard the welfare of children.

The implications of these three principles are truly onerous for the practitioner who is called upon to make complex judgements decisions, and recommendations. He or she requires skills to conduct an objective, reliable assessment. But words like 'needs' and 'health' constitute a veritable minefield, given such problems as definition of terms, the subjectivity and ethnocentrism that bedevil the value judgements of child-rearing issues, and the uncertainties inherent in estimating the risks of leaving children in certain homes (or taking them into care). We shall certainly return to these matters.

But what else does the Children Act enjoin the worker to take into account? Undoubtedly, support for children and families becomes a priority. Local authorities have a duty to promote the upbringing of *children in need* by their families so far as is consistent with their welfare (see Appendix II). 'Children in need' becomes a 'technical' term which covers *children who need services to secure a reasonable standard of health and development*. It includes children who are disabled.

Because *protection* of children, quite rightly, is such a major preoccupation of the law, the issue of the *welfare balance* can create a considerable intellectual, emotional and moral tension for the professional. The Act seeks to protect children both from the harm which can arise from failure or abuse within the family and from the harm which can be caused by unwarranted intervention in family life.

The courts are given wide powers to intervene to protect children at risk of harm within the family. If an assessment of the child is needed to decide whether significant harm is likely and it is clear that there is not an emergency calling for an emergency protection order, the Act allows an application for an order for an assessment which can last up to seven days (see Appendix III – Protective orders).

The Act states that the court shall have regard in particular to the child's welfare as defined in the welfare checklist below:

Welfare checklist [s.1(3)]
(a) the ascertainable wishes and feelings of the child concerned (considered in the light of the child's age and understanding)
(b) the child's physical, emotional and educational needs
(c) the likely effect on the child of any change in circumstances
(d) the child's age, sex, background and any characteristics that the court considers relevant
(e) any harm the child has suffered, or is at risk of suffering
(f) how capable each of the child's parents, and any other person in relation to whom the court considers the question to be relevant, is of meeting the child's needs
(g) the range of powers available to the court under this Act in the proceedings in question.

The Child's Wishes and Feelings

Communicating with the child is emphasized as his or her views in proceedings are seen to be of great significance. The welfare checklist to which the court is to have regard in reaching decisions about the child is headed by the *child's wishes and feelings* and this highlights the great importance attached to the latter. When a court determines any question with respect to the upbringing of a child, it has regard, in particular, to the ascertainable wishes and feelings of the child concerned (considered in the light of his/her age and understanding). Thus there is a greater emphasis than in earlier legislation on consulting children and finding out their views. The courts, according to Judith Masson (1990), should not merely suggest that a child is too young to be consulted nor should they rely on what a parent says the child wants. Guardians Ad Litem in care proceedings attempt to discover the views of children as young as three years old.

So how does one find out what the child wants? As with all persons, the major methods used are observation, questioning and being given a sympathetic 'hearing'. Interviewing, because of the opportunity it gives to 'ask them', 'question them' and, by no means least, 'listen to them', becomes a prime instrument of assessment, investigation, intervention and evaluation. Verbal report, based upon clinical conversations, may be a fairly good predictor of real-life behaviour, but it can also be very misleading, and therefore, unreliable. Do not rely entirely on it (and that means the interview) for your data. Clients, including children, may not notice things, they may misperceive events, they may forget significant details and emphasize irrelevant points.

Embarrassment or guilt may lead to errors of commission and omission in information-giving. If the crucial behaviour consists of overlearned responses, the client may be quite unaware ('unconscious') of his or her actions. So go and look for yourself and/or train clients to observe, so that you can see things through their informed eyes.

Even then, you may observe patterns of behaviour which misrepresent the 'true' state of affairs. Your 'snapshots' may be contaminated by an observer effect; people and situations change as you observe them. Clients may play a part, knowing full well what you are looking for. The meaning of behaviours may not be apparent if you are not fully aware of the nuances of context and background of certain relationships and interactions. You may over-generalize observations to make 'traits', 'tendencies' or 'deep-seated motives' out of what are merely situation-specific actions. I have had to make assessments during 'access' visits of parents to children, which (by their very nature of venue, supervision and purpose) seem artificial and fraught for all concerned.

Interviewing children

Young children tend to be talkative but are sometimes limited in their ability to reflect insightfully about their experiences; adolescents are usually introspective (reflective) but have a way of becoming monosyllabic when asked personal questions. This poses a problem for the would-be interviewer.

Children are not always very good at expressing their fears, frustrations or uncertainties. They cannot always tell their parents, let alone a comparative stranger, how they feel. But they have a language that adults can learn to translate – the language of behaviour and fantasy. What they do (in a direct sense in everyday life) and say (indirectly through play or story-telling) can be most revealing.

It is easy to forget that children are not simply little adults and it can therefore come as a surprise when they don't interview like adults. They often fidget, become alarmingly restless in their movements, tic, look out of the window, or fiddle endlessly with a button, when they find the interview uncomfortable. And there may be many good, objective reasons for their discomfort, and for the series of blank looks or 'don't knows' that meet the interviewer's queries. Style is important: a patronizing, insincere tone will soon be picked up and responded to negatively; an artificial (this is my voice for children) style is also counterproductive.

The child may not comprehend the question, especially when he or she is cognitively immature, and the question is too abstract or complex. As you will see in Chapter 4, children's understanding of social nuances, moral issues or causal relationships are age-related. They are likely to have difficulty with questions that are not specific, in other words, questions framed in terms that are open-ended and global. The double-barrelled question (where two different answers are required from one question), or questions laced in jargon, are likely to floor even the older child. A child may simply not know the answer to the question. Interviewers and questionnaire designers often wrongly assume that clients must know the answers to their questions, if only they'd speak out.

Children, especially those with low self-esteem, may be afraid to give their opinions because they think the interview is like a test, with right or wrong answers. They may be afraid to say anything out of loyalty to their family and/or fear of the consequences of their answers for themselves and their parents.

They may put too literal an interpretation on questions, and their egocentricity, when young, may prevent them from seeing another's point of view. Then again, they may be at a stage of intellectual development which does not yet allow them to recognize or understand the connections between people or events you are seeking.

Shyness about the topic of investigation may also inhibit responses to questions. All of these emotions – fear, embarrassment, loyalty, and others – require a delicate approach in the interview, the establishment of rapport, and carefully judged reassurance where necessary.

Adjuncts to the child interview

Play with dolls, miniatures, puppets, paint, water and/or sand makes use of children's familiar and natural mode of expression. Play should occur preferably in a special playroom. It provides a background for the practitioner to discuss children's problems with them.

Theories of the importance of play in childhood go a long way back. The first person to advocate studying the play of children in order to understand and educate them was Jean Jacques Rousseau. There have been several theories put forward to explain the meaning and utility of play in childhood; they generally emphasize its function as a means of preparation for the future, as a natural process of learning and as a means of release from tensions and of excess physical energies. In many ways, play for children is life itself. They use it in order to develop their personality and their ability to get on with other children.

Sigmund Freud's daughter, Anna Freud, used children's play in a manner analogous to the use of dreams with adults. Play was analysed so as to uncover unconscious conflicts. This involved the interpretation of the symbolic meanings and the unconscious motivations underlying drawings, paintings, games and other forms of imaginative play. She transposed classical psychoanalytical theory into a system of child analysis. There have been several offshoots of psychoanalytical play therapy and also systems of play assessment and therapy which are not in this mould at all, for example, those used in behaviour therapy. (See also page 150.)

The advantage of using so-called *projective techniques* (which include play, puppets, dramatic creations, completing stories or sentences) for assessment, is that they involve relatively unstructured tasks that permit an almost unlimited variety of responses. The client has to fall back on his or her own resources rather than stereotyped, socially-desirable answers. The techniques (as psychometric instruments) have their critics, but are invaluable if used cautiously as aids to communicating with children. The caution refers to interpreting the protocols – the child's statements about feelings and attitudes toward various members of the family. It is thought that children identify with the central characters in their stories, project their own feelings (especially unacceptable or difficult-to-acknowledge impulses or attitudes) onto the fantasy figures, and attribute various motives and ideas that are essentially their own, into the play or other creative situations and plots.

Where the child is too loyal, too frightened or ashamed, or too inarticulate to speak about feelings or painful events in the family, it may be possible to express these things in an evolving story about a boy or girl of similar age. The therapist makes up the basic structure, leaving spaces for the child to fill in. Thus you can begin: 'Once upon a time there was a boy/girl. What did he/she most like doing?' . . . 'What did he/she not like doing?' . . . (The therapist gradually introduces, among neutral themes, topics such as secrets, fears, worries, preoccupations, family tensions, parental behaviours, and so on.)

Sentence completions are useful:
'*I like to* . . .'
'*What I most dislike* . . .'
'*My best friend* . . .'
'*I wish* . . .'
'*My dad* . . .'
'*My mum* . . .'
'*If only* . . .'
'*In my home the nicest thing is* . . .'
'*The worst thing is* . . .'

With stories told as a response to pictures, the therapist needs (as always) to be cautious about interpretation. There is a tendency to find what one hopes to find or to superimpose our 'theories' onto the projective protocols. The safest use of these instruments is as a means of eliciting *clues* to important themes, which are then investigated further. With these caveats in mind, play, drama (with puppets or miniatures) or stories are undoubtedly an invaluable adjunct to work with children. The professional would do well to have a store of miniatures, drawing materials and pictures available. There is also available a wide range of imaginative techniques for exploring children's attitudes, personal attributes and family relationships. The Bene-Anthony test of family attitudes is a good example of the latter.

Children as witnesses

Children who disclose events of physical and sexual abuse may be called upon to appear in court to give evidence about the circumstances. Until recently, the 'received wisdom' was that children were less reliable and less accurate witnesses than adults. A review of the research literature by Spencer and Flin (1990) examined the evidence under several headings:

- the reliability or otherwise of children's memories;
- children's egocentricity;
- their suggestibility;
- their difficulties in distinguishing facts from fantasy;

- their tendency to make false allegations;
- their failure to understand the importance of telling the truth in court.

Spencer and Flin concluded that the evidence on the reliability or otherwise of children's memories depends upon how children are questioned; for example, how soon after an incident they are able to give an account of it. The most accurate account is likely to be that taken immediately after an event.

The authors considered the question of children's egocentricity in terms of their alleged lack of concern for the effects of their behaviour on others, and their lack of concern for details which have no direct personal significance for themselves. They confirm that very young children (say four and under) are not readily able to take the point of view of other people, but comment that this is a separate issue from whether children attempt to tell accurately what they experienced. As to the second allegation, they point out that a preoccupation with matters concerning them personally is characteristic of both adults and children, and that there is no evidence that older children are more self-centred than adults.

Like adults, children can be *suggestible;* this risk is reduced if the interviewer takes the following precautions:

▷ explicitly tells the child that the interviewer does not know what occurred;
▷ gives the child unambiguous and comprehensible instructions at the start of the interview;
▷ explicitly instructs the child to say 'I don't know' if unsure of the answer to a question;
▷ avoids repeating questions;
▷ generally avoids leading questions, but if these are necessary, knows how and when to use them;
▷ interviews the child 'on home ground' if possible.

There were inadequate grounds (that is, only limited empirical research studies) upon which to base any conclusions about children's inability to distinguish fact from fantasy. It appears, however, that young children cannot imagine accurately and in detail sexual activity which they have not experienced. The authors underline the importance of careful interviewing, so that imagined experience can be distinguished from reality.

Children's tendency to make false allegations has been more extensively studied. Jones and McGraw (1987) analysed 576 reports of suspected sexual abuse made to the Social Services Department of Denver, Colorado. They concluded that of the 439 cases where there was sufficient information to judge whether or not sexual abuse had occurred, only two per cent of reports were fictitious reports made by children.

With regard to children's understanding of the importance of telling the truth in court, children as young as five or six do understand the meanings of such terms as 'telling a lie', even if like many adults, they cannot define specifically the nature of 'truth'. Children from six to ten years also understand the importance of telling the truth in court, in the sense of recognizing the implications of falsehood for innocent people.

The review of current research concludes that if there is sensitive interviewing soon after the event, a child's evidence is likely to be accurate. Other studies lend support to this conclusion (see Further Reading).

Assessing 'Children in Need'

This chapter is not simply about assessment, but specifically about the assessment of *children in need* (see checklists in Appendix IV). 'Children in need' in today's legislation is a phrase with a formal definition. A child is taken to be in need if (a) he/she is unlikely to achieve or maintain, or to have the opportunity of achieving or maintaining, a reasonable standard of health or development without the provision for him/her of specified services by a local authority (see Part III of the Act and Appendix II); or (b) he/she is likely to be significantly impaired, or further impaired, without provision of such services; or (c) he/she is disabled. A child is disabled if he/she is blind, deaf or dumb, or suffers from mental disorder of any kind or is substantially handicapped by illness, injury, or congenital deformity. 'Development' means physical, intellectual, emotional, social or behavioural development; and 'health' means physical or mental health.

In this last sentence lies a major part of the professional's dilemma. What is a reasonable standard of development? And what constitutes physical or mental health let alone their impairment? The word 'need' is also difficult to define precisely! As we saw earlier, it appears in the Act within the list of terms defining the child's welfare (that is, his or her 'physical, emotional and educational needs'). Masson (1990) notes that the emphasis should be on an *objective* assessment of the needs of the individual child, but there is a danger that subjectivity in the form of preference for particular life styles might be introduced here. After all, we often owe allegiance to (in the sense of valuing) the way that we were brought up, the traditions of the culture we belong to, and the ideas we have evolved about child rearing. It is important to see the *reasons* given for identifying particular needs. Rational arguments for a point of view are required, not personal sentiment or prejudice.

Professionals carrying out an assessment obviously need a sound empirical knowledge base for their recommendations and decisions (see Schaffer, 1990). It is important to be clear about what questions are being posed in the assessment; what is its purpose and, therefore, your objectives. For example, the needs of children which are potentially at risk (if not responded to consistently) are of two kinds:

- *survival* functions such as the need for food, shelter and physical care, and
- *psychosocial* functions, including the child's requirements of love, security, attention, new experiences, acceptance, education, praise, recognition and belongingness.

Infants and children – if they are to survive – must also acquire vast amounts of information about the environment they inhabit. One of the main objectives of this training is the preparation of children for their future. It is doubtful whether any child – in our far from ideal world – has all of his or her individual needs satisfied by parents. This, in part, is why the term 'good enough parenting' has entered the professional vocabulary. The Children Act uses the concept of 'reasonable parents'. In referring to care orders, Section 31 specifies that the care must be not 'what it would be reasonable to expect a parent to give'.

If an assessment of these matters is to be trusted, then the methods or indicators used, and their application, should meet certain criteria:

☐ They should have the appropriate coverage – breadth and specificity. Observations, for example, should be of a *representative* sample of the client's behaviour occurring in specified situations.

☐ They should provide indicators or measures that are fair. This point is related to the one above. The assessment should not apply to a biased or narrow aspect of the clients' activities or attitudes. Nor should one use tests or questions that are culture-bound (ethnocentric) and which therefore discriminate unfairly against particular persons.

☐ They should provide accurate indicators or measures. This means that they should be reliable (and, if circumstances allow, repeatable). They should also be translated into precise statements and descriptions as opposed to vague, global terminology.

☐ They should provide indicators or measures that are relevant. Relevance is critical if assessments are to be valid. In other words, assessments should measure or indicate what they purport to measure/indicate.

☐ They should be practicable to use. There is little point in using unwieldy, time-consuming, esoteric methods.

☐ They should be ethical. This is a *sine qua non* of all one's practice.

Given sound and serious concerns, a request for a formal assessment to help establish basic facts about a child's condition and circumstances may be necessary (see Appendix III). The professional may have a nagging concern about a child who is failing to thrive or cope and/or the parents may be ignorant or unwilling to face up to possible harm to their child because of the state of his or her health or development. *At least* the professional must have 'reasonable cause to suspect that the child is suffering or is likely to suffer, significant harm' [s.43(1) (a)].

When is a child being harmed?

The concept of harm is defined in Part IV of the Children Act by Section 31(9) to mean ill-treatment *or* the impairment of physical or mental health or development. 'Development', as already noted, refers to physical, intellectual, emotional, social or behavioural development, and 'ill treatment' includes sexual abuse and forms of ill-treatment which are not only physical. Impairment of health or development therefore also covers any case of neglect: poor nutrition, low standards of hygiene, poor emotional care through failure to seek treatment for an illness or condition.

Whatever the nature of the harm, the court has to decide whether the harm is, in itself, *significant*. This relates to the seriousness of the harm *and* its implications for the child. The court must also consider whether the child is suffering harm *currently* or whether he or she is *likely* to suffer it. Likelihood, according to White (1991), means that harm is higher than a mere possibility but not as high as 'more likely than not'.

Section 31 of the Act requires the court to be satisfied, before making a care or supervision order and before applying the principles in Section 1 of the Act, that certain criteria (referred to as 'threshold criteria') exist in the child's circumstances (see *Figure 1.1*).

The central concept of the criteria is harm. But even if the threshold criteria are met, the court may still decide not to make a care or supervision order. It has to take into account the checklist in Section 1(3) (see page 4) and, in particular, the range of orders available to the court, which include the orders under Section 8 of the Act. These orders can be made whether or not the threshold criteria are satisfied.

The child assessment order

When an assessment is necessary and the parents/caregivers refuse to agree the applicant may seek a child assessment order lasting up to seven days [s.43]. A proposal to apply for a child assessment order [s.43(1)], and the arrangements to be discussed with the court for the assessment, could be considered at a case conference according to local child protection procedures. The person who has

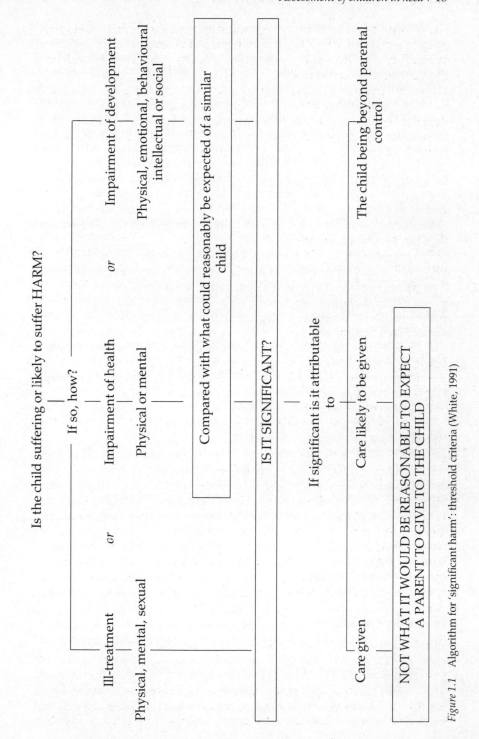

Is the child suffering or likely to suffer HARM?

If so, how?

Ill-treatment   or   Impairment of health   or   Impairment of development

Physical, mental, sexual   Physical or mental   Physical, emotional, behavioural intellectual or social

Compared with what could reasonably be expected of a similar child

IS IT SIGNIFICANT?

If significant is it attributable to

Care given   Care likely to be given   The child being beyond parental control

NOT WHAT IT WOULD BE REASONABLE TO EXPECT A PARENT TO GIVE TO THE CHILD

Figure 1.1   Algorithm for 'significant harm': threshold criteria (White, 1991)

expressed concern about the child to the Local Authority and Social Services Department or to the National Society for the Prevention of Cruelty to Children (NSPCC) (the only agencies which can apply for a child assessment order) will have to contribute to the conference's considerations.

The child's parents or carers should always be told that a child assessment order may be applied for if they persist in refusing to cooperate. They should also be informed of the legal effect and detailed implications of the order, and the court procedure that would be followed. Parents will need information about the purpose of an assessment. Some parents, although willing to cooperate with the terms of an assessment, will have fears about the possible removal of their child as a result. Although this can apply in exceptional circumstances, it is not the intention of an assessment, and this needs to be made clear.

The question that still begs an answer is that very difficult one: At what point can it be said that a child is actually being *harmed* by the neglect of needs or the presence of unskilled, insensitive or inexperienced parenting? After all, it is not the cases of explicitly malicious abuse or extreme neglect that create the agonizing debates about what constitutes harm. The harm being done is obvious. It is the more subtle and ambiguous consequences for the child's well-being that flow from parental ignorance, inexperience, emotional inadequacies or lack of resourcefulness, that evade confident classification. (I pursue this issue further in Chapter 2.)

It is important to remember that where the question of whether harm suffered by a child is *significant*, his or her health or development is 'compared with that which could reasonably be expected of a similar child' [s.31(10)]. According to the Lord Chancellor, a similar child is a child with the same physical attributes as the child concerned, not a child of the same background (Hansard, H. L., Vol. 503, col. 354). But as Judith Masson (1990) observes, this ignores the fact that social and environmental factors contribute very significantly to what can be achieved.

She observes that the definition of significant harm crops up in various places in the Act and, in this sense, is constructed like a Russian doll. The contexts within which significant harm is mentioned include child assessment orders under Section 43, emergency protection orders under Section 44, the police power to remove a child under Section 46, the local authority's duty to investigate under Section 47, and detention in secure accommodation under Section 25.

When are children psychologically 'disturbed'?

The difficulties of objectively specifying a reasonable standard of health or development or what constitutes physical or mental impairment have already been discussed. One particularly fraught area is that of mental health. Parents' enjoyment of their children is likely to diminish rapidly and give way to anxious concern, and perhaps anger and resentment, when they show signs of abnormal or deviant behaviour and emotion. Parents and teachers begin to worry about youngsters in their care when their actions persist in being:

- *not understandable*, that is when their moods, attitudes or behaviours defy good sense and lack reason or meaning;
- *unpredictable*, such that there is a Jekyll-and-Hyde-like quality of changeability, disconcerting switches in mood;
- *rebellious and uncontrollable* in the sense that adults are unable to impose their authority and/or their youngsters seem unwilling or unable to control their own behaviour.

Few parents (or teachers) have not observed undesirable forms of behaviour in a particular child or adolescent at one time or another, and they tend to be resigned about such manifestations. ('Well, that's what you'd expect, isn't it, of a toddler (or teenager?)'.) It is when such actions are *frequent* and *intense* that real concern is felt.

At what point is it inappropriate to be philosophical about children's behavioural difficulties? When should your mental 'alarm bells' begin to ring? When do you cease saying to parents, 'Ah well, she'll grow out of it'? At the most general level you might ask yourself:

▷ What are the consequences – benign or unfavourable – of the child's actions?
▷ Does the child's style of life prevent her from leading a contented life in which she is able to enjoy social relationships, and play and work (learn) effectively?
▷ Does the child's behaviour, in terms of his development towards maturity, represent a retrogressive trend – as when he resorts to thumb-sucking and temper tantrums as a way of deflecting mother's attention from the 'rival' baby sister?

By the way, you can substitute *parent* for *child* in most of these questions to assess the seriousness of parents' problems – a matter taken up in the next chapter – and this also applies to the supplementary questions listed below:

▷ Is the child withdrawn, regressed or 'frozen' in his/her emotional and social expression?
▷ Does the child get excessively miserable, embarrassed, shy, hostile, anxious or morbidly guilty?
▷ Does he/she give vent to anger too readily?
▷ Is his/her tolerance of frustration too low?
▷ Is he/she flexible in the face of failure?

▷ Does he/she find it difficult to cope with novel or difficult situations?

▷ Does he/she experience difficulty in establishing affectionate, lasting relationships with adults and peers?

▷ Does he/she fail to learn from experience (for example, from disciplinary situations)?

▷ Does he/she find it impossible to get on with most teachers or other adults in authority?

Your answers to these questions could be important 'diagnostically' (that is, for indicating seriousness), because problem behaviours have unfavourable consequences for the youngster and/or those in contact with him or her. Generally speaking, there is an association between intense and prolonged feelings of unhappiness and psychological disorder; there is a loss of a sense of well-being.

Abnormalities of mental health in childhood in the form of emotional or behavioural disorders, are (in the main) matters of degree. Problems represent, most often, exaggerations, deficiencies or handicapping combinations of behaviours, emotions or attitudes common to all people. We judge the seriousness of problems in terms of their disabling and/or distressing consequences – for the individual, and for others, and in terms of the risk they constitute to the optimal development of the child. Some two per cent of all children in the United Kingdom have emotional and behavioural problems of an intensity sufficient to be disabling. The extreme, and rare, mental illnesses (for example, disintegrative psychosis) are described in Chapter 6.

FURTHER READING

Dent, H. (1986) An experimental study of the effectiveness of different techniques of questioning mental handicapped child witnesses. *British Journal of Clinical Psychology, 25*, 13–17. [Useful information in a much neglected area.]

Dent, H. and Flin, R. A. (1992) *Children as Witnesses*. Chichester: John Wiley. [A review of developments in child witness research and practice.]

Schaefer, C. E., Gitlin, K. and Sandgrun, A. (Eds) (1991) *Play, Diagnosis and Assessment*. New York: Wiley. [A useful book on play therapy, including play 'scales' which cover developmental progress, diagnostics, parent–child interaction and peer interaction.]

Vizard, E. (1991) Interviewing children suspected of being sexually abused. In R. Hollins and K. Howells (Eds) *Clinical Approach to Sex Offenders and their Victims*. Chichester: John Wiley. [The use of anatomically correct dolls as aids to sexual abuse disclosure.]

Other references on child abuse can be found in Further Reading in Chapter 3.

2 *Assessment of parenting*

With the birth (or adoption) of the first child, the tasks of the parents, the roles they occupy, their orientation toward the future, all change profoundly. This simple step into parenthood, so often taken by biological parents as an inadvertent 'slip up', provides a severe test for the parents. The inevitable changes will alter their relationship and may place stresses upon it until a new equilibrium can be established in their lives. The heightened emotional intimacy and interdependence of members of small, intimate nuclear families can place a great burden on some parents, most particularly the mother, and also on the children. Parents are the crucial and therefore (potentially) the weak link in the chain of rearing and training children – a process called socialization.

Taking care of young children is likely to be overwhelming for some parents. It requires considerable maturity to shift one's orientation from being mainly adult-centred to being primarily child-centred. The responsibility of a total commitment to a baby – especially for young parents used to having their freedom and responsibility only for themselves – may seem awesome and, sometimes, depressing.

Responsibility as parents goes hand in hand with parental respons-iveness (that is, caring attitudes) toward a child. More than the protection and nurturance of a helpless infant is at stake. There is also further responsibility – the all-important transmission of culture. This cannot be left to chance. The welfare of the individual and the continuity of the culture depend upon there being a satisfactory means of inducting the new generation into society's mores, attitudes and skills and to ensure that they, in turn, will satisfactorily hand on the culture and assume the role of another generation of parents. The concept of parental responsibility is enshrined in legislation, notably in the Children Act.

Parental Responsibility: The Legal Framework

The term 'parental responsibility' refers to 'all the rights, duties, powers, responsibilities and authority which by law a parent of a child has in relation to the child and his property' [s.3(1)]. Where the father and mother of the child were married to each other at the time of the child's birth or have subsequently married (the meaning of this is extended by Section 1 of the Family Law Reform Act 1987), they both have parental responsibility for the child; otherwise only the mother has parental responsibility [s.2(1)–(3)]. If people have parental responsibility by virtue of their status as married parents, they never lose it save on the making of an adoption order [Sched 10, para 3].

The *unmarried father* can acquire parental responsibility by:
- obtaining a parental responsibility order [s.4(1)(a)];
- means of a formal agreement with the mother [s.4(1)(b)];
- being granted a residence order [s.12(1)];
- being appointed a guardian [s.5].

Anyone can acquire parental responsibility by:
- being granted a residence order [s.12(2)];
- being appointed a guardian [s.5];
- having an emergency protection order in their favour although it is limited to taking reasonable steps to safeguard or promote the welfare of the child [s.44(4) (c) and (5)];
- having an adoption order made in their favour.

The *local authority* can acquire parental responsibility by:
- having a care order in force with respect to the child [s.33(3)].

If a person has acquired parental responsibility as the result of a formal agreement or court order, it can be brought to an end:
- by a successful application to the court by a person with parental responsibility;
- with the leave of the court, on the application of the child [s.4(3)]. (Leaflets are available which explain children's rights under the Act in simple language.)

Otherwise it comes to an end once the child reaches the age of eighteen.

If a person has acquired parental responsibility as the result of a residence order, a successful application for the discharge of the order brings the parental responsibility to an end [s.12(2)]. Otherwise it ends on the child reaching the age of 16 (18 in exceptional circumstances).

This then is the legal framework for parental responsibility. But what of the human perspective?

The Human Dimension: Parental Responsiveness

Social workers sometimes aid paediatricians and health visitors in cases where infants fail to thrive, in the absence of any organic (physical) illness. They have to explore the social and emotional context in which the child is cared for, and grows up. Parental responsiveness is a complex and many-sided phenomenon, but there are at least three different elements which make for what one might assess to be *sensitive* responsiveness: the tendency to react *promptly*, *consistently*, and *appropriately*, to their offspring. A social worker or health visitor would be concerned if parents continually failed to show these reactions in response to their child's hunger, pain, crying or other communications and actions.

Parental responsiveness is important in something as apparently basic as providing sustenance to a baby. Typically, feeding times must be adapted to the cycles of hunger and satisfaction expressed by the infant and responded to by the parent. During the feeding sessions, carers should preferably be calm, and sensitive enough to respond from moment-to-moment to changes in the baby's behaviour. For example, they commonly respond to pauses in the child's sucking at the breast or bottle by jiggling the baby. They will gaze back at the baby and talk to it. They will be alert to the child's changing needs for nourishment as it matures, by altering its diet.

The interactions between parents and children (particularly the early ones) are of crucial significance in the child's development. And parenting is not simply a matter of being *reactive*; it is also about being proactive – initiating play, pre-empting accidents and facilitating learning, by imaginative, resourceful care. Personal factors can interfere with these intricate processes. To take the extreme case: a mother suffering from depression may find it difficult to 'tune in' to the child in a sufficiently sensitive manner to be able to construct with him/her a mutually beneficial and stimulating sequence of interaction. Psychologists have observed infants under conditions in which their mothers simulated depression and found their behaviour to be markedly affected. Mismatching through the adult's faulty timing, may well have drastic consequences if continuously experienced as part of the child's daily life.

Parenting Skills

The Children Act describes parents' ability to raise their child to moral, physical and emotional health. This demands a series of far-from-simple skills – part common sense, part intuition and part empathy (the ability to see things from another's point of view). All parents should provide for the basic survival needs of their children, namely safety, shelter, space (which includes space to play, and particularly for older children, privacy), food, income, physical care and health care. The child's physical care can be rated for its adequacy on *Table 2.1*. Responsible parents also provide love, security, attention, new experiences, acceptance, education, praise and recognition in order to meet their children's vital psychosocial needs. *Table 2.2* can be used to assess the quality of parental care.

Table 2.1 The child's physical care

Rate the quality of care in the boxes provided: Excellent (E), Good (G), Adequate (A), Poor (P), or Inadequate (I).

Physical needs	Rating	Some guiding questions
1. Safety	☐	• Is the child protected from danger (for example, poisons/medicines locked away; training to avoid accidents, dangerous situations; children not left alone at night)?
2. Food	☐	• What, and how often, does the child eat and drink? • Who usually feeds the child? • What times are the meals? • Are there problems feeding the child?
3. Shelter	☐	• Does the child have reasonable accommodation (for example, a warm, dry bed; some privacy; a place for his/her property; a place to play)?
4. Rest	☐	• What time does the child go to bed? • How much sleep does he/she get? • Where does he/she sleep? Alone? • Does he/she have difficulties in (a) sleeping? (b) staying in bed?
5. Cleanliness	☐	• Is the child taught personal hygiene (for example, wash hands after toilet)? • Are cuts and bruises attended to after a fall? • Is the child encouraged to wash, bath, clean hair? Are they done for him/her? How often?
6. Appearance	☐	• Is the child reasonably/appropriately clothed (for example, warm/tidy)? • Does the child smell? • Is he/she grubby?

Table 2.2 The quality of parental care

Rate the quality of care in the boxes provided: Excellent (E), Good (G), Adequate (A), Poor (P), or Inadequate (I).

Emotional needs	Rating	Some defining criteria
1. Affection	☐	Affection includes physical contact, admiration, touching, holding, comforting, making allowances, being tender, showing concern, communicating.
2. Security	☐	Security means continuity of care, a predictable environment, consistent controls, settled patterns of care and daily routines, fair and understandable rules, harmonious family relationships, the feeling that one's home and family are always there.
3. Responsibility	☐	Responsibility involves discipline appropriate to the child's stage of development, providing a model to emulate/imitate, indicating limits, insisting on concern for others.
4. Independence	☐	Independence implies making opportunities for the child to do more unaided and make decisions, first about small things but gradually about larger matters.
5. Responsiveness	☐	Responsiveness means prompt, consistent, appropriate actions to meet the child's needs.
6. Stimulation	☐	Stimulation means encouraging curiosity and exploratory behaviour, by praising, by responding to questions and play, by promoting training/educational opportunities and new experiences.

It is worth noting that although society delegates its most crucial functions to the family, there is little formal education or training offered to would-be parents; even the informal learning and experience once available to older children caring for younger siblings in large families, or the help from the experienced members of the extended family and from relatives living nearby, may not be available to the relatively small and isolated nuclear family (mother, father, children).

What is important is the general social climate in the home – the attitudes and feelings of the parents – which form a background to the application of specific child-rearing methods. Feeding and toileting and the like are important elements of the child's daily activities, but it is the social interactions they mediate – the manner in which parents undertake these tasks – that give them significance. It is how the young child is looked after that is crucial; and it is the social and psychological context of the care which matters, rather than its chronology and mechanics. Effective parents tend to be those who care for their children with a sense of confidence, doing what, at the time, they and the community believe is right for the child.

When things do go wrong, as sometimes happens when a temperamentally difficult infant (see page 40) or a handicapped child makes heavy demands on parents, remedies are available as we shall see. Many parents can be trained in the necessary skills – child care and behaviour management. More often than not they have skills they're not even aware of. To this end every family can make use of its combined store of skills so that members can usefully share and learn from each other. Broadly speaking, these skills fall into seven categories: relationship; social; communication; problem-solving; coping; study and work skills.

A far more difficult task is to encourage those feelings that come so readily to most parents, but which are absent or distorted in some. In the way that success breeds success and failure breeds failure, good parenting facilitates good parenting in the next generation, and poor parenting generates poor parenting (see Rutter and Madge, 1976). Fortunately, when it comes to the last part of that 'rule', there are – as with most aspects of child rearing – many exceptions.

Parent–Child Attachment

The question of sensitive or insensitive responsiveness has been linked, in part, with the quality of the emotional 'bond' or 'attachment' that forms between the parent and baby. Obviously, the infant's survival depends upon a loving and long-term commitment by adult caregivers. Social workers and health visitors are on the lookout for signs of rejection, neglect and abuse.

When all goes well – and it usually does – a 'bond' is cemented between a mother (say) and her infant; a relationship implying unconditional love, self-sacrifice and caring attitudes which, for the mother's part, are quite likely to last a lifetime. Put briefly, the doctrine of mother-to-infant bonding suggests that in some mammalian species, including our own, mothers become bonded to their infants through close contact – skin-to-skin – during a short critical period, soon after birth. This is an awesome claim, considering that no other adult human behaviour, and a complex pattern of behaviour and attitude at that, is explained in such 'ethological' terms (that is, in the language of animal behaviour).

The close-contact, critical-period bonding theory is said to be justified on two grounds: one is rooted in studies of animal behaviour; the other has to do with observations of human mothers, comparing those who have had little or no contact with their newborn babies, with those who have extended contact.

I have commented elsewhere (see Further Reading) how liberalizing ideas in the field of child care – for example, 'maternal deprivation' theory – can become oppressive when elevated into prescriptive dogmas. The eminently realistic and humane idea of allowing a mother and her new baby to get to know one another early on by means of frequent and intimate social interaction, becomes intrusive and unrealistic when the permissive 'ought' of physical contact is transformed into an authoritarian 'must' – whatever the condition of the mother or her offspring. Mothers-to-be, often exhausted and hypersensitive to potential dangers, may be undermined by the fear that if they do not have contact with their babies soon after delivery, they may not fall in love with them.

Maternal bonding

This is not the place to review the complex and detailed studies of bonding. However there seems to be no reliable evidence that skin-to-skin contact is necessary for the development of mother love, and, what is more significant, mother-to-infant attachment does not depend on such contact occurring during a sensitive period of short duration after the birth of the baby (see Further Reading).

Of course, relationships have to have a beginning – close mother–infant contact is decidedly desirable whenever possible. Mothers tend to like it and lactation is facilitated. Where better to begin than at the very beginning, with the newborn child placed in its mother's arms? Mutual awareness and familiarity have an opportunity to develop. What we are talking about is foundational learning, learning how to relate to (and love) a stranger, a baby. It would seem that this learning comes quickly for some but for others more slowly; the range of individual differences is wide.

The period after birth, with its heightened emotional arousal and excited expectation and fulfilment of a new family member, may have tremendous significance for all members of the family. Remember that parental bonds and relationships have their own complex, many-sided developmental histories, stretching over many years. Among the factors which can influence the way a mother behaves and relates to her offspring are her age, her cultural and social background, her own experience of being parented, her personality, her previous experience with babies and her experiences during pregnancy and birth.

Insensitivity to cultural values in clinical and social work practice can lead to much individual suffering if methods used offend against cherished cultural and/or religious beliefs. For some ethnic groups, bonding ideas, if applied insensitively by doctors and nurses, may have disturbing repercussions. In some Asian families, birth is a less personal event than in European families. The baby is thought to be bonded to the family group rather than to the mother in particular. Unless hospital staff are sensitive to ethnic differences in behaviour and attitudes after birth, these parents could feel intense conflict over 'bonding procedures'.

It has been suggested that separation of the mother and infant for several weeks immediately after birth may not only irreversibly damage the subsequent mother–child relationship, but also predis-poses such mothers to child abuse. In fact, the evidence for such far-reaching claims is simply not available; these notions do not stand up to painstaking enquiry and investigation (see Further Reading).

Allaying parents' fears
The practical advice to parents who have had an enforced separation – at whatever time – from their babies or older children is: 'Do not spend time worrying needlessly'. Adult bonding (and, indeed, child-to-parent attachments) need not be impaired, in the case of those separations in the maternity hospital, or when mothers have to go out to work, or *wish* to do so, unless they talk themselves into a crisis.

Guilt is usually the enemy! Parents are afraid of damaging their relationships with their children. It is true that where a separation occurs, young children may be upset for a short time, but they will soon recover if parents appear their usual selves and avoid fussing over them in nervous expectation of the worst. We know that a child's separation from its caregiver does not inevitably result in maladjustment; far from it. Brief separations are fairly common for all children and seem to have little in the way of long-term adverse effects. The key issue is to provide good and stable substitute care during the absence/s and, in the case of hospitalization, to prepare children for what lies ahead (many hospitals do this with commend-able sensitivity), arrange for a person to stay with the young child or make regular visits to the older one.

It is reassuring to realize that there are variations in the way that maternal feelings arise and grow. Mothers generally expect to have positive maternal feelings towards their infants at the time of birth. Indeed, some mothers *do* report an instant love towards their newborn babies. Others report that they feel nothing. However, you can reassure mothers that they do not need to worry if they initially feel detached from their babies, as this appears to be a fairly common occurrence. Some 40 per cent of mothers of first-borns have been found to express an initial indifference to their infants, a state of mind which soon evaporates as they get to know their offspring.

When subjective and objective reports of the development of mother love are scrutinized, it becomes apparent that the growth of maternal attachment is usually a gradual process.

Paternal bonding

Paternal love puts a large question mark over the bonding doctrine, for it implies that a father's love is of a lower order and quality than the mother's. Yet it is not always the female that cares for the baby. This is so even in some animal species: male marmosets, to take just one example, carry the infant at all times except when it is feeding.

Most human fathers develop a strong love for their offspring, even if they were nowhere near the delivery room when they were born. First-time fathers tend to begin developing a bond to their newborn baby by the first three days after the birth and often earlier; they develop a feeling of preoccupation, absorption and interest ('engross-ment'). There are no clear indications that the father's early contact with the newborn facilitates this engrossment. Nevertheless, the opportunity for father and infant to get to know one another early on would seem to be a good idea, especially as contemporary western society is witnessing a massive increase in the number of single-parent families, and in some it is the father who is the caregiver (see Sluckin and Herbert, 1986, for a review of the evidence).

Fostering and adoption

It is mysterious that the bonding doctrine, in its fundamentalist version, held (holds?) such sway, given that foster or adoptive parents usually form warm attachments to their charges whom they have not seen as babies at all. It could be said that it is possible to look after children satisfactorily without ever becoming attached to them, but how many adoptive or foster parents would say that they felt no bond with their child?

Not only is there no 'blood bond' between adoptive mother and the child, but she has missed out vital weeks, months and sometimes years of exposure to the youngster. Not surprisingly, there is nothing to suggest that adoptive parents are in any way inferior in their familial or parental roles than biological parents. A painstaking study of children who had been in care throughout their early years, followed them up on leaving care. One group of children was adopted, another returned to their families. It was found that the latter did less well than the adopted children, both in the initial stages of settling in and in their subsequent progress. The reason lay primarily in the attitudes of the two sets of parents: the adoptive group 'worked' harder at being parents, possibly for the very reason that the child was not their own, in a genetic sense.

The attitude of some people to adoption in this country in the 18th and early 19th centuries was very different from the one shared by most of us today. We gather from George Eliot's novel, *Silas Marner*, that adoption was only permissible and likely to succeed if it came about by chance, not intent. George Eliot, in her usual insightful manner, made the point that the 'blood bond' is less important that the bonds forged by long-term tender care and affection. And she has been shown to be correct.

Researchers provide evidence that adoption is notable for its high 'success rate', both in absolute terms, and relative to other forms of substitute care. Like any other parents, adopters have their share of difficult children with whom they will need to learn to deal. (Appendix III contains more details about family placements.)

Bonding in cases of multiple births

Bearing in mind the strength and flexibility of mother love, it should, theoretically, make no difference to the mother's feeling towards each child whether she gives birth to a singleton or twins or triplets. However, one must remember that in the case of multiple births, the babies are often premature and underweight at birth and need very special attention, if not special care, during their first few weeks. Even in the case of a normal delivery, one of the babies may be more vulnerable than the other(s). From the time of birth, infants can signal information about their needs. Where the mother perceives the signal accurately and responds appropriately, the mother–infant relationship is characterized by 'synchrony' which facilitates the baby's development and is a source of satisfaction to the mother.

It could be argued that in multiple births, synchrony is more difficult to achieve as the mother may be physically and emotionally too exhausted to adapt herself to the rhythms of two or more babies. However, we know that the majority of multiple birth mothers not only learn to love their babies dearly, but also learn to respect the babies' individual differences. However, problems can arise if a mother finds herself spending more time initially with the weakly baby. She may experience a sense of guilt and may blame herself for not giving each an equal amount of attention, thinking that this may adversely affect present and subsequent relationships.

A systems approach to bonding issues

The family can be conceptualized as a 'system' with its individual members as elements or sub-units within it. Whatever happens to one or more of its elements – say, a mother's physical or mental illness, a father's unemployment, or serious marital disharmony – may affect the entire system. This is sometimes forgotten in the 'encapsulation' of the mother–infant relationship in the literature, that is to say the exclusive attention focused on mother and child to the neglect of other members of the family.

Taking care of infants and young children is likely to be more debilitating and/or demoralizing for some parents than for others, especially in unfavourable circumstances (for example, illness, poverty, poor housing). The identification of advantageous and 'faulty' patterns of family life, and providing community, medical and social support, should theoretically allow for the remediation and, better still, prevention of problems. Let us look, for a moment, at these problems. We shall return, in Chapter 8, to look at them more fully.

Difficulties in the bonding process

The term 'emotional abuse' has been added to the concept of 'physical abuse'; it is less tangible and even more difficult to diagnose or 'prove'. It reflects difficulties of a serious kind in parent–child attachment (bonding) and is defined in terms of neglect of needs referred to earlier such as:

- physical care and protection;
- affection and approval;
- stimulation and teaching;
- discipline and controls which are consistent and appropriate to the child's age and development;
- opportunity and encouragement to acquire gradual autonomy, that is, for the child to take gradual control over his or her own life.

Emotional abuse is 'signposted' by parental indifference, the outward and visible sign, all too often, of a deep-seated emotional rejection of the child.

Parental rejection

There cannot be many professionals who have not worked with parents whose concern for their children is minimal and whose attitudes are casual, *laissez-faire*, lax or even feckless. For some, rejection means callous and indifferent neglect or positive hostility from the parents; but it may also be more subtle. Children come to believe that they are worthless, that their very existence makes their parents unhappy. The child is ignored, there may be inadequate physical care, the child lacks stimulation, physical contact, security. The child is thus denied emotional warmth and love as well as protection, support and discipline. Parents' negative attitudes may lead to abusive threats, constant criticism and scapegoating. With older children, this is sometimes accompanied by ridicule and denigration of all the child's efforts to please. Some apply the term 'emotional abuse' also to over-protection.

The concept of emotional abuse is in danger of being over-inclusive and far too vague. It is therefore an advantage to have more tangible indicators to pinpoint its presence.

Indicator 1 entails punishment of positive 'operant' behaviour such as smiling, mobility, manipulation;

Indicator 2 is behaviour which results in discouragement of parent–infant bonding (for example, pushing children away every time they seek proximity, comfort and affection);

Indicator 3 involves the punishment of self-esteem as when parents endlessly criticize their child;

Indicator 4 is parental behaviour leading to the punishing of those interpersonal skills (for example, friendliness) which are vital for acceptance in environments outside the home, for example, school, peer groups.

It should not be forgotten that emotional abuse is also associated with physical and sexual abuse (see also Chapter 10).

Psychiatric illness and maternal bonding

Psychiatric illness is frequently mentioned as putting mother and baby at risk. Yet little detailed work has been done on the mother–baby relationship during the mother's psychiatric disorder. Practical competence is often relatively intact, at least at the crude level at which it has been measured, but social activities such as play and touching are more frequently disrupted. Sadly, research designs are not usually of a standard to allow confident generalizations or conclusions in this area. It does seem, however, that different aspects of maternal psychopathology may interfere with the mother–baby relationship in different ways. An ill mother's rejection of her baby is a common concern among nursing staff and doctors. Rejection of the infant might occur in several ways: negative thoughts about the child; a wish that the child had never been born or could be changed in some fundamental way (for example, by being of the opposite sex); denial that the child is hers or even that she has given birth at all.

Manic patients commonly show a marked disorganization of practical care. They may, however, relate warmly to the infant but only for short periods, and then, inconsistently. Mothers with chronic schizophrenia show poor practical competence and deficits in their organization of daily routines to an even more marked degree than manic mothers. Their babies are often placed in the care of the Local Authority Social Services. Mothers with depression frequently report a lack of feeling which may involve the infant. They may express concern about their lack of love for the baby, and commonly experience an inability to cope. (Sutton and Herbert, 1992, have published a resource pack for assessing and helping clients with such mental health problems.)

As yet, there has been insufficient research to disentangle the effects of psychiatric illness, maternal attitudes and behaviour, and the various aspects of treatment. Perhaps an important prerequisite for future progress is to stop considering normal and abnormal bonding as two discrete categories and to consider separately the components of the bonding process and their relation to psychiatric disorders. Bonding problems are complex phenomena involving different levels of analysis: family, marital, intra-personal, inter-personal and behavioural (see Further Reading).

Interviewing Parents

There are many studies which point out the consistent and persistent biasing of maternal reports in the direction of cultural stereotypes. The idealized picture of the happy family is one of the most potent in modern society, and any failure to live up to that image rebounds on the parents, particularly on the mother. Sigmund Freud ensured that the 'sins' of the children would be visited on the parents. Not surprisingly, parents complaining about 'deviant' behaviours of their children are very conscious that the complaints reflect back on them. An interview with a mother generally reflects an extremely ego-involved reporter.

The finding of bias in maternal reports is particularly high when they are giving retrospective reports; the passage of time dims the memory and what memory cannot provide, imagination elaborates – an elaboration that is in a direction that is socially desirable. Reports of *current* beliefs and practices are more accurate and reliable. The parent presumably finds it more difficult (certainly not impossible) to falsify the present; it is much easier to rewrite history. Reliability studies have shown that there are wide discrepancies between the reports of the same mother at different times and of the same mother with a different interviewer.

How, then, can one improve the reliability of parental reports? According to the evidence, if the mother is asked for a statement on current beliefs and practices, then the reports reach a satisfactory level of validity and reliability. When parents are asked to *describe* rather than *interpret*, reliability and validity measures can reach satisfactory levels of accuracy. As a check on maternal and paternal reports, professsionals systematically seek out information from different sources, noting areas of concordance and discordance.

To this end, you need to have a penetrating, but discreet, look at the significant people who play a part in your client's life. The interview should include a series of guided conversations which involve asking questions and careful and sensitive listening (listening with the 'third ear' as it has been called) to answers and spontaneous offerings. It is critical in assessing parents' behaviour that one should observe them in interaction and conversation with their children. Selma Fraiberg (1980), on the basis of her work on the Child Development Project in Michigan, is committed to having the baby physically present in therapeutic work on parent–infant issues. As she puts it: 'The baby, as the patient who couldn't talk, could nevertheless engage in an eloquent dialogue with his family and us. Without words, he could tell us how he was feeling about the world and himself, whether he was valued, understood, satisfied, whether he was going through a rough time . . .'. *Table 2.3* (stage 1 of the ASPIRE model – see also page 134) can be used as a guide to the information typically required in an assessment interview.

The collaborative relationship

It is important to consider what perspective or 'style' of help will be offered. Professionals may ascribe to the *expert model*, or to the *partnership* or *collaborative model*. In the expert model – and this is very much a medical perspective – professionals view themselves as in charge because of their monopoly (or near monopoly) of expertise and responsibility. The professional is therefore the decision-maker while the client is relatively passive, the recipient of advice or 'prescriptions' (for example, about health or how to manage children).

This matter of perspective is a crucial one! When things go badly wrong, our society gets an irresistible urge to find something or someone to blame. And when they go wrong with children, or with the relationships between parents and their children, the finger is almost always pointed at the mother. The literature on childhood psychological problems is full of over-protective, dominating or rejecting mothers – a litany of negative attitudes.

In the collaborative relationship (as described by Webster-Stratton and Herbert, 1993), the professional works *with* the parents by actively soliciting their ideas and feelings, understanding their cultural context, and jointly involving them in the process of sharing their experiences, discussing ideas, and problem-solving. The

Table 2.3 Aspire checklist

Stage 1: Assessment

---

1. Conduct the assessment. This involves:
   - using counselling and listening skills;
   - establishing a respecting relationship;
   - listening to the clients' views of difficulties;
   - listening to others' views of difficulties;
   - reducing stress by adopting a calm manner.

2. Clarify 'What do we together see as the problem(s)?'
   How does the client (child or caregiver) view his or her own needs?

3. Gather information.
   The background to the difficulty should be elicited sensitively, including an estimate, in particular, of how reliable this information is.

   (a) Personal history:
   - the child's personal circumstances;
   - date of birth and family circumstances;
   - major 'life events';
   - family circumstances in present situation.

   (b) Circumstances related to the difficulty:
   - parents' relationship;
   - child's separation anxieties;
   - fears about school;
   - fears about friends, loneliness;
   - other traumatic/difficult experiences may include physical abuse, sexual abuse, sibling rivalry, school failure;
   - specific factors relating to onset of present and previous episodes.

   (c) Present state:
   - circumstances leading to referral;
   - extent of current distress;
   - difficulties in terms of: affect (feelings), behaviour (actions), cognitions (thoughts, memories).

   (d) The needs and values of the family/carers:
   Take cultural considerations into account. If the above approach is too Eurocentric, what are the crucial factors, as the clients perceive them? Negotiate common ground.

4. Consider other factors affecting the assessment.
   - social issues, such as cultural expectations;
   - additional stresses, such as unemployment, poverty, racism;
   - impact of ill health (child's or carer's).

5. Discuss and agree priorities.
   Take into account urgency of situation, resources, importance of enabling people to feel that they have hope and some control. Agree together with the client which of the problems are to be addressed first.

6. Share the assessment.
   - attempt to address the question, 'Why have these problems occurred?';
   - clarify the nature of the disorder and help those involved to make sense of what is happening to them;
   - answer questions about the problem where you have the relevant knowledge;
   - clarify the extent of help available.

---

professional does not set him/herself up as the 'expert', dispensing advice or lectures to parents about how they *should* parent more effectively; rather, he or she invites parents to help write the 'script' for the intervention programme. The professional's role, then, as collaborator, is to understand the perspective of the parent and of the family as a system. More specifically, the professional aims to clarify issues, to summarize important ideas and themes raised by the parents, to teach and interpret in a way which is culturally sensitive and, finally, to suggest and illustrate possible alternative approaches or choices when parents request assistance and when misunderstandings occur.

The process of creating a partnership between the parents and the professional has the effect of giving dignity, respect and self-empowerment to parents, who are often seeking help for their children's problems at a time of vulnerability and low self-confidence and who may be experiencing intense feelings of guilt, self-blame and/or stress. The collaborative process has the double-edged advantage of reducing attrition rates (increasing motivation and commitment, reducing resistance) and giving both parents and the professional a 'stake in the outcome' of the intervention efforts. On the other hand, controlling or hierarchical modes of therapy, in which the therapist makes decisions *for* parents without inviting their input, may result in a low level of commitment, dependency, resentment, low self-efficacy and increased resistance. In fact, if parents are not given appropriate ways to participate, they may see no alternative but to drop out as a method of gaining control.

FURTHER READING

Barber, D. (1978) *One Parent Families*. Sevenoaks: Hodder & Stoughton. [Single parenting is fairly commonplace today. What are the advantages and disadvantages?]

Bowlby, J. (1988) *A Secure Base*. London: Routledge. [The importance of secure attachment.]

Fratter, J. (1991) Permanent family placement: a decade of experience. In *B.A.A.F. Research Studies 8*. [Issues and research data fully discussed.]

Lamb, M. E. (Ed.) (1981) *The Role of the Father in Child Development*. New York: John Wiley. [Fathers have been neglected as well as neglectful. This book addresses these issues.]

Shaw, M. (1986) Substitute parenting. In W. Sluckin and M. Herbert (Eds) *Parental Behaviour*. Oxford: Basil Blackwell. [A review of the main issues raised by adoption and fostering with reference to empirical studies.]

Sluckin, W., Herbert, M. and Sluckin, A. (1983) *Maternal Bonding*. Oxford: Basil Blackwell. [A critical but constructive review of the bonding theories.]

3 Taking the family into account

Many of the problems affecting parents and their children are the problems of the family *as a family*, and need to be construed as such. The family has, in a sense, a life of its own. It is a dynamic institution, that is to say, movement is essential to the development of children and, indeed adults. The same can be said of family life. Both individuals and families have their life (or developmental) tasks to accomplish. These give a particular 'feel' or atmosphere to a family: the members have different and changing roles which, in turn, change the 'personality' of the family as time goes by; they have their successes and failures which reflect on the family; alliances form, dissolve and reform.

The family thus has its own life cycle from 'infancy' to 'old age' with associated changes in its size, 'shape' and function. As children grow into adolescents, they bring new elements into the family system. The peer group gains more influence; the youngster learns that friends' families work by different standards and rules; the teenage culture introduces its values with regard to sex, religion, politics and drugs.

Parents too, are changing. Families are not impervious to social change. Fourteen per cent are now single-parent families; many are reconstituted families (step-families) because 36 per cent of marriages are re-marriages. In 1989, 27 per cent of births occurred outside marriage. In contrast to an earlier generation, the experience of family life within, say, a classroom of today's children, will be extremely varied – the differences in patterns of parenting and home life far from homogeneous.

Family therapists see the total network of family transactions as greater than the sum of its parts: hence their rejection of the parents' labelling of a problem simply as 'my son's/daughter's problem'. The family system is viewed as the functioning of three subsystems – spouses; parents and children; children alone – all contained within a defined *boundary* and, in turn, operating within a given social and cultural context.

Problems within the family with which you are likely to deal are those involving relationships (for example, sibling rivalry and jealousy, parental over-protection, marital discord); lack of knowledge (for example, ignorance of what to expect of children at different ages); disagreements over the sharing of finite resources (such as money, time, attention); conflict (for example, over policies such as rules, discipline, routines). Helping parents to resolve conflicts with adolescents is a valuable contribution to happier family life, as is the reduction of aggravation brought about by planning 'around the clock' rules and routines for the toddler – with regard to dressing, meals, visiting, shopping and going to bed.

Establishing Problem Priorities

Those workers with mandatory obligations will doubtless have their own guidelines on priorities. But it is still useful to assess what the clients' top priorities are for bringing about change. Yours and their hierarchy of tasks might be influenced by the following considerations with regard to the problem(s):

- their annoyance value;
- their actual/potential dangerousness;
- their interference with the life of the family or its individual members;
- their accessibility to change (improvement) and intervention;
- their frequency, intensity and magnitude (that is, their pervasiveness);
- their disabling implications;
- the 'costs' of change in terms of resources (time, money, etc.) and possible consequences for the well-being of other people close to the client;
- the ethical acceptability of the desired outcome;
- the availability of the necessary skills and resources on your part or the part of your agency to provide help.

The Family as a System

Systemic thinking has influenced the manner in which practitioners seek explanations for the problems of family life. The *simpler* forms of behavioural theory are reductionist and linear: a direct link is sought between cause and effect, between stimulus and response; children are described in terms of their responses to the environmental forces impinging on them. Contrasting with this model, is the systems version of family therapy. The General Systems or Cybernetic paradigm was originally conceived by Von Bertalanffy in the late 1920s in an attempt to understand living organisms in a holistic way; but it was in the 1970s that theorists applied it to work with families. The systems approach embraces the concept of circular/reciprocal causation. What we have is a recursive sequence in which each action can be considered as the consequence of the action preceding it and the cause of the action following it. No single element in the sequence controls the operation of the sequence as a whole, because it is itself governed by the operation of the other elements in the system.

Thus any individual in a family system is affected by the activities of other members of the family – activities which his or her actions or decisions, in turn, influence. Systems theorists, in contemporary practice, concentrate not only on the individual but on the system of relationships in which he or she acts out his or her life. The focus of help, in the light of this interactional frame of reference, is not prejudged as the child who was referred to the clinic. The unit of attention is defined as the whole family (or one of its subsystems).

The family life map is a useful visual device for bringing together the life events, transitions and developmental tasks of different members of a family living together (see *Figure 3.1*). All salient elements are listed; not only those which potentially may generate conflict (the clash of discordant goals), but also those which may be used to mobilize emotional support within the family. Empirical studies have shown that such support is critical in helping individuals overcome their difficulties.

The family as a small group can be observed and assessed on a variety of dimensions: patterns of communication, processes of decision-making, cohesion, and dysfunctional patterns, to mention only a few.

Family cohesion
Family cohesion has a marked effect on the psychological well-being of family members and can be measured by the presence of the following factors:

▷ Members spend a fair amount of time in shared activity.
▷ Withdrawal, avoidance and segregated (separate) activities are rare.
▷ Interactions that are warm are common and interactions that are hostile are infrequent among members.
▷ There is full and accurate communication between members of the family.
▷ Valuations of other members of the family are generally favourable; critical judgements are rare.
▷ Individuals tend to perceive other members as having favourable views of them.
▷ Members are visibly affectionate.
▷ They show high levels of satisfaction and morale, and are optimistic about the future stability of the family group.

When these features are absent, the family members who are particularly at risk are those already vulnerable for other reasons: the young, the elderly, those coping with stress such as hospitalization and alcohol dependence.

	TIM: 22 months of age	ANNE: age 10 years	PETER: age 14 years	MOTHER: age 38	FATHER: age 45	GRANNY: age 66
LIFE TASKS	• develop motor skills	• cope with academic demands at school (underachieving)	• adjust to physical changes of puberty	• review her life and commitments	• review commitments in mid-life	• deal with increasing dependence on others
	• develop self-control	• developing her sense of self	• and to sexual awareness	• adjust to loss of youth and (in her perception) 'looks'	• develop new phase in relationship with wife	• come to terms with old age/death
	• elaborate vocabulary	• learn to be part of a team	• cope with the opposite sex (shyness)	• cope with an adolescent as a patient and caring parent	• face physical changes – some limitations on athletic/sexual activity	• cope with loss of peers
	• explore his world – make 'discoveries'		• deepen friendships (intimacy)			
LIFE EVENTS	• parents insists on obedience now	• afraid to go to school (cannot manage maths and other subjects)	• worried about his skin (acne) and the smallness of his penis	• coping with late child – an active toddler	• threat of redundancy	• poor health
	• adjust to temporary separations when mother goes to work	• bullied by a girl in her class	• has a girlfriend – his first	• has taken part-time job to relieve feeling of being trapped	• high blood pressure	• gave up home when bereaved (may have made a mistake)
	• not the centre of attention and 'uncritical deference' as much as previously	• jealous of attention Tim gets (calls him a spoiled brat)	• upset by his parents' quarrels	• feels guilty	• worried about drifting apart from his wife	• enjoys the little one, but
		• worried about father's health	• complains that his mother is always watching him	• bouts of depression	• had a brief affair	• feels 'claustrophobic' with all the activity and squabbles
				• no longer enjoys sex	• feels unattractive	
	TODDLERHOOD	PREPUBESCENCE	ADOLESCENCE	MIDLIFE		RETIREMENT

Figure 3.1 A family life map

Adaptability

This term indicates that a family can modify its roles and relationships in response to particular influences, that is, change can occur when necessary. The family that is functioning well is able to accommodate setbacks and change and has self-corrective properties; the 'healthy' family also has adaptive mechanisms that allow it not only to survive and protect its members, but also to 'bounce back' when problems occur.

An investment in more than one relationship

The system is a set of intersecting relationships: mother–father, mother–child, father–child, sibling–sibling, etc. It follows from such a definition, that to be closely involved with, say, one's wife, but uninterested in one's child; or, conversely, to be close to one's child but not to one's partner, is a sign that the family is not functioning well as a system. The goal for such a family may be a 'proper' balance of investments.

A sense of boundaries

Boundaries are defined by 'rules' which specify an individual's role within the family, what subsystem he or she belongs to, and the appropriate behaviours which such membership entails. Boundaries can be clear (easily recognized and acceptable rules), diffuse (ambiguous and chaotic because rules are unstable or absent), or rigid (inflexible, unadaptable). Family therapy is often especially concerned with families that have weak boundaries or reversed territories between generations. For instance, parent can play child, and/or child can move into the role of parent. Family members define boundaries and base these (*inter alia*) on prescriptions for generation and gender.

Boundaries apply also in distinctions between 'family' and 'not family'. In a family that is functioning well, family relationships should neither prevent outside contact nor force outside contact as an escape. The attitude toward the outside society should be 'open and hopeful'.

Homeostasis

This term describes the 'steady state' of the 'organism' (for our purposes the family) indicating that the various subsystems are in balance and the whole system is in harmony with the environment. To achieve and maintain homeostasis in the face of change and stress, a system, it is hypothesized, must have the following characteristics:

☐ The family should be *open*, which means, as we saw above, that family members have a high level of exchange with the outside community, as compared with systems which are *closed*, and which have very little exchange with the community outside their boundaries.

☐ The family should make use of *feedback* processes which reflect its ability to 'recognize' the consequences of its actions. For example, the family that is functioning well is capable of monitoring its progress toward family goals and correcting (modifying) its actions to bring itself back on track, if necessary.

Dysfunctional patterns

By way of contrast, dysfunctional families may display the following attributes:

- Chaotic family organization; little or no organization makes the management of change or coping with stress extremely difficult.
- Overly rigid organization which inhibits change when change is necessary, or leads to a stereotyped, and therefore inappropriate, reaction to events.
- Too great a distance between members of the family, potentially leading to emotional isolation and physical deprivation.
- Excessive closeness between members of the family, potentially leading to over-identification and loss of individuality.
- An inability to work through conflicts, solve problems or make decisions.
- An inability on the part of parents to form a coalition and to work together, to the detriment of the marriage and/or children.
- An alliance across the generations which disrupts family life, as when a grandparent interferes with the mother's child-rearing plans and actions.
- Poor communication between members.
- A failure to respond appropriately to each other's feelings.

The Parent–Child Attachment System

There is another application of the term 'system', this time to 'dyadic' relationships. Theorists have found it useful to conceive of, say, the mother and child, while they are interacting with each other, as a single 'attachment system'. This system is almost always at work, especially in the early part of a child's life. Mother and baby are seldom out of each other's minds. What happens to one has a 'ripple' effect on the other; matters that strongly affect a mother usually have some sort of repercussion on her baby. We cannot analyse a child's so-called problems, for example, without also describing the mother's behaviour towards her child. I can illustrate this in a very simple manner, by describing a little incident in the waiting room at the Child and Family Centre where I used to work. I had gone there to fetch five-year-old Colin to take him to the playroom. He was referred (as a 'timid, clingy, nervous child') by the family doctor for our help. As I extended my hand, explaining to Colin who I was, where we were going and where his mother would be, Colin came forward, smiling at me. As we turned to go, his mother jumped up, anxiously saying, 'Oh I don't think he'll go on his own; he doesn't like leaving me'. Colin immediately turned to his mother, hung on to her legs and began to cry.

In many ways, children's behaviour can have as much effect on their parents' actions as their parents' behaviour has on them. So when parents meet extremely difficult, temperamental or inborn factors – a powerful individuality in their offspring – from a very tender age, they can be overwhelmed for a time, and change the direction and manner in which they intended to bring up their child. Without support for vulnerable parents, these adverse temperamental attributes predispose infants to later behaviour problems (see *Table 3.1*).

Some of the ways in which a child may contribute (wittingly or unwittingly) to a family's inability to cope with conflict, have been described by family theorists:

▷ parent–child coalition, where one parent attacks the other, using one of the children as an ally;
▷ triangulation, where both parents attempt to induce a child to take their side;
▷ go-between, where a child is used to transmit messages and feelings;
▷ whipping-boy, where one parent, instead of making a direct attack on the other, uses their child as a scapegoat;
▷ child as weapon, where one parent attacks the other using the child as a weapon;
▷ sibling transfer, where the children agree to divert the parents from arguing;
▷ pacification, where one child acts as peacemaker;
▷ detour through illness, where children learn that disagreements between parents may be reduced when they are ill.

Family Violence

The picture of the family as a haven of care and safety is shattered more frequently than the public cares to think about. Child abuse is one of the most common causes of death in young children in Britain today, with at least two children dying at the hands of their parents and relatives every week. This grim statistic highlights the fact that not enough is being done to protect children; many abusive or neglectful families are without social work support. As a result, many children grow up physically and emotionally scarred for life.

Table 3.1 Temperament

Research has shown that very early in life babies can be classified according to their 'temperament' – inborn or constitutional attributes of personality. They include characteristics such as:

Activity level: which can range from very fidgety and active to relatively still and passive.

Quality of mood: this may range from predominantly positive, happy, contented to mainly negative, fretful, miserable.

Approach versus withdrawal tendencies: the child, when exposed to new features of the environment, reacts positively or negatively to particular types of stimulation (for example, touch or taste); or reacts positively or negatively to new people.

Rhythmicity: habits of eating, sleeping, bowel movements, etc. relatively predictable rather than erratic or unpredictable.

Adaptability: child settles down relatively easily versus resistance to change when exposed to new routines or situations.

Threshold of responsiveness: child is hypersensitive to sounds, touch, etc. versus relatively insensitive.

Intensity of reaction: some babies may cry loudly and intensely; others react more moderately to stimuli.

Distractability: some children attend to things for considerable periods of time; others flit from one thing to another.

Persistence: some babies are very 'single-minded' and stick to 'goals' with great persistence.

One group of babies (about ten per cent of those studied by Thomas, Chess and Birch, 1968) was described as 'difficult' (and unkindly, in some instances, as 'mother killers') because of the combination of aversive attributes they possessed. They were predisposed to develop behaviour problems of a serious kind later in life.

Research shows that child abuse and neglect are, in the main, preventable. For example, the majority of cases of physical abuse involve relatively minor physical injuries; and most of these take place in what parents perceive to be *disciplinary encounters.* This allows us to set a realistic, but optimistic, agenda for child abuse interventions. Neil Frude (1991) is of the opinion that a high level of concern, both by the public and by professionals, with regard to the serious and dramatic injuries sustained by *relatively* few children, may prove to have the most welcome effect of increasing the general community support available for the very large number of troubled parents and their children. However, this is unlikely to happen if undue attention is drawn to those parents who systematically and sadistically torture their children. Frude is concerned that this distorted image of the abusing parent may lead to the withdrawal of any sympathy towards *all* parents involved in non-accidental injury and their stigmatization as 'monsters', 'inhuman', and 'a race apart'.

An understandable public concern should not blind us to the individuality of parents who abuse, and the normality of some of their predicaments. This is *not* to condone abuse, but to argue for keeping a sense of proportion. David Wolfe (1987) states that the conceptualization of physical abuse as impulsive, yet not necessarily malicious, forms a major basis for contending that abusive parents are not marked by major forms of psychopathology, but rather demonstrate critical defects within the boundless possibilities of what can go wrong for any parents in the course of rearing children. In some homes, violence is accepted as the 'norm'. One needs to consider potentially explosive situations such as a socially isolated, inexperienced, single parent, often living in poor accommodation and trying to manage a persistently difficult, crying baby. Fortunately, there is a great deal that can be done to help parents with these so-called disciplinary problems (see Part II).

Factors involved in family violence

Although a history of parental mishandling and abuse in the previous generation may play a part in a particular case of maltreatment, this is of limited relevance to the practitioner. In the 'here and now', which is the overriding concern of social and health workers, it is sometimes the child's, sometimes the parent's behaviour (and it frequently takes an aggressive form) that triggers an *incident* which, in turn, leads to an aggressive counter-attack by other members of the family. Certainly, it has been found that abused children harass their peers and parents far more frequently than non-abused children.

The picture which emerges from a plethora of studies of the different forms of aggression expressed between family members, is that family violence is a many-sided phenomenon, caused and maintained by a wide range of mechanisms.

Research literature reveals that certain characteristics are common to those who abuse. They tend to have low self-esteem; a sense of personal incompetence (low self-efficacy); a sense of being un-supported and helpless. Other features include social isolation which, perhaps, is not surprising given their tendency to be aggressive, to show a lack of warmth and empathy, and to suffer from depression.

Among the characteristics which contribute to their predisposition to violence are poor impulse/self-control; misperceptions of the victim; hostile feelings; the experience of marital difficulties; and the likeli-hood of having been victims themselves of abuse in childhood. Both sexes are implicated in family violence. Browne (1988) has identified a list of screening characteristics for child abuse:

Table 3.2 Relative importance of screening characteristics for child abuse (as deter-mined by step-wise discriminant function analysis). (Adapted from Browne, K.D., 1988)

	Abusing families (n = 62) %	Non-abusing families (n = 124) %
1. parent indifferent, intolerant or over-anxious towards child	83.9	21.8
2. history of family violence	51.6	5.6
3. socio-economic problems such as unemployment	85.5	34.7
4. infant premature, low birth weight	24.2	3.2
5. parent abused or neglected as a child	43.5	6.5
6. step-parent or cohabitee present	35.5	4.8
7. single or separated parent	38.7	8.1
8. mother less than 21 years old at the time of birth	40.3	23.4
9. history of mental illness, drug or alcohol addiction	61.3	21.8
10. infant separated from mother for greater than 24 hours post delivery	17.7	5.6
11. infant mentally or physically handicapped	1.6	0.8
12. less than 18 months between birth of children	22.6	15.3
13. infant never breast fed	46.8	40.3

It is important to remember that a correlation does not necessarily imply causation. Correlation is sometimes found between criminality, alcoholism, drug abuse and low intelligence and the various forms of family violence. Obviously, there are many people who drink heavily or have criminal records but never abuse children, wives or grandparents. Causation is a difficult concept; some factors may set the stage (predispose) a person toward abusive behaviours (for example, the childhood experience of being abused oneself), while others trigger or precipitate particular incidents of assault. Many causal agents ('multifactorial causation') operate in cases of family violence, as in so many other areas of family dysfunction.

These factors illustrate why no one theory provides a complete rationale (and certainly not an all-embracing, integrated explanation) for the diversity of dysfunctional attitudes and dangerous actions that constitute the far from homogenous phenomenon called family violence.

Child Abuse

The current definitions of child abuse recommended as criteria for registration throughout England and Wales by the Departments of Health and Social Security (1986) are:

❑ *Physical abuse:* Physical injury to a child. This might be due to excessive corporal punishment. It also includes deliberate poisoning, where there is definite knowledge, or a reasonable suspicion, that the injury was inflicted, or knowingly not prevented.

❑ *Neglect:* The persistent or severe neglect of a child (for example, exposure to dangers such as cold and starvation) which results in serious impairment of the child's health or development, including non-organic failure to thrive.

❑ *Sexual abuse:* The involvement of dependent, developmentally immature children and adolescents in sexual activities they do not truly comprehend, to which they are unable to give informed consent, or which violate social taboos concerning family roles (see page 47).

❑ *Emotional abuse:* The severe adverse effect on the behaviour and emotional development of a child caused by persistent or severe emotional ill-treatment or rejection. As all abuse involves some emotional ill-treatment, this category is used where it is the main or sole form of abuse.

The Children Act provides a framework for the care and protection of children. It introduced new orders for use when children are at risk of significant harm. As discussed in Chapter 1, harm is defined as ill-treatment or the impairment of health or development [s.31(9)]. Ill-treatment includes sexual abuse and forms of ill-treatment which are not physical. Local authorities in England record each child on their Protection Register, in one of the categories presented above, choosing the one which provides the most accurate picture of the situation. Overall 21,200 girls and 19,500 boys in England (theorists believe that a lot go undetected) were considered to require protection from abuse in 1989.

Abusive parents

Parental emotions and responses to stress
A state of heightened arousal in stressful situations is common to many child abusers. It is suggested that an inability to cope well with stress and emotional arousal plays a significant role in incidents of child abuse and neglect. Parents who abuse their children score high on measures of stress, such as the 'Family Stress Checklist' and the 'Parenting Stress Index' (PSI). The PSI is a screening instrument that provides scores related to the parent's sense of attachment, competence, social isolation, relationship with spouse and mental and physical health. In addition to an assessment of life stress events, it also provides scores relating to the child's demands, mood, activity, adaptability and acceptability, as perceived by the parent.

Frodi and Lamb (1980) showed videotaped scenes of crying and smiling infants to abusive parents and matched controls. It was found that abusers show greater discomfort, irritation and emotional arousal in response to infant cries and smiles. Parents who abuse also showed greater physiological arousal, such as increased blood pressure and heart rate and reported more annoyance, indifference and less sympathy to both the crying and smiling infants.

Knowledge and attitudes to child rearing
Research comparing abusing and non-abusing families reveals markedly different attitudes when it comes to child development. Child abusers have unrealistic and distorted expectations about their children's abilities. They tend to entertain much higher expectations of their children and this influences discipline and punishment. For example, there are unrealistic beliefs such as notions that babies should be able to sit alone at 12 weeks and take their first steps at 40 weeks. More importantly, they may expect their infants to be able to recognize wrong-doing at 52 weeks. A significant proportion of sexual and physical abusive incidents involve senseless attempts by parents to force a child to behave in a manner that is beyond the child's developmental limitations.

Parental perceptions of child behaviour
Parents who abuse tend to have more negative conceptions of their children's behaviour than non-abusing parents; they perceive their children to be more irritable and demanding. This may be related to the fact that abused children are more likely to have health problems,

eating or sleeping disturbances, but it may also be a direct result of the unrealistic expectations often reported for abusing parents.

Parent–child interactions

Observational studies provide evidence that interactive patterns within abusing and non-abusing families differ markedly. Abusive parents are significantly more harsh to their children on a day-to-day basis and are less appropriate in their choice of disciplinary methods as compared with non-abusive parents. Abusing parents show less interactive behaviour, both in terms of sensitivity and responsiveness to their children. They are described as being aversive, negative and controlling. Evidence shows that abused and neglected infants demonstrate an insecure pattern of attachment toward their mother.

It is clearly important to remember the *individual differences* in children and the contexts within which they experience life and its vicissitudes. Certainly the consequences of maltreatment are *not* the same for all children. Nevertheless, findings suggest there are more risks of behaviour problems in children who are both abused and neglected compared with contrast non-abusive groups. Abusing and neglectful parents, together with their children, suffer from pervasive confusion and ambivalence in their relations with each other.

Sibling Abuse

Adult violence to women and children is often thought of as the most common and most problematic aspect of violence in the home. Yet, they are far from being the only, or most common, forms of family violence. For example, violence between siblings is so frequent that the public rarely perceives these events as family violence.

There is cause for concern, especially with regard to the abuse by bullying of a growing number of victims in the home and classroom. Sibling abuse involves an aggressive or violent act directed at one sibling by another; it is the most common form of family violence. The greater the difference in age between siblings, the more likely is the assault and its consequences to approximate the abuse that occurs between adult and child. Sibling abuse is often found in families where there is physical, sexual and emotional abuse.

A large proportion of physical aggression in families consists of occasional, uncontrolled, one-off responses to provocation or frustration, administered in the heat of the moment. This is especially true of what are perceived to be disciplinary encounters or of hostile manifestations of sibling rivalry. Bullying, with its intention to *hurt* the victim, tends to be a systematically repetitive activity, involving physical and/or psychological (often verbal) harm, instigated by one or more persons against another person — one who lacks the power, strength or will to resist. Merciless taunting and teasing may be as damaging over the longer term as physical assaults.

Abuse of Parents

Can we speak of 'parent abuse' or are we stretching the concept of abuse to such ludicrous limits that we debase its already ambiguous meaning? The large majority of parent victims are so ashamed by their victimization that they are reluctant to discuss anything but the most severe incidents; and, when they do report, they, like adolescent victims, are often blamed for being hit. The very notion of children controlling, indeed assaulting, their parents is so alien to our ideas about the power relationships between parents and their offspring that it is difficult to believe that such a reversal, and one so subversive, can actually occur.

The prevalence of child-to-parent violence is difficult enough to assess; the loss of parental authority, impossible. Professionals know of many examples of small children hurting their parents by kicking their shins, pulling their hair and pinching them. But is this abuse? Matters of definition remain unresolved, and this makes a critical review of the evidence difficult. But there is no mistaking the gravity of some acts of aggression.

The majority of offspring who attack a parent are between the ages of 13 and 24, although studies also report children as young as ten years old inflicting injury on their parents. Researchers agree that sons are slightly more likely to be violent or abusive than daughters. Sons' rates of severe violence against a parent increase with age, while the rates for daughters usually decline with age.

Clinical observations of children and adolescents who exert continuing and *extreme* intimidation (including physical abuse) on parents and siblings, indicate that these families usually have some disturbance in their authority structure. Abusing children may develop a grandiose sense of self, feel omnipotent, and expect everyone to respond to them accordingly. The outcome is a series of explosive responses to situations for which no prior family rules exist.

As children approach adolescence and grow stronger, more assertive and rebellious, what were 'merely' difficult situations for parents can become menacing, in some cases, dangerous. In some, fortunately relatively rare cases, the violence is so unrestrained that it results in very serious injury or even the murder of the parent (parricide). When this happens, it is usually an end result of the most dysfunctional relationships within extremely disturbed families. Mothers are most likely to be victims of their children's violence, but fathers are more likely to be victims of older male children.

Sexual Abuse

David Finkelhor (1986) is often quoted for his estimate that 19 per cent of all females and nine per cent of all males have been sexually abused at some time in their lives. Reports have, in fact, ranged from six per cent to 62 per cent for females, and three per cent to 31 per cent for males. Reliable incidence data are simply not available.

Perpetrators are mainly men, but there is an increasing awareness of the role of women (and, indeed, siblings) as sexual abusers; the majority of perpetrators are friends and relatives of the children they victimize. Victims are usually female, although involvement of boys may be under-reported. Almost 40 per cent of children are initially abused prior to age ten, though abuse may continue beyond this age. There are no significant differences in social class with regard to prevalence rates; no ethnic differences appear to be significant; and although physical force is evident in only a minority of cases, threats and coercion are almost universal.

The term sexual abuse includes the following acts: rape; sexual intercourse; buggery (anal penetration); masturbation; digital (finger) penetration; fondling; exhibitionism or flashing; involvement in pornographic activity.

Enquiry into sexual abuse

The following categories of information have been recommended by MacFarlene and Krebs (1986) as areas of enquiry during an interview, to help establish a context for the abuse and to aid in the child's recounting of essential details:

▶ *Who* abused the child? Were others present? Where were significant others when the abuse occurred? Is the child aware of any sexual activities between the abuser and other children? Has the child been abused by anyone else?
▶ *What* happened? (Ask for specific details of the abuse; the interviewer needs to cover all areas of possible abusive activities.)
▶ *Where* did this occur? (For each incident, the interviewer should ask where the abuse occurred.)
▶ *When* did this occur? How often did this occur? (Here children need to be oriented and the interviewer should refer to significant events in time, for example, 'What grade were you in?'; 'Was it hot or cold out?'. Often it is helpful to begin with the first abusive event which may be less traumatizing and then move on to more recent events.)
▶ *How* did the abuser engage the child? Was the child threatened, or asked to keep the abuse a secret? Did the child ever try to tell someone what happened? What made the child decide to tell now? How does the child feel about what happened? What was

the child's experience of the events? What are the child's present or future worries about disclosing the abuse?

Criteria for establishing sexual abuse
It is not within the scope of this book to deal fully with this disturbing and complex issue (see Further Reading). However, it is as well to be alert to possible warning 'signs'. Do seek experienced and expert help as many of these signs in children and adolescents are open to alternative explanations, and are thus vulnerable to misinterpretation as sexual abuse.

Physical warning signs of possible child sexual abuse might be:
- sleeplessness, nightmares and fear of the dark
- bruises, scratches, bite marks
- depression, suicide attempts
- anorexia nervosa
- eating disorders or change in eating habits
- difficulty in walking or sitting
- pregnancy – particularly with reluctance to name the father
- recurring urinary tract problems
- vaginal infections or genital/anal damage
- veneral disease
- bed-wetting
- vague pains and aches
- itching or soreness.

Behavioural warning signs of possible child sexual abuse are:
- lack of trust in adults
- fear of a particular individual
- withdrawal and introversion
- running away from home
- girl takes over the mothering role
- sudden school problems, truanting and falling standards
- low self-esteem and low expectations of others
- stealing
- drug, alcohol or solvent abuse
- display of sexual knowledge beyond the child's years
- sexual drawing
- prostitution
- vulnerability to sexual and emotional exploitation
- revulsion towards sex
- fears of school medical examinations.

Marsha Heiman (1992), in a paper reviewing the literature on judging the validity of sexual abuse allegations, begins with a cautionary tale, or rather, case: the Washington DC 'Morgan' legal dispute. Two experts in the field of abuse lined up on opposite sides to give opinions about the truthfulness of a child's allegations (Svegedy-Maszak, 1989). Both were completely convinced of their own judgement, but neither side was capable of appealing to a scientific body of empirical research which definitively differentiated *bona fide* abuse cases from those which are false.

The fact is that there is no specific test to verify sexual abuse. Validation of child sexual abuse depends almost completely upon investigation by interview of the child (see Chapter 1). It has been claimed that there are crucial indicators or 'credibility enhancers'. Heiman states that the most frequently quoted indicators include the following:

▷ a detailed description of events, with explicit sexual information that is developmentally advanced, containing contextual, distinguishing and affective details;
▷ a verbal description which elaborates a progression of activities over time and may include elements of secrecy, bribery, pressure and/or coercion; consistency in description of major details;
▷ sexual themes, re-enactments and descriptions of sexual events portrayed across modalities (play, drawings, dolls);
▷ changes in functioning with symptoms indicative of stress and/or sexual behaviours inappropriate for age;
▷ events told from a child's perspective;
▷ congruence between affect and description of events;
▷ delayed disclosure, which may be accompanied by retractions;
▷ differentiation of fact from fantasy;
▷ other supporting evidence.

Criticisms have been levelled at the use of any checklist approach, since no single sign is predictive of abuse. Heiman recommends the use of multiple criteria, based on several sources of information:

☐ the history of symptoms (Is there a change in the child's behaviour?);
☐ verbal report (Did the child specifically state he/she was abused?);
☐ phenomenological experience (Does the child describe a set of experiences consistent with those reported by other victims?);
☐ presentational style (Does the child's emotions correspond to his/her verbalizations?);
☐ corroborating evidence (Are there additional sources of information which confirm the child's statements?).

As the practitioner examines each of these sources of information, decisions can be made about the validity of the stated allegations. In some cases, many validating criteria may be present, while in other cases only certain points will be confirmed. It is important, however, to assess criteria within each information domain. More certainty exists and a stronger case can be made for substantiating abuse when multiple criteria are present. Even when definitive conclusions cannot be reached, the decision-making process can be clarified so that treatment recommendations can be provided.

The full legal, moral, technical and social ramifications of these problems go far beyond the scope of this book. What is critical to remember is that children may be able to cope with one-off or short-duration trauma *if* the aftermath is sensitively dealt with by adults (parents and/or the authorities). What is more damaging in the shorter and longer term is the abusive situation that goes on and on (see Chapter 10). As so many emotional, physical and sexual incidents of an abusive kind occur in the child's home, this is precisely what tends to happen.

Psychological measurement

How useful are psychological techniques as a means of detecting sexual abuse and/or the trauma associated with it? Gloria Babiker, in a doctoral study (1992) carried out at the University of Bristol, set out to answer this question comparing three matched groups of children (sexually abused, physically abused and non-abused) in terms of their responses to human figure drawing (HFD), a specially designed word association task (WA) and, in the case of the younger children, anatomical doll play (ACD). All 49 children were living away from home. The findings on univariate analyses were that, while the utility of the WA as a measure received minimal support, none of the tests discriminated adequately between sexually abused children and other children. However, multivariate analysis suggested that combinations of all three measures were significant predictors of correct classification by abuse groups. The anatomical doll test generated the fewest false negative 'judgements', that is to say, judgements that there was no abuse when, in fact, there was a record of abuse. The researcher is cautious about the readiness of these particular measures for routine clinical use; further validational studies are required. Nevertheless, they may well be useful adjuncts to the traditional interview.

Babiker observes that sexual abuse takes place within a socio-cultural context, and diagnostic decisions are greatly influenced by the estimated cost of a false diagnosis. As she puts it:

This cost is determined to a large extent by decisions about the trade-off between the two types of error: the risk of misclassifying children who are being abused and possibly subjecting them to further trauma, versus *the risk of misclassifying children who are not being abused and possibly subjecting them and their family unnecessarily to the stress of intervention* (p. 243).

There was a fairly high trend to false positives in Babiker's tables, that is, the issue of 'diagnosing' the existence of sexual abuse that is not occurring. This is a problem which besets and worries all clinicians and social workers, and a reminder of the need to be as unintrusive as possible while being rigorous in one's investigations – a difficult balance to achieve.

Prevention of sexual abuse

When it comes to prevention, David Finkelhor notes that most sexual child abuse is perpetrated by men. In his opinion, this is, in part, an inevitable consequence of the way men are socialized. To illustrate this, he makes three points:

- Men are raised to channel emotional fulfilment through sex.
- For men, an attractive female is typically one who is smaller, younger and less powerful than they are. Children are at the end of this gradient, which is continually promoted by advertising.
- When a man does not participate in nurturing, he is more likely to be unaware of the pain his sexual advances are causing the child.

Sexual abuse of children will diminish, in his opinion, when men become more involved in taking care of children; when they are able to get emotional gratification outside of sex; and when versions of female beauty change.

The issues of power and control are also gender-related and have a crucial role in sexual abuse. I return to this theme in Chapter 10.

Professional reactions to sexual abuse work

When a case of suspected abuse or neglect comes to light, interviews with parents (and, of course, children) can be particularly difficult for professionals, and require a mixture of great delicacy and assurance. The feelings of the social worker may get in the way of these requirements. Jones *et al.* (1987), in a guide to the interview, list the following common reactions that can beset all professionals:

❑ *Denial* that anything is wrong, often presented as 'all children in that area have those sort of bruises – if we react to this case we shall have all the children on the estate in care' or, 'I have known these people for years and they are really very nice – I don't know what happened but I'm sure they couldn't do anything like that'. Such comments are often valid but do not always fit the facts.

❑ *Anger* with the family for having let the worker down ('I gave them all that time and helped them in so many ways yet still they go and do this – well that's all they're getting from me'), or with a colleague for not having done more.

❑ *Guilt* that more should have been done to help before the incident, or that the worker should have been more skilful or perceptive – 'It's all my fault'.

❏ *Fear* of personal and professional criticism for not having prevented what has happened and of possible damage to future career prospects (often associated with guilt); of getting caught up in procedures over which nobody has control and which may swamp family and worker.

❏ *Despair* that all seems so bleak with nothing apparently possible by way of help; occasionally justified, but such feelings can defeat systematic appraisal of alternatives.

❏ *Horror* that such serious and possibly permanent injuries can be inflicted on a child, freezing consideration of future action.

❏ *Jealousy* of professional colleagues now more intimately involved with a family known for a long time; this may be associated with resentment.

❏ *Resentment* that somebody else is doing the investigation and formulating an assessment, possibly disturbing a carefully nurtured, long-term relationship in the process.

❏ *Omnipotence* – the belief that 'I know best', 'I have the best relationship with the family', or 'I alone know how to deal with this – leave it all to me'. In practice, a multidisciplinary approach is essential, even if one person has most contact with the family.

The authors advise workers to listen more than talk, and to avoid selective gathering of information. Workers need to keep calm and alert and should not confront; it is vital to maintain a neutral, objective attitude. The authors add that it is important to remember that this 'neutral' approach must never imply acceptance of ill-treatment of a child, nor condone such behaviour. After all, it is quite possible to convey empathy and understanding of behaviour which is unacceptable, indeed even illegal, but the worker must never abandon his or her objectivity and must make it explicit and clear. It is emphasized by experienced practitioners that, once suspicions are raised, the child must be interviewed alone. The main reason that children may be reluctant to reveal sexual abuse is thought to be because they so often have tried to tell someone, but were not believed. Work with sexually abused children is discussed in Chapter 10. (See Appendix III for a description of care and supervision orders.)

FURTHER READING

Araji, S. and Finkelhor, D. (1986) Abusers: A review of research. In D. Finkelhor (Ed.) *A Sourcebook on Child Sexual Abuse.* Beverley Hills, C.A.: Sage. [Valuable information about the characteristics of abusers.]

Behavioral Sciences and the Law (1991) Special edition on child abuse, Vol. 9, No. 9, Winter. [Articles on assessment, excuses of molesters, children's secrets, Munchausen Syndrome by Proxy, etc.]

Browne, K., Davies, C. and Stratton, P. (1988) *Early Prediction and Prevention of Child Abuse.* Chichester: John Wiley. [Chapters on various themes such as prevalence, vulnerability, screening, prevention, intervention, family systems, failure-to-thrive.]

Fitzpatrick, C. and Fitzgerald, E. (1991) Sibling sexual abuse: Family characteristics. *Newsletter of the Association for Child Psychology and Psychiatry,* 13, No. 6, 10–13.

Jones, D. and McQuiston, M. (1988) *Interviewing the Sexually Abused Child.* London: Gaskell Psychiatry Series, The Royal College of Psychiatrists. [A valuable guide to the difficult and delicate task of interviewing a sexually abused child.]

Maan, C. (1991) Assessment of sexually abused children with anatomically detailed dolls: A critical review. *Behavioural Sciences and the Law,* 9, 43–45.

4 Normal development

It is important to be familiar with child development. Without this knowledge, you will not be able to assess the 'normality' of a child's behaviour and, of course, the appropriateness of the parent's care. The essence of life is development – hopefully, a forward momentum toward greater maturity and fulfilment – and this presupposes transition and change. These transitional (dynamic) features of life apply not only to individuals, but also to the families within which they reside. Life is all about change – expected and unexpected, welcome and dreaded. A feature of much problem behaviour in childhood (and, indeed, adolescence) is its transitoriness. So mercurial are some of the changes of behaviour in response to the rapid growth and the successive challenges of life, that it is difficult to pinpoint the beginning of serious problems.

Each individual begins a journey through life with a relatively unique and enduring set of psychological tendencies and reveals them in the course of his or her transactions with various social environments such as home, school and playground. It is assumed that inherited biological influences interact with environmental influences as children grow up, with the consequence that they gradually develop characteristic patterns of behaviour – the outward and visible signs of inner moral values, traits, habits, cognitive structures and needs. These patterns become progressively resistant, but certainly not impervious, to change with maturity. It has been said of personality that in some ways we are like all other persons, like some other persons, and like no other person. Each of us is, in many respects, unique.

A normal set of genes (the basic chemical units of heredity) and an appropriate, encouraging environment are both needed for satisfactory personality development and the acquisition of flexible and effective (adaptive) behaviour for dealing with life. (The influence of abnormal genes and disability is summarized on page 89.) Environmental factors can set limits on, or enhance, the individual's achievement of all his or her genetic potential. A youngster well-endowed with intellectual potential, for example, may well be cognitively 'stunted' if starved of stimulation and the opportunity to learn – an issue to be aware of in an assessment of a grossly unstimulating home.

According to Erikson (1965), children's psychosocial needs can be related to developmental tasks. A developmental task arises at a certain period in the life of an individual, successful achievement of which leads to happiness and success with later tasks, while failure leads to unhappiness in the individual, disapproval by society, and difficulty with other tasks. The tasks might be ones such as learning to talk or to control elimination; or they may involve the development of self-control over aggressive and sexual inclinations, acquiring moral attitudes and social skills, adjusting to school life and mastering academic competencies or becoming self-directed and self-confident.

Let us examine what can only be a bird's eye view of the main stages of development, each of which may be the source of difficulties for the child, and by association, the parents. The logical place to begin is with infancy.

Infancy

So much happens to the infant, his or her appearance and skills are so dramatically transformed in the transition from a somewhat amorphous neonate to a distinct personality of a year-and-a-half, that it seems naïve to treat infancy as a unified period. The justification for doing so is the extent of the dependency of human infants during this time, and the implications this has for caregivers in terms of their ability to enhance development. The converse, of course, is the power to disrupt development.

Babies are more competent that was once realized, given the restrictions of the research methodology of earlier times. Normal infants are born with all sensory systems functioning; they are capable at birth of engaging in reciprocating relationships with other persons. Very young babies exhibit a need to be competent, to deal effectively with their own environment. Psychologists consider this need to be related to such motives as mastery, curiosity and achievement. The psychologist, Martin Seligman (1975), suggests that infants begin a 'dance with their environment' that will last throughout childhood. He believes that it is the outcome of this dance that determines their helplessness or mastery. When they make some response, it can either produce a change in the environment or be independent of what changes occur. At some primitive level, infants calculate the correlation between response and outcome. If the correlation is zero, helplessness develops. If the correlation is highly positive or highly negative, this means the response is working and infants learn either to perform that response more frequently or to refrain from performing it, depending on whether the correlated outcome is good or bad.

The most important aspect of infant development in the first months is the capacity for learning. The rate of acquisition of a behavioural repertoire is stunning. Parents, the source of much of the infant's experience, are often concerned about the competency and rates of development of their offspring. Are they normal, slow or advanced? *Figure 4.1* provides a guide to some of the milestones which are of interest to parents.

It is generally agreed that the infant's first human relationships form the foundation stones of his or her developing personality. Healthy adjustment depends upon the adequate satisfaction of the infant's needs for interactions such as nurturant care, warm and affectionate communication, attention, play and other stimulation which flow from the feeling and attitude of love. In addition, parents have the opportunity to influence the child's behaviour in ways that can contribute toward the development of competence. Particular kinds of activity (for example, play and storytime) lend themselves well to the provision of creative, stimulating interactions between parents and children. Children who develop a relatively high degree of competence generally have mothers who tend to demonstrate and explain things at the child's instigation rather than their own. Help and guidance are thus orientated around the child's interests and, at times, determined by the child himself or herself. Children of lower developmental competence, on the other hand, experience more didactic handling from their mothers, whose respect for the child's own interests is more limited and discouraging.

Security and insecurity in infants

From the time of birth, infants can signal information about their needs. Where the parent (say mother) perceives the signals accurately and responds appropriately, the mother–infant relationship is said to be characterized by 'synchrony' which facilitates the baby's development and is a source of satisfaction to the mother. It is postulated that those children whose parents respond to their signals and communications promptly and appropriately throughout infancy develop confidence in their parents' availability and will have the security to use them as a base from which to explore their environment. Some parents may be too immature or preoccupied by personal problems to do this. Insecure children tend to be anxious about their parents' availability and show little confidence in their reactions to the world. Securely and insecurely attached one-year-old infants have been investigated in laboratory situations (Ainsworth *et al.*, 1978). Mary Ainsworth emphasizes that multiple criteria are necessary in measuring infant-to-parent attachment. However the so-called 'strange situation' is a particularly useful indicator.

Episode 1: the mother and baby are first introduced to the experimental room.
Episode 2: the baby explores the room with the mother present.

Most infants, by the approximate age (or between the ages) on the pointer:

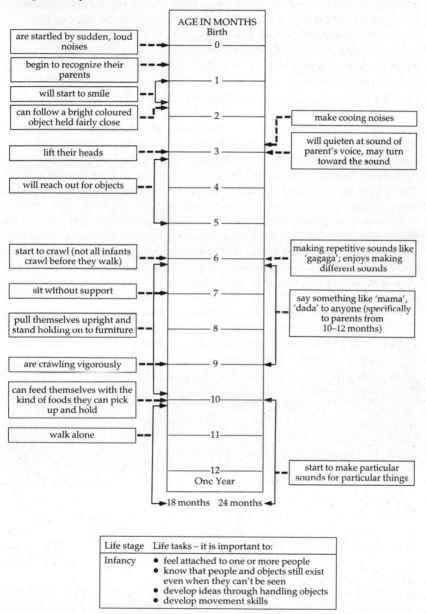

Figure 4.1 Child development and life tasks (birth to one year plus)

Episode 3: the stranger enters, talks to the mother, and then approaches the baby.
Episode 4: the baby and stranger are left alone in the room together.
Episode 5: the mother returns and the stranger leaves, so that the baby is reunited with the mother.
Episode 6: the baby is left alone in the room.
Episode 7: the stranger enters the room and the baby is alone with the stranger.
Episode 8: the mother again returns and the stranger leaves.

Ainsworth's 'strange situation' exposes a child to three potentially upsetting experiences: separation from the caregiver, contact with a stranger, and unfamiliar surroundings. The episodes are arranged so that the effect of these experiences may be observed separately, and also together, since during episodes 4 and 7, all occur simultaneously. The sequence of episodes in the procedure is fixed. The child's reactions to separation and the presence of a stranger are viewed in the context of the child's willingness to explore the unfamiliar environment. That is, it is possible to determine how seriously the cumulating stress experiences affect a child's natural tendency to explore and play with the toys and other objects in the strange situation.

The largest group of infants (almost 70 per cent of Ainsworth's sample) were classified as Group B and had a securely attached pattern of behaviour. These infants actively explored the new environment when in the presence of their mothers, and they showed no distress at the novelty of the situation. Upon reunion with their mothers after separation, the infants greeted them with affection and delight. They did not necessarily cry when the mother first left the room. Rather, they often seemed to realize that the mother would still be accessible to them if they needed her. In general, these infants used their mother as a secure base from which to explore the room and interact with the stranger. Even when they become distressed after the mother left (which generally occurred after the second separation, during episode 6), Group B children were able to recover quickly by actively seeking contact with her on reunion and maintaining this contact for some time. These babies were relatively easy to comfort, even by the end of the experiment when they were most upset, and they quickly returned to exploration of the room after they were comforted.

Group C children were quite distressed upon each separation from the mother, and were quite difficult to comfort upon reunion. In fact, these children resisted comfort and contact from their mothers, even though (unlike the Group A children) they did show considerable separation anxiety. Their behaviour showed an angry ambivalence, in the sense that they objected to being left alone, but they refused to be consoled when rejoined with their mothers. On the one hand, they were overly preoccupied with the mother and, on the other, they could not be consoled by her. They seemed to experience a lack of confidence in other people (including the caregiver), as well as in new situations. These children were the ones least likely to play with the toys in the room or to interact with the stranger.

Group A children – at 20 per cent, a sizeable minority of Ainsworth's sample – actually avoided their mothers during the reunion episodes. It was during the reunions that these children showed greatest negative feeling in the sense of an absence of proximity-seeking toward their mothers. The avoidant babies not only did not seek contact with their mother during reunion, but sometimes looked away from her when she approached. This is a phenomenon called gaze aversion and is a common response to an approaching stranger, but hardly to a returning mother. The avoidant infants were also not particularly upset upon initial separation from their mothers. They did become distressed after being left alone for a while, but were comforted as easily by the stranger as by the mother. Even their play with toys often showed an emotionless, superficial and rigid quality.

Erik Erikson (1965) theorizes that, during the early months and years of life, a baby learns whether the world is a good and satisfying place to live in or a source of pain, misery, frustration and uncertainty. Because human infants are so totally dependent for so long, they need to know that they can depend on the outside world. If their needs are met by the significant people in their lives, they are thought to develop a 'basic trust' in the world and evolve a nucleus of self-trust which is indispensable to later development. Trust might be said to be demonstrated in the ease with which babies feed, in the depth of their sleep, and in the relaxation of their bowels. Later on, it is shown when infants will let their mother out of their sight without undue anxiety or rage. Babies who smile easily are also thought to demonstrate trust. What hinders the development of a perception of a predictable and trustworthy world in which children can seek their independence, are social and physical conditions which interfere with their sense of personal adequacy and/or their acquisition of skills.

Jay Belsky argues (Belsky and Nezworski, 1988) that there has been a 'virtual revolution' in our understanding of early development, and, in particular, a recognition that certain attributes that indicate differences between individuals, measured within the first year of life, are capable of anticipating or predicting later developments in the child. For example, the measurement of the child's sense of security in its relationship to its mother at the end of the first year of life, has been found to predict the infant's likely competence when it is old enough to go to school.

There is also a clear link between early insecure attachment and later development of behaviour problems, bringing attachment research into the domain of the clinic. It is hypothesized that many conduct problems are strategies for gaining the attention or proximity of caregivers who are unresponsive to the child's prosocial communications (Belsky and Nezworski, 1988). It is important to remember that early patterns of behaviour do not necessarily persist and they are not necessarily indicators of a serious rift in the relationship between parent and child. However, they are worthy of following up in an assessment.

The basic assumption is not that the relationship between parent/s and baby inevitably or comprehensively influences later development, but rather that the infant's initial (and foundational) experience of this relationship anticipates much that is of significance in later social development. This occurs because the experience affects the infant's expectations and ideas about cause and effect (what psychologists call 'attributions') with regard to other relationships, and also has a significant impact on the infant's feelings about him or herself.

The Toddler

Toddlerhood – a period of intense exploration and discovery for the child – is a fascinating, tiring and sometimes difficult time for parents. Just look at *Figure 4.2* to see some of the momentous developmental events that are taking place.

Language development

Parent–child relationships are vital in the development of language and a host of other skills. We begin with language as it is foundational to *other* aspects of social training and is one of the crucial developmental or life tasks of toddlerhood. Babies vocalize from birth. Although we do not usually describe their early crying as language, it is certainly a vital form of communication. The earliest evidence of language is usually taken to be the production of a child's first recognizable word. 'Normal' children may produce their first word at any age between seven months and two years or even later; but even before the first word is uttered, much development will have occurred which is relevant to language. The child will have established a high degree of communicative skill, with the use of gesture and facial expression, and will be having 'conversations' with caregivers. These early conversations consist of talking on the adult's part, and vocalizations, movements, smiles and gestures on the part of the child.

Language, virtually from its beginning, is lawfully patterned. Children don't just learn words and sentences; they learn rules. At all

Most children, by the
approximate age (or between
the ages) on the pointer:

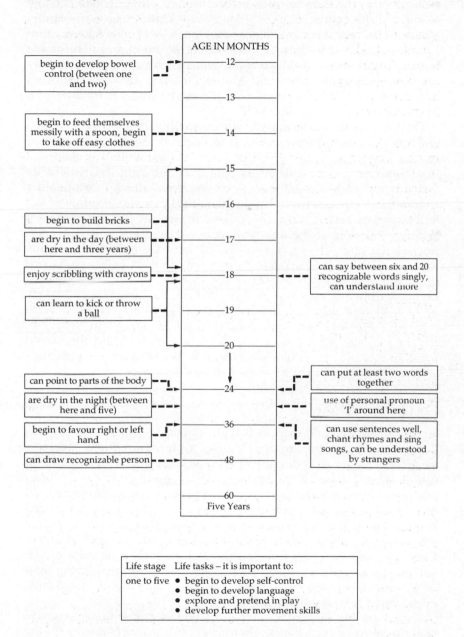

Figure 4.2 Child development and life tasks (one to five years)

stages of language development, understanding exceeds, and precedes, production. Children can understand certain words and respond appropriately to them before they use them spontaneously in speech; this is true also for grammatical features of many kinds, and it is also true for phonological development (the development of speech sounds). Children can appreciate phonological distinctions before putting those distinctions into practice, for example, they may say 'tum' instead of 'come'. Of course, language development does not manifest itself in isolation; it depends on, and largely parallels, cognitive and social development.

With regard to intellectual development and the manner in which children think about their world, Jean Piaget is the seminal influence to this day. According to Piaget (1953), the child's intellectual development, conceptualized as stages of thinking, is marked by increasingly sophisticated mental actions ('operations') for adapting to his or her environment. Language is the supreme example of the human's potential for mastering the environment. The ability to form and use symbols is the key feature of what Piaget calls the 'pre-operational stage' (two to seven years). Symbols (or 'internal mental representations') are organized into different symbol systems, which are developed in every aspect of life, for example, in the areas of number, drawing, music, dance, modelling. Language, again, is one of the most obvious and immediately useful symbol systems. Current research stresses that the proper unit of study in language development is not so much the child as the child and the parent together. What the child says cannot be studied meaningfully without consideration of what the parent says as well.

Coercive behaviour

Another task of childhood is the development of impulse control. Before the age of two, children largely fail to differentiate what *they* do, from what an *adult* does; in other words they do not comprehend causal agency. The development of the cognitive ability to differentiate between *self* and *other* leads to a gradual recognition of causal relationships and an increasing desire for influence over things and people. This increasing awareness of self-identity not uncommonly leads to a 'negativistic crisis' around the age of two (Patterson, 1982). Children who have previously accepted assistance in their efforts without fuss, insist on doing things themselves and displaying their own competence; they also resist parental request and commands, often with much sound and fury.

Two-year-olds display high rates of whining, crying, yelling and many other coercive actions. There is usually a steady decline in the frequency of such behaviours, from a high point shortly before the age of three, down to more moderate levels at the age of school entrance. By the age of four, there are substantial reductions in negative commands, destructiveness and attempts to lash out at others.

Of course, some children remain, or become, particularly unruly and defiant; they take their antagonism to an unbearable extreme. The perennial problem for the social worker assessing the seriousness of non-compliance, is the ubiquity of disobedience as a 'problem' of childhood. It is, in a sense, a 'normal' response to the 'rigours' of socialization; indeed, up to a point, disobedience – representing (as it does) the striving for independence – is undoubtedly adaptive and its complete absence would be a matter of concern. But what is that 'point' at which non-compliance is thought to be excessive, counter-productive and thus maladaptive? Forehand's and Atkeson's (1977) review of the scanty normative data that is available, indicates that compliance to parental commands for normal preschool samples ranges from approximately 60 to 80 per cent. *Frequency, intensity* and *duration* of the problem (for example, defiance) become the watchwords of assessment.

Not infrequently, the parent or teacher will take the line of least resistance and give in to the child's disobedience. This comes as a result of the child's coercive response (for example, a temper tantrum) to the parent's attempts to insist. Conceding to the child's non-compliance, gives the child positive reinforcement for his/her coercive actions and they are likely to recur again in similar circumstances. A child's oppositional behaviour is also often maintained by parental attention. Such attention can come in a variety of forms: getting 'wound up', verbal reprimands (scolding, nagging), pleading with the child, or simply trying to be caring and understanding by discussing the misdemeanour at too great a length. This is referred to by learning theorists as the 'positive reinforcer trap'.

The parent's pattern of capitulation is, in turn, reinforced by the termination of the victorious child's upsetting tantrum. This process of reciprocal reinforcement by the removal of aversive stimuli has been described as the 'negative reinforcer trap'. In most cases, oppositional behaviour is probably maintained by a combination of both positive and negative reinforcement. Where such patterns are frequent and intense and persist over time, there is a danger of negative, mutually coercive patterns of family life becoming ingrained.

In preschool children, we can expect some 15 per cent to have mild emotional and behavioural problems; seven per cent to have moderate to severe problems. Sixty per cent of three-year-olds identified as having mental health problems still have them at eight years of age – a good argument for early screening and intervention.

The impressionable age

It is commonly believed that the child's first five or so years of life constitute a 'critical' or 'sensitive' period, when they show a heightened susceptibility to the effects of their environment and are therefore vulnerable to adverse experiences and learning situations. The young have always been said to be more easily influenced, more impressionable, than their elders. In addition, these early effects are thought to be lasting. In the writings of Plato, the Bible and the Jesuits in the past, and, more recently, the psychoanalysts, there is a belief that 'character' is so set by about the age of six or seven, that whatever happens to a child thereafter is but a ripple on the surface.

What precisely are the facts, as opposed to the speculations, about the after-effects of early experience and learning? The psychologists, Alan and Ann Clarke (1976) reviewed the available evidence concerning early experience and its effects, and were able to identify certain consistencies in the research findings. They suggest that there is little reason to suppose that infants learn and remember more easily than adults. In fact, experiments suggest that infants and young children are strikingly inferior to adults in many dimensions of learning. The long-term effects of short, traumatic incidents seem to be negligible, both in animals and in young human beings, and the specific effects of an infant's experiences before the age of seven months appear to be of very short duration. Only when early learning is, by repetition, continually reinforced, do long-term effects appear.

This must be reassuring to parents who worry a great deal about 'mistakes' they have made in dealing with their child, or about severe emotional upsets the child has suffered. However, it is no reason to be complacent. Some trauma and disasters are so intense in their effects that a one-off experience is sufficient to produce what is called a 'post traumatic stress disorder' (see Yule, 1991). Whatever the intensity level, the important thing is to deal sensitively, knowledgeably and sensibly with trauma in order to prevent (potentially transitory) negative experiences being repeated to a point at which their ill-effects become chronic.

The School-Going Child

According to Erikson, the period of playschool and 'proper' school coincides with *psychological* developments which facilitate the requirements of the child's early education. The period from approximately four to five years is notable for the development of the child's sense of initiative; it is a period of vigorous reality testing, imitation of adult patterns of behaviour and imaginative play. Overly strict discipline, interference, over-protection and the like can disrupt or delay the successful achievement of these attributes, making for poor spontaneity and uncertain testing and appreciation of realities (see *Table 4.1*).

Acquiring a sense of duty and accomplishment is the next developmental task facing the child. This occurs between the ages of six and 11 years, when the child puts aside much of the fantasy and play life and undertakes 'real' tasks at school, and develops academic and social skills. Excessive demands, or competition and personal limitations which lead to persistent failure, can make a crisis of this important stage – resulting in feelings of inferiority and poor work habits.

What of cognitive development at this stage of life? As children, at about four years of age, emerge from what Piaget called 'pre-conceptual thinking', their ability to classify, order and quantify gradually develops. Their thinking is still 'intuitive', however, as they remain unaware of the principles which underlie these abilities. But they have the intellectual equipment necessary for classroom activity; and, by the age of five, the average child has a vocabulary of some 6,000 words and knowledge of hundreds of rules of grammar. During the next stage of 'concrete operations', these principles become more explicit, so children can explain their logical reasoning in a satisfactory manner. This transition from the pre-operational to concrete operational stage takes place at around the age of seven; it has been the subject of much research and educational discussion.

The opportunity to mix with a wide variety of people – the peer group and adults (teachers) who present different points of view – widens markedly the child's appreciation of social roles and expectations; the development of social awareness is profound during the years of attending school. As always, development occurs at various levels which are interrelated. Thus cognitive (intellectual) development goes hand in hand with social maturing.

Social cognition

Intellectual understanding forms the underpinning of social understanding; both underlie moral judgements. Socially skilled children typically show higher levels of social understanding than those who lack social skills. Some elements of social cognition are:

▷ *Empathy and role taking.* This is the ability to see things from the other person's point of view, that is, to empathize with them or to feel for them.
▷ *Self-control.* Low self-control is characterized by impulsive behaviour, the apparent absence of thought between impulse and action.
▷ *Social problem-solving.* This refers to the process of generating feasible courses of action, considering the various outcomes, and planning how to achieve the preferred outcome in a given social situation.

Table 4.1 Parental care checklist (school-age period)

Place a tick in the appropriate column.

Does the parent/caregiver:

	Always	Usually	Sometimes	Seldom	Never
1. Encourage the child's ideas?					
2. 'Listen' carefully so as to understand?					
3. Communicate clearly to the child?					
4. Respect his/her privacy?					
5. Set an example for the child?					
6. Provide guidance at appropriate times?					
7. Share (family news/appropriate decisions)?					
8. Respect the child's views?					
9. Acknowledge the child's efforts?					
10. Demonstrate emotional support (by comforting or encouraging)?					
11. Keep confidences?					
12. Make eye contact during conversation?					
13. Address the child by name?					
14. Remember the child's birthday?					
15. Talk to the child about family matters?					
16. Discuss (when appropriate) religion, politics, sex, education, death, etc.?					
17. Teach the child appropriate social skills?					
18. Accept the child's friends?					
19. Manage, resolve (fairly) any conflicts between children?					
20. Set reasonable limits and stick to them?					

Robert Selman (1980), author of *The Growth of Interpersonal Understanding*, is one of the most influential thinkers in this field. He devised a series of stories that describe relationships and dilemmas within relationships. Children hear, or read, these stories and are then asked to say what the characters in the story should do or would do. Based on their comments, Selman proposed five stages or levels in children's ability to adopt a social point of view or perspective (see *Table 4.2*). These levels of social understanding are loosely related to particular ages, but there is a good deal of individual variation in the time it takes a child to move through each level.

Moral awareness

Prior to the age of five, children certainly feel 'bad' when they have transgressed, but primarily because of fears of external parental punishment or disapproval. But, at about four or five years of age, the locus of anxiety or fear comes from within and children feel guilt when they have transgressed. This can be seen as the beginning of moral awareness. Moral awareness and behaviour have at least four components:

☐ *Resistance to temptation.* The 'braking' or inhibitory mechanism that works against committing misdemeanours even when the individual is not being observed.
☐ *Guilt.* The acute emotional discomfort which we all have experienced, both as child and adult. Guilt follows transgression and may lead to confession, reparation or self-blame.
☐ *Altruism.* This refers to various prosocial acts, often described as unselfishness, such as kindness, helpfulness, generosity, sympathy, empathy and service to others.
☐ *Moral belief and insight.* This covers all aspects of what people think and say about morality, including their willingness to blame others who do wrong.

Each of these components is complex, and related one to the other in a complex manner. Moral development refers to the processes by which children adopt principles that lead them to judge certain behaviours as 'right' and others as 'wrong'; and to the process by which children come to govern their own actions in terms of these principles. If people are to live together in society, they need to share certain assumptions of what is right and what is wrong.

Parents cannot always be on the spot to check their children's actions. Eventually their voices and other voices (for example, those of teachers, religious leaders and friends who exemplify or enunciate moral and social values) are internalized by the child so that the child has the choice of heeding his or her own voice from within – the voice of conscience. Many theorists draw a distinction between social

Table 4.2 Selman's five levels of social understanding (adapted from Selman, 1980)

Approximate age	Level of social understanding	Characteristics of child's social understanding
3–6	0	The child is capable of taking only an egocentric perspective. He or she may realize that other people experience things differently in a physical sense, but cannot yet appreciate that other people feel or think in a different manner from him or herself.
5–9	1	The child is now capable of taking a subjective differentiated perspective. He or she appreciates that other people feel and think differently and is aware that people may act differently from how they feel, but does not yet realize that other people also perceive the same things about him or her.
7–12	2	The child is now capable of adopting a self-reflective and reciprocal perspective. He or she appreciates that there is two-way traffic in social relationships/interactions – that each member of a pair knows the other may think differently (I know that you know that I know). Relationships are perceived as being truly reciprocal.
10–15	3	The child is capable of adopting a third-person and mutual perspective. At this stage (early formal operations) he or she is able to stand apart from a relationship (i.e outside it), and view it as if he or she were a third person. Relationships involve mutual coordinations, mutual satisfactions.
12–adult	4	The child is now capable of adopting an in-depth and societal-symbolic perspective. The young person understands that other people's actions are influenced by their upbringing, by their personalities, and by social forces. He or she is able to take these factors into account.

values (norms or conventions) and moral rules. The former may vary from culture to culture and from society to society; they are also subject to radical changes as the years pass by. Moral rules are seen to be timeless, universal and foundational, in the sense that they are concerned with basic principles of truth and justice.

When children, after many years of development, have internalized the rules and values, they are usually able to restrain themselves from doing wrong even when no one else will 'find out'. If they give way to temptation, they are likely to feel guilty afterwards. Not only can they be relied upon to keep the rules without constant supervision, but they will, in turn, teach the rules to their offspring. At the same time, they will endeavour to ensure that there are sanctions for people who break the rules.

People's consciences are not equally strong. Going back to those early commands and prohibitions which are the foundation stones of conscience, it is apparent that some toddlers obey them more readily and consistently than others; and some parents convey them more effectively and constructively than others.

Piaget believed that an ability to keep rules goes together with a mature understanding of those rules. The theorist, Lawrence Kohlberg, would be in wholehearted agreement, believing that the person who understands justice is more likely to practise it. Kohlberg (1976) devised a series of dilemmas in order to explore a child's or young person's reasoning about difficult moral issues, such as the value of human life or the reasons for doing 'right' things. He argues that moral development progresses through a number of levels, with different stages at each level. At the lower stages, moral reasoning is characterized by its concrete nature and egocentricity; at the higher stages, moral reasoning is guided by abstract notions such as 'justice' and 'rights' and is much more social in orientation. In the former ('preconventional' morality) the child judges what is wrong on the basis of what is punished. Obedience is respected for its own sake. The child obeys because adults have superior power. In the latter ('principled' morality) the young person develops, and is loyal to, his or her own chosen ethical principles.

A learning theory perspective

Learning theorists base their investigations of conscience development upon the assumption that there is nothing about moral learning to distinguish it qualitatively from other forms of learning. They consider that behaviours indicative of guilt such as confession, self-criticism and apology, are learned responses which have been found to be instrumental in reducing the anxiety that follows some transgression of the rules. Learning theory (as opposed to the broader perspective adopted by social learning theorists) does not account sufficiently for the fact that punishment and reward are mediated by human agents (for example, parents and teachers) and are not simply the impersonal consequences of behaviour. The individual's relationship to this agent is a crucial factor in moral development. For instance, the words of a mother, whose child wishes to emulate and please her, will carry much more force than those of a person for whom the child feels nothing or, worse, disrespect.

Encouraging social understanding and adaptive behaviour

Factors that facilitate the development of social understanding and adaptive behaviours include:

- strong ties of affection between parents and children;
- firm moral demands made by parents on their offspring;
- consistent use of sanctions (setting limits);
- techniques of punishment that are psychological rather than physical (such as methods that signify or threaten withdrawal of approval), provoking anxiety or guilt rather than acting out anger;
- an intensive use of reasoning and explanations (inductive methods);
- giving responsibility to the young person.

The balancing of these components is perhaps best illustrated in the philosophy of what, on the basis of her investigations, Diana Baumrind (1971) calls the 'authoritative' parent. The mother, for example, attempts to direct her child's activities in a rational manner, determined by the issues involved in particular disciplinary situations. She encourages verbal give-and-take and shares with the child the reasoning behind her policy. She values both the child's self-expression and his or her so-called 'instrumental attributes' (respect for authority, work and the like). She appreciates both independent self-will and disciplined conformity. Therefore, this kind of parent exerts firm control at points where she and the child diverge in viewpoint, but does not suppress him or her with restrictions. She recognizes her own special rights as an adult, but also the child's individual interests and special ways. All in all, she enhances her child's social awareness and understanding.

There is abundant evidence to show that aggressive behaviour in children can be related to broad (long-term) attitudes and child-rearing practices. A combination of lax discipline, especially with regard to children's acts of aggression, combined with hostile attitudes in the parents, produces very aggressive and poorly controlled behaviour in the offspring.

Mental health problems in middle childhood – children around the age of ten – are likely to 'stick' if untreated. Between 50 and 75 per cent (depending on diagnosis) still have problems at 14 years of age.

Adolescence

The major task of the adolescent stage, according to many contemporary psychologists, is the young person's need to shape and consolidate his or her own identity as a unique and mature person. According to Erikson, the period from 12 to 15 years is a time when adolescents clarify who they are and what their role in life is to be. This is thought to be a vital precursor to true intimacy and depth in personal relationships. This period begins with teenagers' intense concern for discovering their individual nature, and ends when they have established a coherent sense of self and personal identity. Society may make for difficulties for the early adolescent by failing to provide clearly defined or valued roles and standards for the young person. Indeed, it gives ambiguous messages about when childhood ends and adolescence, as young adulthood, begins; or for that matter, when adolescence ends and independent adulthood begins. If the physiological changes of puberty are most commonly taken as the onset of adolescence, then it is sociological phenomena such as status, duties, privileges, the end of education and the right to marry and enjoy economic independence, which are most frequently taken as the termination of adolescence. During the past half century or so, adolescence in western societies has become a progressively longer span of years – indeed as long as ten years in duration. This reflects the mixed feelings we have about the decision as to when, in law or social custom, a young person is grown-up and responsible: old enough to drink in a pub, mature enough to manage a bank account, to indulge in sexual intercourse, to get married, to vote, or to be held responsible for a criminal act.

The physical and psychological changes that take place at 12 (on average) in girls, and 14 in boys, are due to the action of hormones, and are quite dramatic; growth in virtually all parts of the body is sharply accelerated. During so-called transitional periods like adolescence, individuals are in the marginal position of having lost an established and accustomed status, but of not yet having acquired the new status toward which developmental changes are driving them.

The self-image

How young people perceive themselves depends very much on how others see them; but it depends most of all on how they *think* others see them – which could, of course, be different from the way in which they are actually perceived. Most particularly, children accept into their self-image what they believe to be their parents' view of them; and this can have long-term consequences. If your client believes that their parents' opinion is negative or critical (even if this is not really the case), they may exhibit insecurity and low self-esteem. If people believe things to be real, they are real in their consequences. This applies with force to the delicate area of a person's self-image.

The development of identity doesn't always proceed smoothly (see *Figure 4.3*). But what evidence we have, calls into question Erikson's belief that adolescents *usually* suffer a crisis over their identity. Most teenagers actually have a positive, but not unrealistically-inflated, self-image.

There is a growing altruism and idealism to be seen in many young people. These different facets are gradually integrated into the adolescent personality. Self-esteem is a vital element for healthy 'adjustment'. When there is a large gap between the teenager's self-concept ('myself as I am') and his or her idealized self ('myself as I would like to be'), there is also likely to be anxiety and over-sensitiveness.

A sheep in wolf's clothing?

Parents worry about the imminence of adolescence and small wonder, given that this period has such a bad reputation – largely due to the 'jaundiced' writings of clinicians. But then clinicians only tend to see people who come to clinics; and people – adolescents in this case – who attend clinics would not be there if they did not have problems. Would a wide cross-section of adolescents, drawn in large numbers from the general population, present problems of sufficient seriousness or in sufficient numbers to give adolescence a 'bad name'?

Adolescence, while certainly not immune from its share of pain for those growing up (and for those guiding the growing up process), is usually not the scourge of folklore. It is something of a sheep – albeit an unruly sheep – in wolf's clothing. For one thing, the problems and hurdles of growing up do not all arrive at one and the same time.

The more serious psychological, or psychiatric, conditions are probably slightly more common during adolescence than during middle childhood, but the difference is not very great, and most adolescents do not manifest psychiatric disorders. Nevertheless, some 10 to 15 per cent of adolescents do experience significant psychological difficulties. The category, referred to by psychologists as 'emotional disorders', is manifested by about two-and-a-half per cent of pre-adolescent children and this figure increases somewhat by adolescence. It has been found that boys and girls are about equally prone to these kind of problems which, for most children, manifest themselves briefly and then become minimal or disappear completely.

This is all very well, but you might well wish to know whether there are any *typical* adolescent problems, typical in the sense that they reflect stresses and strains which emerge from that 'in between' status – between late childhood and early adult life. Surveys of adolescents between 14 and 16 years of age indicate that their particular problems include uncertainty about self-image, lack of financial independence, lack of perceived significance in relation to adults and peers, and anxieties about coping with challenges such as sex, alcohol and fighting. Among the 17 to 19-year-olds, worries are about financial dependence if unemployed, lack of status, racial conflict (for ethnic minorities), and potential involvement with the police (males only). In a sense, these are commonplace problems – even though they are potentially distressing. There certainly are serious psychiatric disorders, such as schizophrenia and anorexia or bulimia nervosa, whose onset is particularly associated with the teenage years.

We can witness in the transition from childhood to adulthood an upsurge of moodiness and feelings of misery. These, as we can see in *Figure 4.3*, are influenced significantly by the progress, or lack of progress, they are making in arriving at a stable sense of identity. Adolescents are often tormented by ideas which are self-critical, worries about the future, and fears about such matters as attending school or becoming involved in social activities. Many of these anxieties relate to the state of their self-esteem.

It is reassuring to realize that, although the *rates* of unhappy feelings and self-depreciation reach a peak during adolescence, the *majority* of teenagers generally seem to be happy and confident and are not the victims of serious depression or of other emotional disturbance. In fact, adolescence does not quite live up to its reputation. This may help those of your clients who are bracing themselves with trepidation for their child's 'run-up' to the 'teens'.

Strengths

The reason why adolescent development is, relatively speaking, so unremarkable in the personal disturbance it causes, is that there are many strength-giving continuities in this period. The adolescent builds on what has gone before; coping skills developed when younger are not necessarily redundant. Many of the changes of this stage of development represent pluses, not minuses; they take the form of increased capacities of various kinds. It is as well to remember these pluses when considering how much to advise parents to 'let go'. It may be helpful to note the results of surveys of young people aged 14 to 19 years.

The aspirations of people of 14 to 16 years include:
• enjoyment of social interaction with peer group and with the opposite sex;
• having access to stimulating and exciting activities;
• being accorded significance and being listened to.

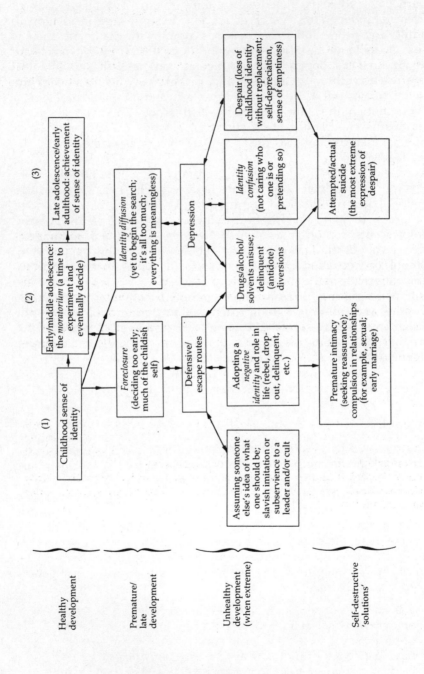

Figure 4.3 Vicissitudes of identity development (based on Erikson's theories)

The satisfactions of young people of 17 to 19 years include:
- greater independence from parental constraints;
- increasing confidence and a stronger sense of identity;
- greater financial independence (if employed).

Disabled adolescents have particular hurdles to overcome as they negotiate young adulthood. Anderson and Clarke (1982) describe the experiences of disabled adolescents and the problems they encounter in connection with:

- aspects of their education – the frequent wish to attend ordinary schools;
- some aspects of their social life – friendship and the use of leisure time;
- relationships with the opposite sex – fears and aspirations;
- the transition from school to adult life;
- fears and aspirations about employment or the lack of it.

Erikson has written about the interplay of 'ego' and 'alter' which is so critical in personality development – namely, the achievement of a balance between the poles of recognizing and accommodating the needs of others as opposed to imposing self-centred demands on other people. An extreme lack of reciprocity between self and others (in either direction) gives rise to emotional and social maladjustment. However by the end of adolescence, most people have managed to attain this balance and go on to become integrated (albeit sometimes uneasily) in the society in which they live.

FURTHER READING

Berryman, J., Hargreaves, D., Herbert, M. and Taylor Davies, A. (1991) *Developmental Psychology and You*. Leicester: BPS Books (The British Psychological Society) and Routledge. [An easy-to-read introduction to development with many illustrations and exercises.]
Cromer, R. (1991) *Language and Thought in Normal and Handicapped Children*. Oxford: Basil Blackwell. [Invaluable aid to those working with handicapped children.]

5 Children with disabilities

Children with disabilities, and their families, constitute a significant proportion of the clients with whom social work and health professionals work. These individuals are best thought of not as 'disabled children', but as *children who have to contend with a disability*. They experience a wide range of physical and learning disabilities (and thus handicaps), as well as problems due to mental illness and sensory impairments. The Children Act can be viewed and implemented in positive and promotional ways for such youngsters. It places a clear, positive and separate duty on local authorities (this means the local Social Services Departments) to provide services with the purpose of:

▷ minimizing the effect on children with disabilities in the area of their disabilities; and
▷ giving such children the chance to lead lives which are as normal as possible (see paragraph 6 of Schedule 2).

In addition to the Children Act, the 1981 and 1988 Education Acts require an active search for children who need extra services. This involves a more precise definition of who is, and who is not, a 'special case'. But, to make life difficult, it is questionable whether children with developmental impairments can be neatly distinguished from 'normal' children by their pattern of behaviour, functional deficit or their neuropsychological profile (Hall, 1992). There is, in fact, a *spectrum of impairment*.

Definitions of Disability

The Children Act states that a child is disabled 'if he is blind, deaf or dumb or suffers from mental disorder of any kind or is substantially and permanently handicapped by illness, injury or congenital deformity or such other disability as may be prescribed' [s.17(11)]. It has taken over a decade of debate before terminology relating to abnormality, dysfunction and disadvantage could be codified in the World Health Organization's (WHO) *International Classification of Impairments, Disabilities and Handicaps* (1980). Definitions contain a functional *and* structural component, summarized as follows:

▶ *Impairment* in the context of health experience is any loss or abnormality of psychological, physiological or anatomical structure or function.

▶ *Disability* is viewed as the limitation of personal activity consequent upon impairment – any restriction or lack (resulting from an impairment) of ability to perform an activity in the manner or within the range considered normal for a human being.

▶ *Handicap* is the resulting personal and social disadvantage that limits or prevents the fulfilment of a role that is normal (depending on age, sex, social and cultural factors) for that individual.

In law, for the first time, children with disabilities will be treated first and foremost as children with *particular* needs, and will be entitled to the same general level of social services as other children in need, to enable them to live as normal a life as possible. Approximately 21,000 children under 16 years of age were registered as substantially and permanently handicapped in England in the 1980s. The most common conditions leading to disability are intellectual impairment (2 to 3 per cent of children); visual impairment (2 to 3.5 per cent) and hearing impairment (about 1.6 per cent). Motor disabilities affecting motor coordination, locomotion and manipulation are frequently associated with disease and injury. Certain diseases are particularly disabling because of their chronicity and/or the debilitating and restrictive nature of their effects. Among these are congenital heart disease (prevalence 0.2 to 0.7 per cent); diabetes (1.8 per cent); asthma (2 to 5 per cent); epilepsy (0.26 to 0.46 per cent); cerebral palsy (0.14 to 0.5 per cent); rheumatoid arthritis (0.1 to 0.3 per cent); kidney disease (0.008 per cent) and muscular dystrophy (0.006 per cent).

The incidence of any disability depends on a wide range of factors, perhaps the most important being the manner in which the disability is defined. This is the issue which arises out of the concept of 'children in need' [s.17(10)]: how is the child who is disabled identified as disabled, and shown to be different from the child who is not disabled?

Our definitions of disability and handicap are subject to many influences: the knowledge that we have and the views and attitudes of the society in which we live. Whatever definition is adopted, it is important to realize that there is, as we have seen, no 'true' definition of disability or handicap and no definitive cut-off point. Not surprisingly, many social workers may be faced with children who appear to be disabled or handicapped in some way, but who have slipped through the surveillance net of other professionals.

Is Further Developmental Assessment Necessary?

A knowledge of child development and disability is essential if you need to make an on-the-spot, if preliminary, assessment. If you suspect that the child is showing evidence of a delay in development, then a more formal assessment may be necessary. Over 100 developmental screening tests have been devised (see Meisels, 1988) for various purposes. They provide a profile of the child's skills, for example, the identification of motor skills, expressive language, eye–hand coordination, cognitive and social skills (see *Table 5.1*). Instruments like the Bayley or Griffiths tests are subject to criticism because, *inter alia*, they do not reliably predict later ability. However, they do provide a guide to the level of, and inequalities across, the range of developmental areas. They indicate marked *delays* in development.

Other screening tests facilitate the detection and early treatment of permanently disabling disorders such as cerebral palsy, autism and mental handicap (now referred to, in a less stigmatizing way, in educational and health circles as 'learning difficulty' or 'learning disability'). These conditions are not cured by early treatment, but quality of life may be enhanced with appropriate help. Vicky Lewis (1987) has written an invaluable guide to how disabled children develop and cope with life. The philosophy behind work with children who are disabled is much more positive than it used to be in the past. Attention is given to the child's needs as a person and to the development of his or her assets and abilities. Families, too, are involved much more in decisions and planning; they too have their own individual needs. All professionals who work with families of disabled children will know how well some families cope with the most distressing problems, whereas others are devastated by disabilities that, in purely physical terms, are far less severe.

Where there is a need for a formal assessment, it is vital to communicate clearly and honestly with the family, seeking the parents' permission. Parents may be particularly worried by this kind of procedure and will require painstaking reassurance that the intention is to enhance the life and abilities of their child. They should understand that the objective of the assessment is to learn more about the child's needs, with the intention of providing services which encourage his/her development and which provide support to the parents in carrying out their responsibilities.

If parents refuse to allow a child about whom there is serious concern to be assessed, this can be an ominous sign of a potential emergency, and will usually justify an application for an emergency protection order [s.44(4)] under the 'frustrated access' condition (see Appendix III).

Parents who resist making the child available to professionals

Table 5.1 Some screening tests

Tests of mental ability/developmental status
Bayley Scales of Infant Development (2 months–2½ years)
British Ability Scales (2½–17 years)
Wechsler Preschool and Primary Scale of Intelligence (WPPSI) (4–6½ years)
Merrill-Palmer Preschool Performance Tests (1½–5¼ years)
McCarthy Scales of Infant Development (2½–8½ years)
Wechsler Intelligence Scale for Children (WISC) (6½–16 years)
Stanford-Binet Intelligence Scale (2 years–adult)
Griffiths Scales (0–8 years)
Gesell Developmental Schedule (4 weeks–6 years)
Vineland Social Maturity Scale (3 months–30 years)
Stycar Developmental Sequences (1 month–5 years)
The Miller Assessment for Preschoolers (MAP) (2 years 9 months–5 years 8 months)

Specialized tests
Goldberg General Health Questionnaire (mothers at risk for mental health problems is one screening application)
Hiskey-Nebraska Test of Learning Aptitude (hearing defects) (3–17 years)
Snijders-Oomen Non-verbal Intelligence Scale (2½–7 years) (all forms of verbal communication handicap)
Leiter International Performance Scale (communication defects and multiple handicap) (2–16 years)
Raven's Progressive Matrices (non-verbal abilities)
Williams Intelligence Test (vision defects) (5–15 years)
Reynell-Zinkin Scales (vision defects) (0–5 years)
Columbia Mental Maturity Scale (verbal and physical handicaps) (3–10 years)
Frostig Developmental Test of Visual Perception (learning disabilities) (4–8 years)
Bender Gestalt Test (visual motor perception) (4 years and over)
Stott-Moyes-Henderson Test of Motor Impairment (motor disability, clumsiness) (5–14 years)
Bene-Anthony Family Relations Test
Scars *et al* Child-rearing Practice Scales

Language and vocabulary tests
Reynell Developmental Language Scale (1½–6 years)
British Picture Vocabulary Scale (2½–18 years)
Peabody Picture Vocabulary Test (2½–18 years)
Stycar Language Test (up to 7 years)

Behaviour problems checklists
Behaviour Screening Questionnaire (3-year-olds) (Richman and Graham)
Children's Behaviour Checklist (2–4, 4–7 years) (Achenbach and Edelbrock)
Hewett Behaviour Checklist (9 months–2 years)
Rutter Scales (School-age children)

Attainment tests
Neale Analysis of Reading Ability (6–12 years)
Wide Range Achievement Test (5 years–adult)
Schonell Reading Test

appointed by the Social Services Department, may be agreeable to the child being examined by the family doctor in a familiar environment, or by an independent professional.

The health professional's records may be scrutinized as part of the investigation. The court will expect to be given details of the investigation and how it arose. This means – as always – that accurate and objective record keeping and writing are vital (see Herbert, 1991a; Sutton and Herbert, 1992). *Table 5.2* can be used as a check to indicate the presence or absence of disability. Each category of disability is subdivided into three levels to indicate the degree of disability. The services required can also be divided into three categories: direct help for the child; development of parenting skills; supplementing of parental resources.

As an aid to effective service provision and planning, the Children Act requires Social Service Departments to maintain a register of disabled children in their area [s.2(2)]. If this is to be of real value in planning services and of benefit to individuals, it needs to be complete, clearly defined and should not include duplication with other registers.

Special Educational Needs

The 1981 Education Act refers to a separate category of children with special educational needs. An important change from past practice in educational procedure, is the aim to integrate children with special needs into ordinary schools wherever possible. Being educated with 'normal' children is, for many people involved with disabled children, synonymous with the term integration. The movement in the direction of more normal environments for children with various types of impairment is not a uniform movement; some authorities are still placing children in special schools. Research tends to show that substantial educational gains are made when the child is placed in a mainstream school *with suitable support.*

The 1981 Education Act also gives parents the right to take part in assessments of their child and in decisions regarding school place-ment. The Warnock Report that preceded the Act spoke of parents as partners. Following an assessment, a *statement* of special educational need is provided for each child between the ages of two and nineteen. The statement sets out the educational provision for the child as required. Parents have the right to appeal against this statement if they disagree with it; they must be notified of a person to whom they can turn for advice.

Table 5.2 Disability checklist

Hearing

moderate to severe: hearing difficulties even with hearing aids; has or is likely to have persisting difficulty with language and communication sufficient to impair development

profound: little or no hearing, with little or no benefit from hearing aids

Vision

moderate to severe: partially sighted, visual difficulties sufficient to impair everyday activities and/or development despite the use of aids

profound: blind, no useful vision

Speech and/or Language

moderate to severe: difficulties communicating through speech and language, and as a result unable to participate in the normal activities of a child of their age

profound: no meaningful speech or language, therefore unlikely to use speech as the primary means of communication

Physical

moderate to severe: physical difficulty (for example, motor) or chronic illness resulting in long-term impairment of health or development, even with the provision of drugs, diet or aids

profound: difficulties with all basic functions, of such severity that assistance is likely to be required

Learning

moderate to severe: a permanent learning impairment sufficient to prevent the child from fulfilling roles or performing activities which are generally understood to be within the capacity of children of that age and cultural background

profound: profound or multiple learning difficulties

Behavioural and Emotional

moderate to severe: emotional and/or behavioural difficulties likely to be long-term, and be such as to impair the quality of the child's life, resulting in underachievement in normal social contexts (for example, school or workplace), with failure of social development and integration

profound: emotional and/or behavioural difficulties likely to be so severe in the long-term that they seriously impair the quality of the child's life, resulting in inability to function in normal social contexts or constituting a risk to themselves or others

The Development of Disability

How does the development of children who are disabled compare with the development of those who are not? The development of children who are disabled may be described as delayed, abnormal, compensatory or absent.

Delayed development is simply slower development than in the case of the normal child, but the same stages are passed through and the same processes are involved; although the child who is disabled may ultimately reach a less advanced stage.

Abnormal development refers to situations when the process of development is different from normal, and the resulting behaviours or developments are not seen in normal children.

Compensatory development refers to situations where development takes a different route from that taken by normal children, although the end point is the same.

Absence of development refers to cases in which the child who is disabled fails to develop in a particular area.

It should be noted that aspects of the disabled child's development may be normal, and can fall within the range of variation reported for non-disabled children. Within any form of impairment, any or all of the developmental variations above may occur, since the impairment may affect different areas of development in different ways. Disabilities have their origins at different stages of development: prenatally (before birth); perinatally (around the time of birth); and postnatally (after birth). The earlier a handicap originates, the more severe it tends to be. About 35 per cent of all handicapping conditions which are identified in the first 12 months of life, actually originate in the first 12 weeks of pregnancy. Some 71 per cent of those children who suffer a severe impairment at the age of seven years, have a defect which originated either before birth or around the time of birth.

Physical Disability

Blindness

Blindness has both legal and educational definitions – in terms of how clearly persons can see (their visual acuity). The legal definition states that a person is blind either if he or she has a central vision acuity of 3/60 or less in the better eye with correcting glasses, or if his or her central visual acuity is better than 3/60 and there is a peripheral field defect such that the widest angle that the visual field subtends is no greater than 20 degrees, that is, less than a sixteenth of the peripheral field.

Partially-sighted people are those with visual acuities between 3/60 and 6/60 in the better eye after necessary medical or surgical treatment has been given and compensating lenses provided. Indeed, most so-called blind children can see something, even though their vision may be very restricted.

The method most commonly used for assessing visual acuity is the Snellen chart, the chart of letters or digits of decreasing size well known to anyone who has visited an optician. This measures distance vision under controlled conditions.

Knowledge of a child's visual strengths and weaknesses is important because of their implications for his or her development and education. Educational definitions of sightedness describe what a child can or cannot do, and what he or she is capable of doing, with help (what is called a 'functional' criterion). A child who has peripheral vision but no central vision will not be able to see what is straight ahead, but will be able to see things off to the side. This child will be unable to read print but probably will be quite mobile. By way of contrast, a child with only central vision (as if looking through a long tube) may be very cautious in movement, but able to read print. The notions of blindness and deafness (and, indeed, other disabilities) mean different things to different people. The ambiguities can lead to confusion in the minds of parents. Today, more and more professionals are classifying children on such a *functional* basis: how the child can use his or her remaining vision or hearing to further their progress.

In as many as half the cases of congenital blindness, causation is unknown. Most children who have some form of visual defect have something wrong with an eye or both eyes. The deficit may be due to atrophy of the optic nerve or some form of brain damage. All in all, visual difficulties (often referred to nowadays as 'partial sightedness' rather than blindness) arise from a wide range of causes.

Deafness

Like visual handicap, hearing deficits are seldom absolute. They are made up of a wide variety of conditions of differing seriousness. There are, in fact, very wide ranges in the severity of hearing problems. Whether a child can hear high notes as well as he or she can hear low notes is significant because it has implications for the development of speech, for whether or not a hearing aid would be useful, and for educational practice. Hearing deficits can thus affect the child in different ways. Professionals are very conscious of the risks that an undetected hearing impairment can present to a child's early linguistic development. This is why they recommend that all children be tested for hearing deficits in the first year of life. Sadly, it is difficult to make accurate hearing assessments of very young children. At a later stage, when assessments are reliable, surveys suggest that about nine in 10,000 school children are either deaf or have partial hearing.

The number of children who are identified as having a hearing impairment increases with age as it becomes easier to identify deafness. Deafness is slightly more common in boys than girls. Causation is not known in a third to a half of cases. It can be caused by damage to different anatomical areas of the ear. The ear is divided into three parts: the external ear, the middle ear and the inner ear. The two main types of hearing loss are conductive and sensori-neural which result from pathology of, or damage to, the middle or the inner ear respectively. It is important to distinguish between them. The deficit associated with a conductive disorder seldom involves total hearing loss and is usually amenable to medical treatment in a way that is reversible. Sensori-neural deafness is more common and more severe. It involves damage to the sensory hair cells of the cochlea or the auditory nerve and is usually irreversible. A sensori-neural loss can occur prenatally, perinatally or postnatally. Forty to 60 per cent of cases of sensori-neural deafness have genetic causes.

Deafness is graded along two scales: intensity and frequency. Intensity is measured in decibels (dB) or units of sound. Intensity is a measure of the power of the sound. Our ears are exposed to sound covering a very wide range of sound pressure, which the ear perceives primarily as changes in loudness. A scale called the decibel scale has been adopted for expressing sound pressure and, thus, sound power. It consists of a 140 decibel range. The normal threshold for hearing pure tones (the quietest audible sound) is 0 dB.

Frequency is measured in units of Hertz (Hz) and the range for the normal ear is from about 20 to 20,000 Hz. The frequencies which are most important for speech discrimination fall between 200 and 8,000 Hz. Low frequency sounds have low pitch; as frequency increases, pitch becomes progressively higher. Any particular sound has the property of intensity *and* frequency.

How the child is functioning educationally and socially with his or her hearing difficulty, is more important than the loss itself. Children with very similar audiograms may have different educational needs. Michael Nolan and Ivan Tucker (1988) state that while one child may be severely handicapped by an 80 dB hearing loss, another may progress in a close to normal way. Much depends on the family and professional support, and a good deal on the child's personal qualities.

Cerebral palsy

Cerebral palsy is a disorder of locomotion and posture resulting from a permanent, non-progressive defect or lesion of the immature brain. Even though two children may both have cerebral palsy, the differences between them may be much greater than their similarities. In addition to motor problems, which can range from hardly noticeable to almost total physical helplessness, there may be difficulties (or a combination of difficulties) in vision, hearing, speech and intellectual ability. A sizeable proportion of children with cerebral palsy may also suffer from fits. Several types of motor problem have been identified:

A group described as *'spastic'* whose movements seem stiff and rigid due to a failure of the muscles to relax. This is the most common problem in cerebral palsy resulting from damage to the motor cortex. An arm may be held pressed against the body with the forearm bent at right-angles to the upper arm and the hand bent against the forearm. The leg is often bent at the knee and rotates inwards from the hip. The person may walk on the outside of their foot so that, if both legs are involved, a scissored gait results. Balance may be poor because of the odd way weight is distributed. Not all limbs are necessarily affected, although they are in about a third of all cases (*quadriplegia*). About a quarter of cases are *hemiplegic*, having a spastic leg and arm on one side of the body. In *diplegia*, 20 per cent of cases, all the limbs are involved, but the legs are worse than the arms. In 18 per cent of cases, only the legs are affected (*paraplegia*).

A group known as *'athetoid'* suffers an excess of uncontrollable movements which interfere with normal body movements. Movements are of a writhing, lurching nature; uncontrolled facial grimacing and dribbling are common. These disabilities are a result of damage to the basal ganglia. This is the second most common motor problem.

A group known as *'ataxic'* have damage to the cerebellum which results in poor coordination of movement and disturbed balance. Children may appear clumsy and unsteady and may have difficulty locating themselves in space.

Spina bifida

This term refers to a divided or split spine which originates during the second and third months of pregnancy when the spinal column is being formed. Part of the tissue which normally covers the spinal cord fails to fuse over, leaving the cord exposed at that point. This disability affects about 20 babies in every 10,000 births. About one half do not survive the end of the first year. Slightly more girls than boys are affected.

There are several different sorts of spinal damage. The main type is spina bifida cystica which is subdivided into myelomeningocele and meningocele. The former is by far the more serious of the two conditions. It is also the most common, accounting for about 85 per cent of all cases of spina bifida cystica. The primary problems in spina bifida, particularly myelomeningocele, are those of incontinence and paralysis of the legs. In many cases of spina bifida there is an additional problem: hydrocephalus. This is associated with myelo-meningocele and involves an accumulation of cerebrospinal fluid around the brain owing to an obstruction in the normal circulation of this fluid. Unless this obstruction is bypassed by the insertion of a shunt to drain off the excess fluid, the build-up of fluid exerts pressure on the brain and skull, bringing about damage to brain cells and enlargement of the head. Unlike spina bifida which is always congenital, hydrocephalus can be either congenital or the result of some postnatal infection, notably meningitis, where the membrane covering the brain and spinal cord becomes inflamed. A consequence of hydrocephalus may be some degree of intellectual impairment.

Spina bifida can occur anywhere along the spinal column, although it is most common in the lower back, the lumbar region, where the vertebrae close over last. The site of the lesion is important, since in myelomeningocele, nerves which originate below the lesion will usually fail to operate their respective muscles, thus preventing movement. Nerves to the hips, legs and bladder originate in the lumbar region. Below this, in the sacral region, are nerves which innervate the sphincter muscles of the urethra and rectum.

Learning Disability

The term 'mental handicap' is being replaced by the less stigmatizing words 'learning difficulty/disability'. Learning disability is marked by the child's impairment of intellect. Although the problem of learning disability has always been with us, a number of developments in our society have re-emphasized its importance. One is the increasing complexity of society and the demands it makes on its members, and another is the emphasis on compulsory education. Both of these have served to alter the definition of intellectual impairment and to bring within the category persons who previously would not have been considered handicapped.

Intellectually impaired children learn maladaptive behaviours in the same way as children who are not handicapped, but there are some important differences:

• Parents may consider the child to be 'ill' on a long-term basis, and so not expect more reasonable behaviour from their child – 'After all, he is mentally handicapped, we can't expect him to stop banging his head on walls'.

- Because 'mentally handicapped children learn more slowly', procedures which would have been successful if continued, tend to be abandoned because there is so little improvement in the short-term.

Children with learning disabilities are a vulnerable group; 40 per cent of children with an I.Q. below 50 (three to four children per 1,000 aged seven to 16 years) can be expected to have severe mental health problems. What are some of the emotional and behavioural problems displayed by children and adolescents with learning disabilities?

- *'Challenging' behaviour:*
– aggression towards others (for example, biting, hitting);
– aggression/harm/injury towards self (for example, head-banging, self-scratching) – this tends to occur most often in profoundly disabled children;
– screaming or shouting;
– hoarding food;
– obsessive, compulsive preoccupations and actions (for example, touching light switches).

- *Disorders of affect* (for example, mood swings, depression).

- *Emotional distress* common to all people (for example, bereavement, illness, separation anxiety).

Children with disabilities are somewhat vulnerable to abuse because of the demands they make of their carers. Teaching the child new skills and ways of behaving may require a more structured approach than is necessary with the normal child (the Portage system described on page 131 is an example). This structure seems to go against the grain for many parents, who quite understandably prefer to rely on less formal, more intuitive approaches.

Normalization

In recent years, there has been a growing emphasis on the integration of less severely handicapped youngsters into the community and the education system where they rightly belong – a theory and, indeed, a policy referred to as 'normalization'. This move is a result of the influence of humanistic ideas, together with the realization by educators that more than 50 per cent of the jobs in our society do not require schooling beyond primary level. Nevertheless, about one per cent of children are so severely handicapped that they require and, will continue to require, considerable help with many or all basic living skills such as dressing, washing and feeding. A further ten per cent are handicapped to an extent that means they are unlikely as adults to find more than the simplest sorts of employment.

Assessment of intellectual impairment

The Intelligence Quotient (I.Q.) has been the foundation of most classifications of intellectual impairment and, in spite of doubts about comparability, has generally been the basis of much research and many policy decisions. An I.Q. under 70 has usually been accepted for 'mild' impairment, in conjunction with 'social criteria'. A level of I.Q. 55 divides 'mild' from 'severe'. In practice, however, I.Q. 50 has proved more useful and is the most widely used convention in the epidemiological literature. Severe learning disability (I.Q. below 50) appears at a rate of about three children per 1,000 (Fryers, 1984). The 'profound' category has achieved poorer agreement, coming into play for I.Q.s of under 25 or 20. Fryers makes the point that no set of categories and no single system of classification is satisfactory, nor can it ever be, however defined, since the group of people with whom we are concerned suffer from a ragbag of disorders, difficulties and needs, and a varying ragbag at that. They have been brought together almost by historical accident of educational development. They do not, and cannot, constitute an entity, except we make it so. Taxonomies are for groups, categories serve the needs of professionals. Individual clients require thorough, multidisciplinary assessment of their individual situation, constantly updated, and a service delivery system which can respond to their changing needs and those of the family.

Causes of learning disabilities

Genetic causes (see *Table 5.3*) include multifactorial, interacting genetic factors; single abnormal gene conditions; and chromosomal abnormalities.

Environmental influences include infections (for example, rubella); trauma (for example, head injury); toxins (for example, alcohol affecting the maternal uterine environment); and asphyxia/brain damage. Some of the common (and uncommon) causes of more moderate levels of learning disability in school children are listed in *Table 5.4*.

Communicating with Disabled Children

Communicating with children with severe learning disabilities requires sensitivity, skill and, sometimes, patience. Sutton and Herbert (1992) make the following suggestions:

▷ Allow plenty of time for the interview.

Table 5.3 Mental handicap and its ramifications (adapted from Fryers, 1984)

Handicapping disorder	Nature of disorder	Detection/ Prevention	Intellectual implications
1. Down's syndrome	Chromosome aberrations present at conception	Amniocentesis can indicate affected foetus	All likely to be intellectually impaired; a majority severely so
2. Patau's syndrome	Autosomal anomalies present at conception	Nil	Occasionally severe, or mild intellectual impairment
3. Edward's syndrome	Autosomal anomalies present at conception	Nil	Occasionally severe, or mild intellectual impairment
4. *Cri du chat* syndrome	Autosomal anomalies present at conception	Nil	Occasionally severe, or mild intellectual impairment
5. Klinefelter's syndrome	Sex chromosome disorder	Nil	Occasionally severe, or mild intellectual impairment
6. Phenylketonuria (PKU)	Defect of protein metabolism	Screening programme after birth; special dietary regime prescribed	Extreme impairment if not treated
7. Galactosaemia	Defect of carbohydrate metabolism	Screening programme after birth; special dietary regime prescribed	Extreme impairment if not treated
8. Tay Sach's Disease	Defect of lipid metabolism	No treatment available Genetic counselling	Extreme impairment
9. Epiloia (tuberous sclerosis)	Causal mechanisms are not clear	No treatment available	Many severely impaired

Table 5.4 Some causes of learning difficulty in school children

- Vision and hearing defects
- Low I.Q. through mild intellectual impairment
- Lack of family support
- Poor teaching
- Poor motivation
- Non-specific ill-health
- Irregular school attendance
- Petit mal epilepsy
- Anticonvulsant medication
- Intracranial space-occupying lesions:
    hydrocephalus
    craniopharyngioma
    other tumours
- Degenerative brain disease
- Motor disorders such as 'clumsiness'
    mild cerebral palsy
    Duchenne muscular dystrophy

▷ Allow plenty of time for helping the person to get to know you and for understanding the situation as far as possible.
▷ Try to meet the person in a setting which is familiar to them.
▷ The following people may be able to help you communicate with these clients: Portage coordinator; speech therapist; parents or carers; interpreters; psychologist; key worker – from hospital, day centre or hostel; specialist social worker; community nurse; teacher; further education tutor.

Verbal communication
▷ Keep questions short.
▷ Deal with one idea at a time.
▷ Keep to one topic at a time.
▷ Check that you have understood correctly. Try to rephrase the same question later on.
▷ Avoid questions starting with 'Why . . .?'.
▷ If you don't understand, say so.
▷ Avoid questions which invite a 'Yes' answer. People with learning disabilities may say 'Yes' to please.
▷ Avoid questions which invite a 'No' answer. People with learning disabilities may say 'No' when they don't understand.
▷ Avoid abstract ideas; give clear examples.
▷ If you are working with an interpreter, take particular care to be clear.

Non-verbal communication
▷ Be aware of your body posture and facial expression.

▷ Be aware of your client's body posture and facial expression. Establish what is 'normal' for them before the interview so that you do not misread the cues.
▷ Remember the possibilities of using British Sign Language or Makaton.
▷ Remember the written word: some people may be able to write but not speak clearly, while others cannot read but can understand the spoken word.

Social Discrimination and its Consequences

It is as well to be sensitive to the effects of social attitudes towards disability which add to the burden of persons suffering mental and/or physical handicaps. According to Goffman (1968), the central feature of the stigmatized individual's situation in life is the absence of 'acceptance': a failure to accord them 'respect and regard'. Discrimination takes many forms and affects not only the disabled child but also the family. The net effect is an increase in stress and strain with people having to contend with factors such as social isolation, physical strain, financial strain and emotional and psychosomatic symptoms.

Social isolation

Clarke *et al.* (1977), on behalf of the Warnock Committee on Special Education, compared a group of disabled children with a group of non-disabled controls. Children with disablement are:

- more likely to play alone;
- slightly more likely to spend time alone with an adult;
- less likely to engage in imaginative play;
- more likely to engage in passive/receptive activity, in listening to others or watching others' activities;
- equally likely to communicate with adults for a similar length of time;
- more likely to communicate less with other children;
- more likely to have one-way, rather than two-way, speech patterns.

Stress on families

There is reasonably firm evidence (see Philp and Duckworth, 1982) that parents of children with disablement are more likely than parents of children without disablement to suffer from stress, anxiety and depression. Baldwin (1976) found that *only* 22 per cent of mothers and 50 per cent of fathers in her sample felt that their physical or mental health had *not* been affected. This is hardly surprising. Hilton Davis

(1993) describes parents' predicament graphically: when children are hurt, ill or disabled, they need physical and personal attention and this has consequences for all members of the family. At a mundane (but, nonetheless, significant) level, one of the parents has to stop working, reading or watching television to see to the child, to cuddle him/her, to kiss a hurt better. If the child is sick, parents become worried, arrangements must be made to look after him/her while one of the parents (if they're a couple) takes the other children to school; or they have to make time to go to the GP. Time may be lost from work, and the children lose some of their usual share of attention. Such difficulties are part of the routine of life for most parents. For parents of chronically ill or disabled children, as Davis points out, these adjustments and priorities are a way of life. Anxiety may be the norm, outside commitments may be impossible, and child care duties are increased and time-consuming. There are numerous appointments with professionals and possibly periods away from home during hospital admissions.

Other factors add to the burden. Families with disabled children are more likely to have poor housing than families without disabled children, in cases like spina bifida where the prevalence of disability has a social class bias (Philp and Duckworth, 1982).

There are often difficulties with transport and mobility. Research suggests that nearly one half of mothers with a disabled child never travel on public transport. Disabled individuals go out infrequently, for short periods, and the types of trip they do make, are largely restricted to essential shopping and visiting friends and relatives. Indoor mobility patterns are also severely limited in comparison with the general public.

The families that adapt most effectively to disablement and chronic illness are those that are cohesive, stable and emotionally expressive. They have low levels of conflict but high levels of honest, open communication. Factors such as depression, ill-health, older age, lack of emotional support and intra-family stress are predictive of personal difficulties in adapting to the child's misfortune and being able to cope effectively with the consequences.

The relationship between the members of the family and those who guide and counsel them, needs to be one of partnership or collaboration in order to share problems and to work together to seek solutions (see Davis, 1993). Such a professional can put families in touch with appropriate resources and support systems (see page 129).

FURTHER READING

Carr, J. (1980) *Helping Your Handicapped Child.* Harmondsworth: Penguin. [Practical guide for hard-pressed parents.]

Eiser, C. (1990) *Chronic Childhood Disease.* Cambridge: Cambridge University Press. [Categories, causes, coping with chronic illnesses of childhood.]

Fraser, W.I. and Murti Rao, J. (1991) Recent studies of mentally handicapped young people's behaviour. *Journal of Child Psychology and Psychiatry, 32,* 79–108. [A self-explanatory title: helpful information about challenging behaviour.]

Hewett, S. (with Newson, J. and Newson, E.) (1970) *The Family and the Handicapped Child.* London: Allen & Unwin. [A sensitive account of family needs and dynamics in caring for a handicapped child.]

Lewis, V. (1987) *Development and Handicap.* Oxford: Basil Blackwell. [A superb book on how children with disabilities develop and can be helped; a book to which the present author is particularly indebted for information about disability.]

Nolan, M. and Tucker, I. G. (1988) *The Hearing Impaired Child and the Family.* London: Souvenir Press. [All the information a family with a hearing impaired child would need to have.]

6 Mental health and psychological problems

The Children Act refers in several places to the child's physical and mental health. Theorists and practitioners (as we have seen) tend to have difficulties over the definition of physical disability, so it is hardly surprising that they become somewhat vague when they are asked to define positive mental health. It is easier to describe the abnormalities of mental life than it is to define effective psychological adjustment. In adults, this is usually taken to mean self-awareness, maturity of judgement and emotional development, self-actualization (that is, realizing one's potential), insight, altruism, and so on. But, by definition, the child, whose 'self-concept' is unformed and immature, cannot meet these criteria, which – it has to be said – are value judgements. Mental health has been described as the facility to work and love effectively. Among the criteria that can be applied to children's mental health, is their ability to form affectionate relationships with their parents, brothers and sisters, and other children. An additional measure of mental health is children's ability to tackle life's tasks with reasonable efficiency, adjusting to the increasingly complex demands – social, emotional and intellectual – which are made upon them as they grow older.

If we ask parents what they would wish for, above all else, for their children, many would probably answer 'happiness'. Generally speaking, there is an association between intense and prolonged feelings of unhappiness and other evidence of emotional problems. It is a characteristic of certain mental disorders in adults and problem behaviours in children, that the individual feels a loss of his or her sense of well-being or contentment. Whether the attainment of fairly consistent happiness is a sign of positive mental health, is much more debatable.

Assessing Emotional and Behavioural Problems

Ultimately, the professional judgement of a child's psychological health or well-being is made in individual terms, taking into account the child's unique personality, his or her particular circumstances and all the opportunities, disappointments and stresses associated with them. It is the task of the practitioner to ascertain where children stand on the developmental 'scale' – whether their progress and mental and physical status are appropriate to their age, retarded or advanced. In the light of this background information, the practitioner has to decide whether or not the child requires help. This involves asking a series of questions:

(1) Is the child's adjustive (adaptive, coping) behaviour appropriate to his or her age, intelligence and social situation?
(2) Is the environment making reasonable demands of the child?
(3) Is the environment satisfying the crucial needs of the child – that is to say, the needs that are vital at his or her particular stage of development?

Psychological problems may have unfavourable social and personal consequences for the child (for example, the consequences of phobic anxiety), for the family (for example, defiance) and sometimes, for the wider community (for example, vandalism). It is necessary to distinguish between antisocial acts, the adverse repercussions of which are felt primarily by others, and anti-aesthetic acts, forms of pleasurable self-indulgence judged by others to be harmful to those who engage in them. There are, broadly speaking, three classes of problematic behaviour:

- behaviour that is excessive (for example, screaming or hitting). These kinds of behaviour are called 'behavioural excesses';
- behaviour that is 'normal' or 'appropriate' of itself, but which occurs in restricted or inappropriate contexts (for example, conforming, but conforming to the norms of the delinquent gang rather than the family);
- behaviour that indicates that something is absent from, or poorly represented in, the child's behavioural repertoire (for example, incontinence, poor social skills, low self-esteem). These kinds of behaviour are called 'behavioural deficits.'

Minor variations of emotional and behavioural problems can be identified in most 'well-adjusted' children; for example, the majority of children are shy at one time or another. Some, however, display a constant and anxious avoidance of social situations. In other words, normality and abnormality are the extremes of a continuum; normality merges almost imperceptibly into abnormality. There are no absolute symptoms of psychological maladjustment in children, no recourse to the laboratory tests or X-rays which are so helpful in making a definitive medical diagnosis. We are not dealing with disease as medical persons understand it.

As mentioned above, emotional or behavioural problems, signs of psychological maladjustment are, by and large, exaggerations of, deficiencies in, or handicapping combinations of, behavioural or emotional patterns that are common to all children. Typical examples might be phobic anxiety, social ineptitude and the awkward combination of poor concentration and underachievement. When it comes to serious psychological disturbance, the prevalence rate is 10 to 15 per cent. Children who are ill have a rate of psychological disorder of 20 to 25 per cent. If the child is, in addition, disabled, the rate of disturbance (emotional and behaviour problems) rises to 30 to 35 per cent – a factor that adds to family burdens.

Continuity of Behaviour Problems

Do children who are 'normal' or, conversely, 'disturbed' (psychologically) at, say, six or seven years of age tend to be so at adolescence or even as far forward as adulthood? Several studies have investigated the intercorrelations among behavioural or personality ratings over the years – an exercise fraught with methodological and interpretive problems. Nevertheless, the view that emerges from long-term longitudinal (prospective) studies is that many individuals retain a great capacity for change; the outcomes of the events of early childhood are continually transformed by later experiences, making the course of human development more open than many theorists in the past ever believed possible.

The problems which decline in frequency with age – looked at in the community of children at large – are elimination (toilet training) problems, speech problems, fears, and thumb sucking. Problems such as insufficient appetite and lying reach a peak early and then subside. Many problems show high frequencies round about, or just before, school-starting age, then decline in prevalence, and rise again at puberty. Among these are restless sleep, disturbing dreams, physical timidity, irritability, attention-demanding, over-dependence, sombreness, jealousy and, in boys, food-finickiness.

Behaviours which decline at a later stage, and at a slower rate, than most others, include over-activity, destructiveness and tempers. In fact, one-third of boys still have temper explosions at 13. In their *severe* forms, these and other types of aggressive, antisocial behaviour constitute a constellation of problems referred to as *conduct disorders*. They involve physical and verbal aggressiveness, disruptiveness, irresponsibility, non-compliance and poor personal relationships; delinquent activities and early drug and substance misuse and abuse may also feature as part of the syndrome. They tend to persist in a worryingly high proportion of cases into adolescence, and even beyond.

We know that, for the most part, children who attend child and family clinics for *emotional problems* such as fears, phobias, shyness and inhibitions, become reasonably 'well adjusted' adults; they are almost as likely to grow up 'normal' as children drawn at random from the general population. In a sense, these difficulties are the emotional equivalent of 'growing pains'. But that is not to deny that they sometimes persist and reach levels of intensity which cause all-round suffering, and which justify their being described as psychological or psychiatric 'disorders'.

Situation Specificity

Children, and indeed adults, vary their actions to some extent according to the situations – and their perceptions of the situations – in which they find themselves. The term 'situation specificity' refers to the fact that behaviour is not usually manifested on a random basis. The probability of a specific action occurring, varies according to contingencies (circumstances) in the surrounding environment (see *Figure 6.1*). Thus a child who is troublesome may display his or her unacceptable behaviour in the home, the classroom, the playground, or perhaps on the streets of the neighbourhood. The behaviour might be even more situation specific, for example, severe temper trantrums may occur at home, and then only at bedtime and at meal times, with the child being quite cooperative and pleasant at other times of the day.

The findings of several studies suggest that maternal and teacher accounts of child behaviour are only slightly correlated, that is, they do not always agree. This is possibly due to the effects of situational factors. Since mothers and teachers see children in different contexts, which are governed by different rules and sanctions, there is no strong reason to expect that their ratings of behaviour should be identical. This discrepancy often comes as a surprise to parents who may hardly recognize the teacher's description of their son's or daughter's behaviour at school. Although maternal and teacher ratings of particular children are only slightly correlated, there is quite marked stability (consistency) in each of their ratings over time.

Conduct Disorders

The prevalence of the disorder (four to ten per cent of children in Britain and the United States) is probably on the increase. Prevention becomes a vital issue, as these children (particularly 'early starters') are at risk of developing problems later on in life, such as dropping out of school, alcoholism, drug abuse, antisocial personality, marital disruption, interpersonal problems and poor physical health.

Children with conduct disorders (see Herbert 1987b) demonstrate a fundamental inability or unwillingness to adhere to the rules and codes of conduct prescribed by society at its various levels. Such

1. *Antecedent events*
   (possible precipitants)

   Carlton is asked to do
   something or to stop
   doing it.

2. *Behaviour*
   a) Non-compliance.
      He takes no notice; if
      Mother insists, he
      resorts to verbal abuse.

   b) Verbal abuse.
      He makes rude
      comments, criticizes,
      occasionally swears and
      shouts.

3. *Consequences*
   (Possible reinforcers)

   a) Mother shouts at him,
      scolds him or discusses
      at length with him, what
      he has done.

   b) She begs him.

   c) Usually he gets his own
      way.

Specificity of Carlton's responses

Persons: He's rude and
disobedient mainly
with Mother;
occasionally to
Father; never with
Grandmother.

Places: Anywhere (but
notably when
visiting, or at a
supermarket).

Times: Meals in particular
– at the beginning,
usually, of the
family meal.

Situations: Mainly when asked
to do something or
when challenged
over being late for
meals or for bad
manners.
Particularly when
questioned about,
or criticized for not
eating properly,
getting up and
leaving the table.

Figure 6.1 The specificity of behaviour

failures may be related to the failure to learn controls or to the fact that the behavioural standards a child has absorbed do not coincide with the norms of that section of society which enacts and enforces the rules. Because of the provocative and confrontational nature of these youngsters' actions (not infrequently a consequence – in part – of harsh life experiences), they tend to invite punishment and quite frequently are physically abused by their parents or other caregivers.

Antisocial activities tend to disrupt and hinder the acquisition of crucial life skills, and, as we have seen, children with more extreme forms do not necessarily 'outgrow' their problem behaviours. The case histories of delinquents repeatedly indicate the onset of serious antisocial behaviour when they were very young.

Delinquent behaviour

A sizeable number of children with conduct problems become delinquent, as their rule-breaking becomes law-breaking. Delinquency is perhaps the most noteworthy of all activities as an adolescent manifestation. It reaches a peak at 15 years for boys and 14 years for girls. By their twenties, most of the former offenders have gradually become law-abiding members of the community. But the number of young people committing detected and adjudicated crimes in the United Kingdom and the United States has increased markedly. What was once an almost completely male preserve now includes substantial numbers of female offenders. The average age for the first court appearance of juveniles is lower, and there is a marked trend towards more violent offences.

The term 'juvenile delinquent' is merely an administrative term, not a clinical diagnosis. It has to be recognized that relatively minor delinquent activities (for example, petty thefts, vandalism) are surprisingly common in the teens. Such activities tend to be transitory. However, there is a small but hard core of adolescents who habitually break the law, thereby creating enormous social problems of punishment, prevention, and rehabilitation – none of which have satisfactorily reduced the prevalence rates.

Drug abuse

Drug abuse is relatively infrequent among children, but not as rare as it used to be. It becomes more common during the years of adolescence. Most young people who try drugs out of curiosity do not continue to use them regularly. Those who take drugs, tend to do so infrequently and give them up altogether after a year or so.

The terms 'drug abuse; and 'drug misuse' refer to the observation that a particular form of drug-taking is a harmful (abuse) and/or socially unacceptable way of using that substance (misuse). 'Users' are likely to develop 'tolerance' for a drug, which means that their body has adapted to it, so that the youngster has to increase the dosage to maintain the same effect. The body may react with 'withdrawal effects' to the sudden absence of a drug to which it has adapted; withdrawal involves severe physical discomfort. When this occurs, leading to a compulsion to continue taking the drug so as to avoid these symptoms, we speak of 'physical dependence'. The more widespread problem of 'psychological dependence' refers to an irresistible psychological compulsion to repeat the stimulation, pleasure or comfort provided by the drug's effects.

The key factor in drug-taking is opportunity – the availability of drugs and people to tempt and 'prompt'. Users have generally been exposed to drugs by their peers or by people (not infrequently family members) whose values incline towards non-conformity or even deviance. Rebelliousness, low self-esteem, a poor sense of psychological well-being (including depression), and low academic aspirations are among the characteristics commonly found in adolescent drug users. The boredom and hopelessness of unemployment also play their part. Substance abuse (for example, glue-sniffing) presents a similar picture.

What are the signs that may lead you to suspect drug use? It isn't always easy to judge, because some of the signs are not uncommon in adolescence generally. There is often a gradual change in habits and a general lethargy. Other signs include: aggression; loss of interest in school work, sport, hobbies and friends; furtive behaviour and frequent lying; bouts of drowsiness or sleeplessness; unexplained disappearances of money and belongings from the home.

Heroin addicts tend to stop bothering about their appearance, their speech may become halting, and they tend to drop old friends and take up new ones. Users of heroin may receive unexplained messages or telephone calls, followed by immediate and unexplained departures. Spots of blood may be noticed on their clothes, and (most important) needle marks on the back of their hands and the inside of their elbows. There may also be thickened brownish cords under the skin, which are veins, solidified as a result of the injections.

Depression

It is now recognized that children can suffer from a depressive disorder. Depression is quite common in adolescence. The new responsibilities of young adulthood, and the difficulties of sexual adjustment, may bring in their wake feelings of misery and inner turmoil. In some adolescents, these lead on to more serious moods of depression – a sense of helplessness and powerlessness, of events being out of, or beyond, control. Some adolescents even entertain ideas about committing suicide; a small number actually do so. The milder forms of depression may manifest as a lack of physical energy and well-being. In its more severe manifestation, children and adolescents tend to be irritable and bad-tempered, and, when it is at its worst, they sleep poorly, lack an appetite and are always dejected, apathetic and lifeless. The following characteristics are possible signs of depression in your client:

- a demeanour of unhappiness and misery (more persistent and intense than 'the blues' which we all suffer from now and then);
- a marked change in eating and/or sleeping patterns;
- a feeling of helplessness, hopelessness and self-dislike;
- an inability to concentrate and apply oneself to anything; everything (even talking and dressing) seems an effort;
- irritating or aggressive behaviour;
- a sudden change in standards of school work;
- a constant search for distractions and new activities;
- dangerous (but exciting/distracting?) risk-taking (for example, with drugs/alcohol; dangerous driving; delinquent actions).

Depression can be masked in adolescence and is not always easily detected. Another problem is that any item in the list above can occur normally in the adolescent without, in any way, indicating a depressive disorder. Affirmative answers to most of the questions below would indicate the presence of depression and will help you to judge whether or not to seek professional psychiatric advice.

- Do several of the signs (listed above) pertain to the teenager?
- Do they occur frequently?
- Have they persisted for a long time?
- Do they cause *extensive* suffering to him/her?
- Do they stand in the way of his/her development towards maturity?
- Do they get in the way of his/her relationships with peers and/or adults?
- Do they cause distress in others?

Affective disorder (depressive illness) can lead to suicide attempts and is therefore a concern in work with unhappy children and adolescents (see *Table 6.1*).

A Poor Self-Image

Psychological problems are very much bound up with the child's favourable or unfavourable self-perceptions, that is, with his or her self-image. For all the importance of the family and other social contexts within which children proactively shape their lives, and/or are reactively moulded, we should not lose sight of the individual

Table 6.1 Suicide and attempted suicide (adapted from an unpublished paper by John Challenor, 1992, with permission)

A Prevalence

- There are few children under 12 years (however, 'how few' is a moot question because of difficulties of recognizing or defining a 'suicide' or 'attempted suicide' because of children's uncertainties about the meaning of death and professional uncertainties about children's intentions and the possibility that a 'suicide' is an accidental death).

- There is an increased incidence with increasing age:
  – by age 10 to 14 suicide accounts for 2–3% of all deaths
  – by age 15 to 19 suicide accounts for 8–10% of all deaths.

- There is a female to male ratio of around 3:1.

- There are substantially higher rates in adults.

B Some characteristics of children who attempt/commit suicide

- *Emotional characteristics:*
  – irritable
  – impulsive, volatile and erratic
  – quiet and uncommunicative
  – self-perfectionists – self-critical – afraid of making mistakes
  – aggressive
  – friendless
  – sensitive to criticism.

- *Ability and education:* There is some evidence of a correlation between higher than average intelligence and suicide. Nevertheless, suicidal children tend to be poor achievers.

- *Accident-prone children:* The hypothesis that repeated accidents are on a continuum of self-destructive behaviour is poorly supported by available studies.

- *Family background:* Children who commit suicide do have a strong family history of suicide; so the question of modelling (learned behaviour) is raised.

- *Precursors:* Include, in adolescents, rows, reception into care, failure at school, abuse.

and, notably, the intimate core of the personality known as 'self'. While it is true that many of the difficulties with which children have to cope are social – the problems of getting on with parents, with brothers and sisters, with other children of the same age, with teachers – they also need to get on with themselves. Children need to rely on themselves, to get to know themselves, to understand their own limitations and to make the most of their capabilities. In a nutshell, they must see themselves in a realistic manner.

It was Aristotle who suggested that friendly relationships require a certain liking for oneself. Good relationships also need a degree of self-awareness and social sensitivity. The boy or girl's self-image plays a part in all of this; if it has been endlessly subverted by criticism or rejection, they are likely to feel unworthy and inferior, and display gauche and 'off-putting' behaviours which betray defensiveness and over-anxiety.

Consequences of Emotional and Behavioural Problems

Fantasy is one defensive strategy children make use of in order to cope with stressful circumstances. Some not only deny unpleasant reality, but also create the sort of world of fantasy they would like to inhabit. Incidentally, fantasy can be productive, for example, it may provide children with the opportunity to rehearse in imagination the solutions to their problems without entailing the risks of the real situation. Non-productive fantasy is the too persistent indulgence in wish-fulfilling kinds of mental activity. It compensates for a lack of achievement in real life.

Emotional insulation (isolation/dissociation). In this case, the child reduces the tensions of need and anxiety by withdrawing into a shell of numbness and passivity, by lowering expectations and by remaining emotionally uninvolved and detached. Apathy and defeated resignation may be the extreme reactions to stress and frustration of long duration.

Underachievement. Perhaps one of the most serious consequences of emotional and behavioural problems, is the deleterious effect on children's learning in the classroom and hence their achievement. Even when highly intelligent, those pupils with psychological difficulties, tend to have real difficulties in school performance. The greater the number of problems manifested by the child, the poorer, on the whole, is school performance.

Mental Disorder

The term 'childhood onset developmental disorder' is frequently used to cover the serious mental disorders of childhood, conditions which are not always amenable to clear-cut definition or demarcation.

Childhood psychosis

Psychoses are characterized by extreme impairments in perception, memory, thinking and language functions, and the child is fundamentally disorganized, rather than merely emotionally disturbed. Mental functions can be so profoundly disturbed by hallucinations and other symptoms that the individual appears irrational or bizarre, and is incapacitated from participating in everyday activities.

Psychoses of the adult type (schizophrenia and manic depression) are extremely rare before puberty, but occur at a rate of about one per 1,000 by mid-adolescence. In the opinion of many researchers, childhood 'psychosis' like 'mental handicap' or 'brain damage', is too general a term to be of much value in planning precise experimental investigations. Whereas 'schizophrenia' is the name given to a group of mental illnesses which usually develop after the age of puberty, and which have a characteristic pattern of clinical symptoms, and a characteristic course and outcome, there is no justification for finding analogies between it and childhood autism, which simply has as one of its features (like schizophrenia) social withdrawal. This characteristic is shared with many other psychotic conditions.

The term 'disintegrative psychosis' has gained ground and is applied to children who appear to be developing normally for several years, but then become confused and later lose skills, thus 'disintegrating' mentally, showing some of the symptoms described for autism.

Autism

Not all children who are diagnosed as autistic show all of the supposedly 'pathognomonic' behaviours or symptoms. The severity of the behaviours varies, and they generally tend to become less severe as the child gets older. This makes it hard to know where to draw the boundary, to say which children are autistic and which children are not. In the opinion of many, not enough is known about the processes underlying the behaviours which characterize autism to make a definitive description of the condition. The term 'autistic disorder' includes *inter alia*, the following attributes:

☐ Qualitative impairment in reciprocal social interaction.
  – Marked lack of awareness of the existence or feelings of others (for example, treats a person as if he or she were a piece of furniture; does not notice another person's distress; apparently

has no concept of the need of others for privacy).
  – Gross impairment in ability to make peer friendships (for
    example, no interest in making peer friendships; or, despite
    interest in making friends, demonstrates lack of understanding
    of conventions of social interaction – may, for example, read the
    phone book to an uninterested peer).

☐ Impairment of verbal and non-verbal communication and
  imaginative activity.
  – No mode of communication.
  – Markedly abnormal non-verbal communication.
  – Absence of imaginative activity (for example, fantasies, acting
    out adult roles, interest in stories about imaginary events).
  – Marked abnormalities in speech production.

☐ Abnormal repertoire of activities and interests.
  – Stereotyped body movements.
  – Persistent preoccupation with parts of objects.
  – Marked distress over changes in trivial aspects of the
    environment.
  – Unreasonable insistence on following routines in precise detail.

The prevalence rate of childhood autism is three to four per 10,000
children. Many aspects of the causation of autism remain a mystery,
but a number of theorists relate much of the bizarre symptomatology
to deficits and/or abnormalities of cognition and to problems of communication. Autistic children display deficits and abnormalities in
communication prior to the period when language is normally
acquired. Babbling is infrequent and conveys less information than
that of non-autistic infants. However, they often cry and scream to
indicate need. They do not use gestures (as deaf children try to do) as
a substitute for speech, and it has proved difficult to train them to do
so. Their faces show little expression.

As they get older, the language and non-verbal communication
deficits of autistic children become even more pronounced, with
mutism a feature of some 50 per cent of all autistic children. Even
when speech is acquired, there are many oddities such as 'pronoun
reversal' (you for I) and echolalia (repeating what people say often
with notable fidelity).

Table 6.2 Helpful organizations for children with mental and physical disabilities

Association for all Speech Impaired Children
Association for Spina Bifida and Hydrocephalus
British Dyslexia Association
British Epilepsy Association
Downs Children's Association
Gifted Children's Information Centre
Hyperactive Children's Support Group
Muscular Dystrophy Group of Great Britain
National Association for Deaf/Blind and Rubella Handicapped
National Deaf Children's Society
National Physically Handicapped and Able Bodied
National Society for Autistic Children
National Society for Mentally Handicapped Children (MENCAP)
National Society for Phenylketonuria and Allied Disorders
Royal National Institute for the Blind
Royal National Institute for the Deaf
Scottish Society for the Mentally Handicapped
Spastics Society
Spinal Injuries Association
Tuberose Sclerosis Group

FURTHER READING

Herbert, M. (1991) *Clinical Child Psychology: Social Learning, Development and Behaviour*. Chichester: John Wiley. [A comprehensive account of childhood mental health problems.]

Ward, R. (Ed.) *A Descriptive Bibliography of Articles and Books on Black and Ethnic Community Mental Health in Britain*. Mind, South East (24–32 Stephenson Way, London, NW1 2HD).

7 *Analysing causes*

Affectionate relationships within a family and wider social support act as buffers against various forms of psychological problem. Individual coping skills, self-confidence and personal strengths also mitigate the influence of stress and make breakdown or violence less rather than more likely as a response to frustration and misery. On the other hand, individuals have particular vulnerabilities which may, of themselves, have no impact on behavioural adjustment, but which may interact with chronic or acute stress to increase the risk of poor developmental outcomes. What must be taken into account in a causal analysis is the *interaction* of life circumstances and events with the individual strengths and weaknesses a child brings to bear on these environmental influences.

Life Events

The Children Act identifies a number of *social circumstances* which render children as being in need. A Social Services Department is quite likely to identify certain categories for which they hold data on children:

▶ Children separated from their parents (for example, parents divorced, children hospitalized for more than three months, a parent in prison, immigration restrictions).
▶ Privately fostered children.
▶ Children with caring responsibilities (for example, a child with disabled parents).
▶ Unsatisfactory home conditions (for example, where the family is delinquent, homeless or in accommodation for the homeless; or where accommodation is over-crowded).
▶ Children excluded from school.
▶ Other defined adverse life circumstances.

Life stress is usually thought of in two categories: *acute stress*, which is associated with specific life events such as divorce, bereavement, hospitalization, birth of a sibling; and *chronic stress*, which is related, *inter alia*, to long-term physical illness, low social status, a family characterized by psychopathology in the parents, and parental rejection and abuse.

Early research was concerned with identifying the kinds of acute stress that made children vulnerable to the development of behavioural problems. For example:

Hospitalization has been linked to a concurrent increased incidence of disturbance in preschool children. Longer term effects are rare, particularly for short-term hospital admissions of less than one week.

Birth of a sibling has been found to be related to increased preschool behavioural difficulties such as sleeping and toileting problems, and increased tearfulness.

Separation trauma commonly follows the breakup of marriages/ partnerships, death, or being taken into care.

Chronic stress, such as that connected with low social status, poor housing conditions and parental psychopathology, has long been associated with childhood behavioural problems. The evidence suggests that children with only one chronic stress factor do not exhibit an increase in the risk of disturbance compared with children without stress factors operating in their lives. If two or more stressors are present concurrently, the risk of developing behavioural problems is raised over and above the rate that would be expected on the basis of a simple additive model. Chronic stressors exhibit a potentiating or multiplicative influence on each other, in the sense that the effects of two or more stressors experienced simultaneously can exert more influence on the individual than the effects of those same stressors experienced separately.

Michael Rutter (1981) refers to a 'family adversity index' which consists of six variables which, by their interactive effects, contribute powerfully to childhood behavioural problems:

- severe marital discord;
- low social status;
- overcrowding or large family size;
- paternal criminality;
- maternal psychopathology;
- child's admission into the care of welfare services.

Separation and Loss

Much attention has been paid by researchers, because of the vital protective and nurturant functions which depend upon continuity of care, to the short and long-term reactions of children experiencing separation due to the loss of loved ones. The available evidence tells us that the effects of early separation are not always predictable, and certainly not necessarily (as was once thought), permanent. Each and every separation is a unique, complex and many-sided matter, requiring painstaking analysis. The outcome is heavily dependent on the quality and continuity of the substitute care and support available (see Appendix III).

Bereavement

Bereavement or grief behaviour has been defined as the total response pattern, psychological and physiological, displayed by an individual following the loss of a significant person. It has two components: mourning and grief. Mourning refers to the conventional behaviour as determined by the customs of the society; grief is the set of psychological and physiological reactions following loss. Given the crucial nature of emotional attachments of children who, by definition, are dependent on significant others, and given the immaturity of their coping strategies, loss of a parent is a particularly poignant experience. Grief has been described as a 'mental wound' which heals slowly and leaves scars; if people cannot work through the period of grieving, they may suffer lasting emotional damage.

Statistics in the 1980s show that approximately 550 wives became widows, 150 husbands became widowers, 40 young children lost a parent through death and almost 40 children under 14 died each day, in the United Kingdom. It is likely that most children (like most adults) adapt more or less painfully, but successfully, to the loss of these loved ones and the disruption of attachments which make life secure and meaningful. However, many do not cope. The typical signs and symptoms have been summarized as follows:

- worse health and physical distress;
- an inability to surrender the past – expressed, for example, by brooding over memories, sensing the presence of the dead, clinging to possessions, being unable to comprehend the loss, feelings of unreality;
- hostility against others, against fate, or turned in upon oneself.

Children are in double jeopardy when a parent or sibling dies: they suffer the impact of the loved one's absence and the temporary and partial 'loss' of the bereaved and preoccupied parent. This is illustrated in the comments of one of 22 young London widows interviewed by Parkes (1972): 'At first I just couldn't understand it. It didn't seem real. It just didn't seem possible, he was such a strong man. I just couldn't cope for a long while, there was nothing to do for it. My sister and the minister told me to pull myself together, but I said, "What for?". They said I had to for the children, but I still felt there was nothing to do for it' (page 127).

The child's concept of death
Kane (1979) has described the child's understanding of death in terms of the components he or she is cognitively capable of comprehending:

❏ *Realization* (understood by most three-year-olds): Even very young children have an awareness of death.

❏ *Separation* (understood by most five-year-olds): Young children can be very aware that death means separation from their parents, friends or brothers and sisters. This may be the main concept they focus on, and they may be concerned that they will feel lonely, or that their parents will be lonely without them.

❏ *Immobility* (understood by most five-year-olds): The awareness that dead people cannot move can concern some children, who are not also aware that dead people cannot feel, see or hear.

❏ *Irrevocability* (understood by most six-year-olds): The fact that once people die they cannot come back to life again is essential in understanding death. Many children younger than five or six may not realize the finality of the process. Children play games at being shot and dying, but then leap to life the next minute. 'Pretend' death and 'real' death need to be made clear, so that the child realizes that 'real' death means never living again.

❏ *Causality* (understood by most six-year-olds): There is always a physical cause of death. Young children, however, often have unusual or 'magical' ideas about what causes death, for example, a nasty wish, saying something horrible, or being naughty, can sometimes be perceived as having caused illness or death. Children need to understand that it is not such imaginary events that cause death, but that something is wrong with the body which is causing people to die.

❏ *Dysfunctionality* (understood by most six-year-olds): Explanations about death to children should include the cessation of bodily functions, for example, that the body stops breathing, growing, seeing, hearing, thinking and feeling and the heart stops beating. Some children worry they might be able to hear what is happening to themselves but not be able to tell anyone.

❏ *Universality* (understood by most seven-year-olds): That every living organism dies at some time is important in understanding that everyone must die eventually. This idea can comfort some children, who may believe that everyone lives for ever, and that it is unfair that they or someone they are close to are dying.

❏ *Insensitivity* (understood by most eight-year-olds): That a dead person cannot feel anything is often difficult for young children to understand. For example, if they walk on a grave, they may wonder if they are 'hurting' the person under the ground. One way of helping a child who is dying in pain, or who has parents who have been in pain, is to help them to realize they will never feel pain again after death.

❏ *Appearance* (understood by most 12-year-olds): A dead body looks different to a living body and children may be very interested in the physical characteristics of death. They can seem ghoulish sometimes in their desire for detailed descriptions of what a dead person looks like.

The loss of a parent is one of the foremost precursors of depressive problems. Losing a parent of the same sex (particularly for boys) appears to be a significant risk factor for depression. The results of research suggest several risk factors for poor adjustment, including the following:

• mental illness in the surviving parent;
• financial difficulties after the death of the parent;
• the sex of the child and of the surviving parent;
• the stability of the home environment prior to and/or after the death;
• the quality of the marital relationship before the death;
• the coping capacity of the surviving parent;
• the quality of the support system of the family after the death – it was shown that the risk of depression increases in the absence of a close confiding relationship.

The most severe problems are associated with having a mentally ill (more often than not, depressed) mother.

There seems little doubt that counselling support of various kinds mitigates some of the known ill-effects of the trauma of bereavement on physical and mental health. Children are remarkable, *if they have a secure base,* in the way they seem to accept the sad facts of life and death, and get on with living. A simple, straightforward explanation of the death (say) of the grandparent, is better than a dishonest palliative which mystifies the child. An awesome silence about the dead person will not help the child to work through and resolve grief.

Divorce/breakup of partnerships

Bereavement is not, of course, limited to the loss of loved ones through death. The loss of parents, or separation from one of them, due to the termination of relationships, is a common experience in western society today. In Britain, at least one in five children will have experienced divorce by the time they are 16 years old. The philosophy of the Children Act, with its emphasis on continuing parental responsibility by both father *and* mother, seems to be saying, 'If you can't make a success of your marriage/partnership, at least make a success of your divorce/separation'.

It is often said that children hold themselves responsible for the breakup of their parents and tend to feel very guilty about this. In fact such reactions do not seem to be very widespread; much more common is anger towards the parents for separating. Children of all ages frequently express the wish that their parents be reunited, and they blame either, or both of them, for the split.

Most children do not want their parents to separate and they may feel that their father and mother have not taken *their* interests into account. A marital separation may result in children's reappraising their own relationships with their parents and, indeed, questioning the nature of all social relationships. For younger children, in particular, there is the painful realization that relationships may not last forever. Preschool children usually appear to be very sad and frightened when their parents separate, and they become clinging and demanding. Bedtime fears and a refusal to be left alone, even for a few minutes, are not uncommon. Children attending school or nursery may become very anxious about going there, and may protest strongly when left. Vivid fantasies about abandonment, death of parents, and suchlike, are encountered and children often express aggression towards other children.

Many of these reactions are expressions of the child's fear of being abandoned by one or both of the parents. Such fears are likely to be most acute if contact has been lost with a parent. If, however, relationships between parents and child can remain intact and supportive, these fears are usually short-lived.

With older children, grief and sadness remain a prominent feature, but anger becomes more marked. This is usually directed at the parents, especially the one with whom the child is living – which, more often than not, means the mother. Regardless of the actual events leading to the breakdown, she is likely to be blamed by the child for everything that has happened. The absent father is quite likely to be idealized (again, regardless of realities), while the mother is held responsible for driving him away. Children, especially in the age group seven to eight, may express very strong yearnings for their father.

Pre-adolescent children tend to demonstrate less of their inner hurt and distress – which is not to say that it does not exist. Covering up is common, and they seek distractions in play and other activities. It may be difficult to get through to such children; they are loath to talk about what they are feeling because of the pain it causes them. Underneath this apparent detachment is often anger; again, they may align themselves very strongly with one parent and even refuse to see the other.

Adolescents sometimes show overt depression; they appear to 'opt out' of family life and withdraw into other relationships outside the home. Worries about their own relationships, sex and marriage, may surface.

These are the immediate reactions to parental separation. Usually they are seen in an acute form for a matter of months and then, hopefully, begin to subside. Unfortunately, the evidence concerning long-term consequences is very meagre and difficult to evaluate. Researchers have found that those people who experience a broken home in childhood, have only a slightly higher risk of developing psychiatric problems when compared with those from unbroken homes; for those with a comfortable economic background, there is no difference at all in the risk factor.

There is, however, a close relationship between fatherlessness and poverty, and many of the unfavourable consequences of deprivation of a father, are primarily the consequences of financial difficulties. Such worries may deplete the last emotional resources of the mother left alone. Young children need special attention and care, but she may have to seek employment. Finding substitute caregivers can be expensive. Housing, too, is a common and costly problem. Despite these problems, children from broken homes may fare better than youngsters from unhappy, unbroken homes. Delinquency is associated with the breakup of homes where there has been a great deal of parental disharmony; the association is not with the disruption of the home, as such.

From the professional's point of view, if called in to work with a family, it is vital to appreciate that an atmosphere of strife and turmoil in the home prior to separation, is one of the most corrosive influences. This quarrelling is something that children describe as very damaging – especially episodes of hostility between mother and father.

Of the factors that are significant to a benign outcome for children, three are of the utmost significance:

- communication about separation;
- continued good relationship with at least one parent;
- satisfaction with custody and access arrangements.

Most children would like two happily married/partnered parents, but would prefer to live with a single parent rather than two unhappily married ones. It is a natural wish on the part of workers to keep parents and children together; but there are times when 'heroic' work to maintain an intact family is counter to the best interests of all concerned.

Reconstituted Families

Reconstituted families, in which one or both partners have been married before, and are combining two families into one, are a common (and sometimes problem-engendering) phenomenon. In one out of every three marriages today, one or both parents have been married before. The difficulties of being a step-child are legendary; so too are the problems of being a step-parent. Research studies have confirmed the truth of these 'legends'. There is an increased risk of psychological problems in persons whose parents remarry, especially where it is the parent of the same sex as the child who finds a new partner.

There are, of course, many instances of step-parents who have brought great happiness and solace to the children in their new lives. The friction, jealousy and ambivalence which are a common feature of step-child/step-parent relationships can be overcome with empathetic handling – trying to see things from the child's point of view. For example, if the step-child lets herself go, and calls her step-father, 'Daddy', and shows him affection, might she not lose the love of her real father because of her disloyalty?

The step-parent is not immune from inner conflict. To what extent should the step-mum try to be a 'mother' when the child still has a mother? Should a step-father be permitted to discipline the child? These issues of who should be the 'executive' parent or parents, and of boundaries within and around the new family, have been tackled by family therapists like Carter and McGoldrick (1992).

Single-Parent Families

The number of such households is on the increase and lone mothers and fathers tend to have a difficult time of it. The problems are likely to be the same whether parents are on their own involuntarily or from choice – because of death, divorce, separation or through being unmarried.

You are likely to encounter the assumption that children from one-parent families will have more problems than children from two-parent families, but there is little hard evidence to confirm this fear. Children from one-parent homes are no more likely to become delinquents, dropouts, vandals or drug addicts than those from more 'conventional' families. Such problems are related to social and economic conditions and to adverse parental styles (attitudes and behaviours). It is not then a matter of being brought up by a single parent per se that puts children at a disadvantage, but, as we saw earlier, the poverty and other stresses that are only too often associated with single status. The vast majority of one-parent families are headed by women (89.3 per cent in 1983).

Unfortunately, as many working mothers learn, facilities for full-time day care are inadequate in most areas. Reliable arrangements for substitute care for young children so that the single parent may work, can make all the difference between a reasonable standard of living for the family, and a miserable, penny-grabbing, insecure existence. The choice is usually between childminders, day nurseries and cooperative grandparents.

The pressing need of a lone parent is support and they also need good accurate information about children and their development in special circumstances. The *National Council for One Parent Families* and *Gingerbread* are two groups organized to help single parents. The man or woman alone could well need financial, practical and personal help. They may also need emotional support. Problems sometimes arise when parents cling to their children to make up for losing their partners; they may require the child to grow up prematurely or create a kind of emotional claustrophobia in the home. Other single parents may try to support their children by over-compensating for what is missing – either by waiting on them hand and foot, or by letting their children do what they like.

Taking Children into Care

In the past, social workers could decide, with the approval of their senior managers, whether to take a child into care, and once in care, what to do about the child's future. In an institution, the child commonly suffers deprivations which add to the burden of his or her grief over a separation or abuse. Frequently, a shortage of residential staff means that the intensive care required by each child cannot be given. And the rapid turnover of staff means that children's experiences of separation or rejection are repeated over and over again until they cannot trust themselves (or adults) to make the emotional commitments most people take for granted.

Children in care were, only too often, allowed to 'drift'. Studies seem to indicate that if a child remains in local authority care for longer than five weeks, he or she has a very strong chance (two out of three cases) of still being in care two years later. The maintenance of close contact with their families is the best indicator that a child will leave local authority care rapidly. Children and adolescents, even if their chances of returning home are slight, function better psychologically, socially and educationally, if they remain in regular contact with their families. The importance attached to this research is clearly reflected in the 1989 Children Act (see Appendix III on Care Proceedings) which makes it clear that Social Services Departments *must* allow parents reasonable contact with children who are the subject of a care order, and try to promote such contact *unless* (and this is critical) this conduct will put the child's welfare at risk. Parental responsibility does not end following the care order.

The Act emphasizes the rights of children and young people to be consulted about plans for their future. The needs of each child or young person require individualized assessment so that clear and realistic plans for the future can be devised. Involving children in plans for their own futures, gives them some sense of control over their own destinies. Children have a need to understand what is happening or what, in the past, has happened to them. They are dealing not only with confused feelings, but with difficulties in finding meaning with regard to what has happened to them. Some of the questions may be of this kind: 'Why couldn't my mother look after me any more?'; 'Why did this illness happen to me and not my brother?'; 'Why did my nan die?'; 'What is going to happen to me?'. Answering children's questions requires sensitivity, honesty and a feeling for their cognitive and emotional maturity. Sometimes, of course, there are no answers to certain questions, and we have to acknowledge that fact.

Devising a life story book is a valuable way of helping children make sense of the fragmentary and sometimes inaccurate memories they have of their early lives. This can be compiled, added to, corrected and elaborated over time, and visits to former places which are important to the child, or to people whom the youngster used to know, can help fill in gaps. Vera Falhberg (1988) suggests that the life story book, which can be reread at the child's own pace, can help the child:

▷ to share, in an orderly fashion, his/her past with selected others;
▷ to organize past events chronologically;
▷ to accept the past;
▷ to aid ego development;
▷ to increase self-esteem;
▷ to build a sense of trust for the worker who aids in compiling the book;
▷ to facilitate bonding.

Individual Influences

We have looked at stressful life events and circumstances, but an analysis of causal influences is incomplete without a picture of how the typical individual reacts to stress and what differentiates the resilient from the vulnerable child in such circumstances.

Typical reactions to major life events

These are the fairly predictable stages which tend to occur following a disruptive life experience:

❏ *Immobilization*. The individual has a sense of being overwhelmed, of being unable to make plans, to understand or to reason; a kind of paralysis sets in.

❏ *Minimization*. The person may try to cope by minimizing the changes. For example, a girl may make light of the pain she feels following the separation of her mother and father; a youngster may try to trivialize the changes brought about by his new step-mother's entry into the home ('I don't know why everyone makes such a fuss over nothing'). Some persons will deny that a change has occurred.

❏ *Depression*. This is a common experience for adolescents, menopausal women and the elderly; the physical changes of puberty, middle life and old age represent dramatic transitions in life. There may be an upsurge of feelings of misery and inner turmoil, and misery may lead to depression in more vulnerable individuals. This is accompanied by feelings of helplessness and/or powerlessness, of events being out of, or beyond, control. Some clients entertain ideas about committing suicide.

❏ *Letting go*. This is the stage of accepting reality for what it is, of figuratively 'letting go' of the past. For the toddler, this means letting go of the dependency of infancy; for the adolescent – the safety of childhood, total parental nurturance and freedom from responsibility.

❏ *Testing*. The 'letting go' stage provides a bridge to the testing phase, in which the individual may begin testing him or herself *vis-à-vis* the new circumstances – trying out new behaviours, skills and even (to the chagrin, sometimes, of family and friends) new life styles. At this time, quite a lot of anger and irritability can be expressed.

❏ *Search for meaning*. Following the phase of activity and self-testing, is a more gradual movement towards finding meaning and understanding how and why things are different.

❏ *Internalization*. These new meanings are eventually internalized, that is, taken into the 'psyche' and behavioural repertoire of the individual.

Vulnerability and resilience

Who goes under when adverse circumstances prevail? Research from various sources (for example, Werner and Smith, 1977) indicates that resilient children are more active, socially responsive and autonomous than non-resilient youngsters. The family environment of resilient children is characterized by parental support, family closeness, rule-setting, discipline, and a respect for individuality. Thus, a positive social orientation, a positive personal disposition, and a positive family environment are related to resilience in the face of stress. Factors that increase vulnerability include late birth order, poor integrity of the central nervous system, prolonged mother–infant separation, repeated childhood health problems, family and parental discord, a high *cumulative* number of stressful life events, and low parental intelligence.

Attitudes and constructs

Some practitioners (and, indeed, parents) dwell on the past when they look for the whys and wherefores of children's difficulties. It is important to maintain a balance between past and present when trying to find reasons or causes for current behaviour. It is only in rare instances that current problems can be traced to specific past experiences with any degree of confidence. In any event, the past cannot be changed, although one might 'liberate' someone from the past ('laying ghosts to rest' so to speak) by resolving or changing present unhealthy attitudes which are *rooted* there.

Personal Construct Theory focuses on such attitudes. These attitudes can be seen as implicit 'theories' we have about life and people, which give meaning to the world we live in; they provide a frame of reference with which people can make interpretations of life. All individuals are concerned to anticipate (or predict) what will happen to and around them. If you are able to make sense of your world, you can then make the necessary adaptations to changing circumstances. To this end, each and every individual constructs in his or her thought processes, a model of past and present experiences and events. This model can be described as a set of 'goggles' through which the individual construes life. On the basis of these constructions or interpretations, he or she is able to take appropriate or, with faulty constructs, inappropriate actions.

The inventor of this model, George Kelly (1955), uses the metaphor of the person as 'scientist' to illustrate his contention that individuals are constantly trying to understand and predict events. The term 'personal construct system' illustrates the fact that people may resemble one another in their construing processes, but essentially, no one person is a carbon copy of another. Every person lives in a world that is unique to him or her because it is idiosyncratically interpreted and experienced.

Parents evolve a construct system to make sense of the world of children and family life. The constructs used by parents (some developed in the bosom of their family of origin, others elaborated with more recent experiences of actual parenting), give meanings to their offspring's behaviour and facilitate mutually satisfactory interactions. Sadly, some construct systems lead (or mislead) parents into confrontations with their babies. If the crying of a very young baby is construed as wilful naughtiness, and smacking is construed as an appropriate training method or punishment for dealing with naughtiness, a fraught and potentially dangerous situation might arise.

The child, too, actively seeks to make sense of his or her world. It is an important part of your assessment to tease out how the child views those parts of the world that are salient to your quest for understanding. There are techniques (repertory grids) for eliciting child and adult construct systems. There are also active, role-play methods for helping clients to test out the way they perceive (and often self-defeatingly misconstrue) their world. They may be used with those who have low self-esteem, feel persecuted and are socially isolated.

The person is encouraged to explore (by trying out) alternative patterns of behaviour contrasted to his/her own. This is based on a carefully scripted role – a sketch worked out with clients and derived from a compromise between what they are 'actually' like, and how they would like to be. They are invited to practise these patterns in everyday life.

From practice, they gain some experience of how the environment can differ in appearance and 'feel', and how it reacts, when they behave in a different manner.

Practice generates new and more effective skills, supplemented by novel experience from the feedback they have received. The expectation is that by receiving new and helpful forms of feedback from the environment, they will change the self-defeating attitudes that control their behaviour. (An illustration of this technique is given on page 168.)

Self-esteem

Human beings old enough to have acquired even a rudimentary self-image, demonstrate a need to perceive themselves in at least a moderately favourable light. A reasonable agreement between the self-concept ('myself as I am') and the concept of the ideal self ('myself as I would like to be') is an indication of self-esteem, and one of the most important conditions for personal happiness and for satisfaction in life. Marked discrepancies arouse anxiety and can be indicative of psychological problems.

You might ask the client to talk about or to write an account on the theme, 'Myself as I am'; and another account entitled, 'Myself as I would like to be'. These can then be compared and the points of mismatch discussed. This could help in setting realistic and meaningful goals for the client.

There are various ways in which people defend their self-esteem. For example, in some children, a 'don't care', independent attitude may well mask a craving for nurturance and a need for dependency. Other youngsters simply withdraw from competitive situations if they feel at a disadvantage or that they may fail. They may be indecisive and procrastinate in times of stress, putting off actions that have to be faced. These are but a few examples of defensive strategies which are used to protect the 'self' (see Lee and Herbert, 1970).

Unconscious motivation

Psychoanalytic theory stresses 'understanding' and the historical element in problem development. There are sometimes heated debates about the status (and, indeed, viability) of psychoanalysis. There is wide disagreement among distinguished thinkers as to whether it is a science, a myth, a theory, a therapy or a premature synthesis.

Some theorists argue that it is perfectly possible for psychoanalytic investigations to be termed scientific (unless the word 'science' is understood in a very rigid and narrow sense). Sigmund Freud, himself, regarded psychoanalysis as a science.

An eminent psychoanalyst, Charles Rycroft (1970), believes that Freud's work was really semantic (that is, a theory concerned with meanings rather than causes), but, owing to his scientific training and allegiance, Freud formulated his findings in the inappropriate conceptual framework of the physical sciences. Rycroft suggests that if psychoanalysis is recognized as a 'semantic theory' not a causal one, its theory can start where its practice does – in the consulting room. A patient who is suffering from something which he or she does not understand, confronts an analyst who has some knowledge of the unconscious – that is, who knows something of the way in which repudiated wishes, thoughts, feelings and memories can translate themselves into symptoms, fantasies and dreams. The analyst has an understanding of the underlying meaning, the 'grammar and syntax' of the outward manifestations of unconscious conflict and is, therefore, in a position to interpret them into the communal language of consciousness.

The writings of psychoanalysts can (if evaluated carefully and critically) open 'mental doors' for social and health workers to dimensions of experience which are not readily accessible to ordinary common sense. It is assumed that this insight will give clients greater control over their behaviour. Many of our motives are unconscious and it is impossible to come to terms with an 'invisible enemy'. The therapist tries to make the invisible visible, the unconscious conscious, so that reality can be grappled with.

Multifactorial Causation

Social and psychological problems in children (and families) are so complex (see *Figure 7.1*) that a search for simple linear causal explanations (A leads to B; Y causes Z) is usually doomed to failure when tested in a treatment programme or intervention plan.

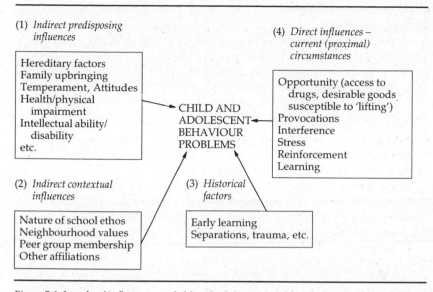

(1) *Indirect predisposing influences*

Hereditary factors
Family upbringing
Temperament, Attitudes
Health/physical
    impairment
Intellectual ability/
    disability
etc.

(4) *Direct influences – current (proximal) circumstances*

Opportunity (access to
    drugs, desirable goods
    susceptible to 'lifting')
Provocations
Interference
Stress
Reinforcement
Learning

CHILD AND ADOLESCENT BEHAVIOUR PROBLEMS

(2) *Indirect contextual influences*

Nature of school ethos
Neighbourhood values
Peer group membership
Other affiliations

(3) *Historical factors*

Early learning
Separations, trauma, etc.

Figure 7.1 Levels of influence on child and adolescent problem behaviour

Social learning theory

Although a great many factors influence the child's behaviour, the process of learning a particular behaviour cannot be explained by these factors alone. It is hypothesized that a major proportion of a child's problematic behaviour is learned, maintained and regulated by its effects upon the natural environment and the feedback the child receives with regard to these consequences. Behaviour does not occur in a vacuum; nor is it a passive process. It is the result of a complex interaction between the individual, with his or her inborn strengths and weaknesses, acting and reacting with an environment which sometimes encourages and sometimes discourages certain actions. An important feature of the social learning model is the acknowledgement of the active role of cognitive variables (complex interpretive, thinking processes) in the way we learn. The part played by understanding in learning is significant.

Parents (and teachers) teach children skills and guide them towards prosocial actions and (when they can) away from antisocial activities. There seems to be a fair amount of latitude in learning conditions for those children with intact central nervous systems, healthy bodies and relatively unvolcanic temperaments. They acquire an understanding of, and willingness to abide by, society's conventions despite parental inconsistency, contradictory demands ('double-binds'), and ambiguous rules. For such children, parental inexperience or poor judgement seem no more than a minor hindrance in the business of growing up.

Nevertheless parents can be said to be informal learning theorists; they use various techniques to teach, influence and change the child in their care. Among those used are material and psychological rewards, praise and encouragement, giving or withholding approval, and psychological punishments such as reproof or disapproval. At its simplest level the rule-of-thumb is as follows:

Acceptable behaviour	+ Reinforcement	= More acceptable behaviour
Acceptable behaviour	+ No reinforcement	= Less acceptable behaviour
Unacceptable behaviour	+ Reinforcement	= More unacceptable behaviour
Unacceptable behaviour	+ No reinforcement	= Less unacceptable behaviour

Behaviour theorists often refer to their assessment – as a simple mnemonic – in ABC terms (sometimes called a 'functional analysis'.)

A stands for *Antecedent events*.

B stands for *Behaviour(s)* – the target behaviour(s) or interactions (also for *Beliefs* – the child's (perhaps parent's) perception or interpretation of what is happening).

C stands for the *Consequences* that flow from these behaviours/ interactions/beliefs.

This linear analysis is elaborated into a recursive sequence such that C's become A's which generate new C's. Target behaviours and/or interactions are chosen for analysis because of their hypothesized significance as problems in the child's (possibly the parent's) repertoire, or in their relationship. Questions to ask are: 'What payoff does the child get for behaving in this way?'; 'What short-term 'solutions' (even if self-defeating in the longer term) do the child's actions provide?'; and 'What purpose does the child's behaviour serve in terms of his or her family life and its psychological and social dynamics?'.

The advantage of encouraging parents/caregivers to keep diaries or ABC sequence records is that such records often indicate the parents' role in maintaining the child's behaviour, most particularly in relation to the consequences of the behaviour. This is most important when parents attribute 'ownership' of the 'problem' entirely to the child, thereby opting out of any responsibility.

A case illustration

Emma Bray (a pseudonym) and her family were referred by their paediatrician because of the child's difficult behaviour, but also because her mother had expressed fears that she might lose her self-control and hurt her.

Emma, aged four, demanded an inordinate amount of individual attention, monopolizing her mother's time wherever she was and whatever she was doing. She clung to her and followed her everywhere, even to the toilet, refusing to let her out of her sight even for a few moments. Emma would not play with other children, including her sister – who had some resentments but no pressing problems as her parents saw it. Emma's behaviour difficulties (including aggression, self-centredness of an extreme kind and other antisocial actions) were rampant and created serious implications for herself and her family. The problems, as our observations confirmed, were real enough, but there were other issues which also required attention.

Those who call themselves systems theorists are agreed in focusing not only on the individual but on the system of relationships in which individuals interact. The value of this 'open-ended' approach is (a) it does not assume that the family is 'the problem'; nor (b) does it jump to the conclusion that the child has 'the problem'. Rather it helps to determine, by careful and systematic assessment, the various aspects and origins of a problem so that appropriate tasks and goals can be planned.

It is a small wonder when we look at Emma's history that we had a many-sided case on our hands: a depressed mother, an unhappy wilful child, a discontented sister, a frustrated and confused father, and a generally miserable, tense family life. Emma had been a difficult and hyperactive child from early in life; from the day of her birth, she would cry day and night. The nights were particularly difficult. Mrs Bray spent much of them nursing her to allow the rest of the family to have some sleep. There were also serious feeding problems. The parents were worried that Emma would starve, so force feeding was necessary for several months. It could take up to three hours to feed the baby. Indeed, she was an unusual child in other ways. She was difficult to amuse, taking only the most fleeting interest in toys. She seldom smiled. Her moods were volatile. When she didn't appear to be depressed and withdrawn, she was often screaming for attention.

Her mother and father found it impossible to enjoy their youngest child as she was so difficult to rear – she hated any change in routine and was predictable only in her unpredictability. Mrs Bray felt guilty for having the child when she had been advised not to, and any nasty remarks in that direction, from anyone, would turn her to the fierce protection of Emma, even though she might secretly agree with the criticisms. Finally, because of the marital tension and lack of her husband's support when dealing with Emma's behaviour, Mrs Bray reached a low point of depression, involving physical and nervous exhaustion. All this further minimized consistent and effective handling of her child.

Emma's demands were usually acceded to following her display of trantrums and disruptive behaviours. Mrs Bray's attention was reinforcing Emma's non-compliant actions. It was quite straight-forward to identify favourable consequences; to take but one example, Emma was being allowed to veto activities she did not like. There were no really unfavourable consequences (penalties) which might serve to diminish Emma's misbehaviour.

What we have then, are several predisposing and precipitating 'causes' of what is essentially a family problem, not just a child's difficult (some would call it 'challenging') behaviour. They include:

- Emma's demanding behaviour from birth (temperamental attributes);
- a physical problem which contributed to eating difficulties and incessant crying;
- the consequent need to nurse Emma a lot, leading to mutual proximity seeking;
- guilt feelings driving Mother to give in to Emma;
- Father's opting out, leading to marital difficulties; adding to Mothers' depression and loss of confidence.

With regard to the direct precipitating influences (triggers) for the performance of problem behaviours, the most significant of these were Mrs Bray's actions. The currency of her commands and threats had been debased; Emma did not trust her words. She had learnt that her wishes (for her mother's undivided attention and 'obedience' to her commands) were likely to be met if she persisted long enough or escalated her coercive behaviours.

Essentially she had learned that certain antisocial behaviours were guaranteed to produce 'payoffs'. Applied in the school situation, this could have aversive consequences for her and reduce her ability to learn.

Because of the endless round of disputations between parents and child, Emma was precluded from much of the usual range of symbolic rewards or social reinforcers which occur in happy and meaningful family communications. Emma, as a volatile, demanding child, had made constant 'assaults' on her mother's self-doubts. This is how Mrs Bray described the situation as she saw it:

'As time went by, Emma has developed into a despot. She shows a general aggression, a degree of wilfulness, and various other unacceptable behaviours. She whines, clings like a limpet, is insecure, and worst of all for me, is incessantly disobedient . . . The situation over the years has deteriorated, compounded by an increasing tiredness on my part. This gradually deepened into general depression for which my doctor prescribed drugs. They didn't

help; in fact feeling slightly drunk and rudderless made coping even more difficult. I was tearful, tense, often unreasonably angry, erratic and emotional, and then silent and withdrawn in turns. The tension in the house was painful . . . I was really desperate. It was an effort to go out, even to the shops. I looked awful, felt awful. Sometimes the loathing for Emma spilled over and I found myself wanting to tell her, "Go away out of my life, I hate you. You've ruined my life". Sometimes I would start then have to bite back the words, remembering that I did love her. Afterwards I would feel consumed with guilt that I could even think these things. And overall was this dreadful sense of failure. Failure as a mother and failure as a wife, even failure as a woman. I have never been so close to a total breakdown.'

As Mrs Bray appeared to bear the brunt of most of Emma's misbehaviour, it might be concluded that Emma's father was able to exercise control over her. This was not so; in fact, Mr Bray's small part in the situation reflects his minimizing of the contact he had with Emma – much to his wife's annoyance. This opting out figured importantly in our analysis and treatment plan.

At a systemic level it was possible to see that Emma served as a convenient scapegoat for various marital and family tensions. Thus, the therapy, while focusing, in part, on the parents' agenda ('a very difficult child'), also attended to issues such as family relationships and Mrs Bray's sense of helplessness (see Chapter 9).

FURTHER READING

Bell, R. and Harper, L. (1977) *Child Effects on Adults*. New Jersey: Erlbaum. [Influence as a two-way process.]

Madge, N. (Ed.) (1983) *Families at Risk*. London: Heinemann. [Self-explanatory.]

Werner, E. E. and Smith R. S. (1982) *Vulnerable, but Invincible. A Longitudinal Study of Resilient Children and Youth*. New York: McGraw-Hill.

PART II

Planning and implementation

The most important instrument in your work with parents and children is yourself. It is essential, therefore, to spend some time preparing yourself before you start work. There are several questions you might ask yourself:

'Why am I involved in this?'
You may be involved in work with parents and children for a variety of reasons. We have all been children and adolescents, and many of us are parents. So we have our own experiences and prejudices; and will be immersed in family matters at both the personal (subjective) and the professional levels. Whatever your reasons for being involved, examine your personal motives and underlying assumptions.

'What is my role?'
The area of child care is value-laden; certain kinds of problems are particularly sensitive (indeed, threatening) to us. The issue of trying to help people change involves important personal, moral and ethical considerations. Practitioners who set out to change people are accused of controlling behaviour. Such allegations imply that clients exist in a vacuum of free will before entering an intervention. Therapists (for example) talk, on the one hand, of liberating clients from some of the unwanted controlling forces in their lives, but assume, on the other hand, a freedom of choice when it comes to accepting an intervention. They tend to say that if a client requires help and requests it, then help should be provided.

'Do I have the right to intervene?'
The difficulty with the comforting principle just enunciated, is that people can be coerced in ways subtle and unsubtle, tangible and intangible, to 'seek' help. Some clients, for example, children, are not in a position to ask for help or (to put it another way) clear enough about the issues (or powerful enough) to reject the offer of help. These matters should be thought through very carefully. Advocacy – speaking up for the child – will be an important part of your work. Indeed, advocacy on behalf of hard-pressed, demoralized mothers

will be another. Other clients, for instance parents, are involuntary recipients of our attention, when we have statutory obligations to make an assessment and/or an intervention. It is notoriously difficult to wear a caring (helping) hat *and* a protecting (controlling) hat at one and the same time. Decisions (as important as an application to take children into care) and the use of powerful therapeutic methods, also involve moral imperatives – a clear understanding of the implications. If these caveats sound rather daunting, then do remember the positives: your potential to help individuals and families in distress and the support you can give to your colleagues.

Inter-Agency Liaison

Working in a team provides an ideal support system. It is important to have people around you to back you up, share ideas, stimulate and challenge you. At times of stress and difficulty, individuals and groups within your agency may be sources of strength to you. You may require supervision from an experienced practitioner if you are learning to use a specialized approach like family therapy or behavioural psychotherapy.

However, no one profession has all the skills with which to remedy the range of problems we have been looking at in Part I. This is the rationale for interdisciplinary teams in some agencies and for making meticulous plans to achieve close inter-agency liaison. Social workers are likely to be heavily engaged, often because of their statutory responsibilities. Members of primary care teams – GPs, nurses and health visitors – are also in the front line. At times, several professionals may be engaged in a family's life and problems; so it is good practice to identify a key worker or case manager who coordinates and monitors a complex situation which, otherwise, might become confused because everyone thinks someone else is doing x, y or z.

Inter-agency liaison and cooperation are essential to those aspects of work with children and families that come under the umbrella of the Children Act. (This is not to say that they are not a prerequisite of all work with people in distress.) Most of the duties under the Act will be met by local authority Social Services Departments. But there are implications for national health service managers and professionals. For example:

- Section 27 requires districts, Special Health Authorities (SHAs) and trusts to collaborate with Social Services Departments in providing support for children and their families.
- Section 85 requires districts, SHAs and trusts to tell the responsible Social Services Department when they provide, or intend to provide, a child with accommodation for at least three consecutive months, and when the child leaves the accommodation.

- Districts, SHAs and trusts will have to meet the requirements of the Children (Secure Accommodation) Regulations 1991 where a child's freedom is restricted other than under the Mental Health Act 1983.

Local education authorities (LEAs) also have duties under the Children Act, for example, with regard to education supervision orders [s.36]. LEAs can apply (*after* consulting the appropriate social services committee) for an education supervision order [s.36(8)]. The court must be satisfied that the child is of compulsory school age and is not being properly educated [s.36(3)]. The child's welfare is the court's paramount consideration [s.1(1)], and there is a presumption of no order unless the court considers that to make an order would be better for the child [s.1(5)].

The supervisor, if appointed, is under a duty to advise, assist and befriend, and give directions to the supervised child and the parents, in such a way as will secure that the child is properly educated [Sched 3, para 12].

The Case Conference

A network meeting or case conference is usual in a child care context so that relevant information can be weighed up and decisions made. The latter is a formal meeting attended by representatives from all the agencies. Increasingly the child's parents are invited to attend – a development encouraged by the Children Act. A plan of action is formulated, for example, to protect a child by seeking a court order. When the meeting decides that the child's family needs support, a key worker will be appointed to coordinate an inter-agency plan to work with the child and the family. The child's name may be entered on the Child Protection Register. The following points are worth remembering when you prepare a report for a case conference or for the courts (see Bromley, 1986):

▷ Specify the sources (for example, direct observations, interviews, case notes) for the comments and conclusions you have arrived at.
▷ Always separate clearly fact from opinion.
▷ Formulate precisely the issues (the objectives, questions, problems) you are addressing.
▷ Provide background information as a context for understanding the previous point.
▷ Offer 'prima facie' explanations (hypotheses, conjectures) for the client's predicament, on the basis of the *evidence*.
▷ Be as parsimonious as possible: first give simple and obvious explanations, and then (if these don't stand up to critical examination) consider more complex and elaborate levels of explanation.

▷ Put forward tentative solutions to the problems, applying the same principles as above.

▷ Consider again evidence that might contradict your explanations and solutions. Hopefully they will stand up to this 'cross-examination'. Whenever you make an assertion say to yourself: 'What is the evidence?'.

▷ Evidence *must* be relevant, admissable, reliable – obtained from credible and competent sources.

▷ Enquire critically into your *sources* of evidence as well as the quality of the evidence itself.

▷ Examine rigorously the internal logic and coherence of your report. Do the explanations lead logically to the intervention/plan of work?

▷ Are the explanations and intervention plan realistic, practical, ethical?

Services and Resources for Families

Pauline Hardiker (1992) makes the point that the Children Act makes a clear distinction between ordinary services and compulsory interventions, and that this is very important in respect of services for children with disabilities. The thresholds (see page 213) identified for state care and supervision relate to compulsory intervention not to ordinary services.

Even when interventions are essential, parental responsibility can be shared with the local authority, and children and parents consulted about their needs and wishes. Support for families is conceived of in terms of services such as domiciliary help, family centres, befriending schemes, day and respite care provision, counselling and accommodation, or help in cash or kind. These support services are best mobilized before interventions of a compulsory nature are considered.

Broadly speaking – despite their individual differences – services have all or some of the following objectives:

▶ Community-based preventive work. Preventing family breakup and reception of children into care by supporting families to alleviate stress, teaching practical skills, and attempting to improve the quality of parent–child relationships; also preventing the deprivation of parental care and the fragmentation of families.

▶ Complementary education (educational outreach). Developing parents' understanding of the educational context of the home and the community, and their educational role in relation to their child. This is the idea of parents as 'complementary educators' – as the first teachers of their children.

▶ Supporting self-help groups. Providing amenities for small self-help groups set up by local people to meet their own needs for friendship, mutual support or child care.

The skills of many specialists and generalists are called upon in providing services, especially where children are disabled.

Health visitors/nurses

Studies suggest that health visitors visit disabled children nearly twice as often per annum as non-disabled children – taken on average. Although mothers feel that health visitors may lack specialist knowledge and information, they enjoy their visits and the support they offer. There are, of course, specialist health visitors who have expertise in particular areas of illness or disability. Nurses and health visitors are in a vital position to ensure that health awareness reaches all sections of the community (Douglas, 1993). Douglas makes the point that child care nurses, community nurses and nurses working in accident and emergency departments have a responsibility to participate in the design and implementation of services for the care of children. In addition, nurses are well placed to be among the earliest to notice a child in need (for example, detecting unusual bruising or behaviour) while caring for them.

Social workers

According to surveys, about one-half of families had received help from social workers in the preceding year. However, over 50 per cent of clients were dissatisfied with this service, complaining that the turnover was too high. In their opinion, social workers were too young, inexperienced or over-worked, with inadequate knowledge of benefits. However, the evidence about the amount and helpfulness of contacts with social workers remains very mixed.

General practitioners

The average GP is likely to have three disabled children in the practice at any one time. The few studies conducted, suggest good relationships exist, with the GP being perceived as supportive.

Hospital doctors

From the evidence that exists on parents' experience with hospitals, it would appear that although the technical proficiency of personnel is high, parents sometimes feel that they rank low in humanity. Parents complained about seeing a different doctor on each visit. Quality assurance schemes in hospitals are attempting to meet these kinds of criticism.

Teachers and psychologists

It has been found that, as the demands for a social response from autistic children are increased, the children are more likely to produce such a response. This kind of observation has encouraged psychologists and teachers (in partnership with parents) to use behavioural and cognitive methods to encourage social behaviour, skills and speech (for example, De Myer *et al.*, 1981).

The role of parents

Davis (1993) makes the point that the psychosocial adaptation of parents should be of central and direct concern to every professional because of the crucial role of the parents in all aspects of the care and treatment of the child. Although professionals do treat children directly, for the most part, it is only through the parents that they have access legally, practically or morally, to the child. Parents often have expertise and supplies of resourcefulness that we ignore at our peril.

There are several schemes available providing help and support for parents of handicapped children. They may take the form of parent groups (for example, MENCAP), training groups with specialist members, or home visits by specialists. The latter is of importance because intellectually impaired children, like all children, perform at their best when relaxed, and in familiar surroundings with familiar people present. Assessment in a hospital, or clinic, can yield quite misleading results.

Usually parents are very reluctant to seek long-term care or to send their child to a residential school. Serious behaviour problems may force this on them. In Baldwin's (1976) study, 76 per cent of parents had never had their child cared for away from home, about 13 per cent had done so once, and 11 per cent had done so several times. Asked if they wanted more short-term care, 74 per cent said no (see Sutton, 1988, for a review of research studies relating to the provision of services).

Parent training is now seen as a standard ingredient for early intervention programmes with children with developmental or intellectual impairments. Home-based assistance is available through the Portage project which began in Wisconsin in 1969. A trained person visits the family at frequent intervals and works with the parents and child. During these visits, the parents and the Portage visitor agree on what skills the child needs to acquire next and how the parents can achieve this by working with the child each day.

Another service of help is the Education of the Developmentally Young (EDY) project started by the Hester Adrian Research Centre at Manchester University. This was designed to teach those working with young handicapped children the skills for modifying the behaviours of these children.

Howlin (1984) has reviewed a number of schemes for parental involvement in the treatment of children with language delays. These range from those centred on children with delays associated with intellectual impairment and autism, through to those involving expressive language delays primarily the result of inadequate or inappropriate stimulation at home. She found that although few of these approaches to treatment had been adequately evaluated, those that involved the parents in home-based activities as part of a *structured learning programme* of remedial help for the children (for example, Portage), were likely to show significant improvements.

Personal and social support

There is evidence that a network of supportive persons (and the quality and intimacy of the support provided) can mitigate the effects of stress. Social isolation is one of the common effects of having a disabled or difficult child. As social networks, ties and contacts promote psychological well-being, it is important for the professional to be familiar with local and national groups and resources and to identify their presence or absence for the client. Knowledge of community resources, having good contacts with other professionals, para-professionals, volunteers and information-providing self-help groups, allows you to 'network' effectively on behalf of your clients – bringing together helpful people.

There are many groups in existence, such as MENCAP, Parentline and Compassionate Friends, who are of inestimable value to people in distress. They provide not only advice and support, but also potential friends.

It is appropriate, also, to seek to involve people whose acceptability to the client has been confirmed, and who can be identified as sources of strength and assistance. Intimate or close relationships of the type provided by primary groups (those people with whom one has face-to-face interaction and a sense of commitment) are the most significant sources of support.

Table II.1 lists questions concerning family and social contacts. These enable clients to indicate supportive people to whom they turn in times of trouble. Such resources help to supplement those resources available from statutory and voluntary services.

Ethnic and Cultural Values

Insensitivity to cultural values in social work and clinical practice can lead to much individual suffering if methods used, or decisions arrived at, offend against cherished cultural and/or religious beliefs. The clients of health and social workers are varied in culture, race, background, religion and age. Legislation concerned with equal

Table II.1 Social support checklist (adapted from Herbert, 1991a)

Tick the appropriate box and give more details where necessary:

Do any of your relatives live nearby?	Yes ☐	
	No ☐	

How often do you seem them?		
Seldom	☐	Other_____
Regularly, but infrequently	☐	_____
Often	☐	_____

Do any of your friends live nearby?	Yes ☐	
	No ☐	

How often do you see them?		
Seldom	☐	Other_____
Regularly, but infrequently	☐	_____
Often	☐	_____

How do you get on with your neighbours?	
Well – great help	☐
Some help	☐
Do not bother with them	☐
Badly – lots of disagreements	☐

How do you spend your leisure time?	_____
	_____

Do you go on family outings?	Yes ☐	Roughly how often?____
	No ☐	_____

To whom do you turn in times of trouble?	
Parents	☐
Partner	☐
Relatives	☐
Friends	☐
Social worker	☐
Health visitor	☐
Doctor	☐
Clergy	☐
Colleagues/workmates	☐
Neighbours	☐
Others (please specify)_____	

opportunities attempts to recognize this diversity explicitly, and to reduce discrimination against minority groups (see the Local Government Management Board's *Maximising Human Resources*, 1990). A way to recognize individual differences and individual needs, is to avoid the temptation to 'lump people together' in anonymous groupings. The practice of talking about 'children who are disabled' as distinct from 'the disabled', about 'families with problems' as distinct from 'problem families', is a move in the right direction.

At an appropriate stage, you might ask the client whether there are aspects of his or her culture or personal circumstances which have implications for the situation or topic under discussion; also demonstrate your wish to learn about the person's culture – insofar as it affects your work together.

As a background to these efforts, you might increase your knowledge of different communities, their cultures, beliefs and practices, by:

- attempting to build individualized and trusting relationships with elders and respected members of different communities;
- supporting attempts to develop 'community guidelines' over matters such as child discipline, that is, guidelines which community leaders have agreed to endorse within their communities;
- developing codes of conduct for occasions when there is the possibility of intergroup differences of opinion.

(Sutton and Herbert, 1992, discuss these issues in relation to an area where prejudice is highly intrusive and destructive – mental health.)

The ASPIRE Model

Planning

At this stage, we return to the ASPIRE model. The first part of the acronym refers to assessment (see page 30). We now move on to the *plan* of work and *implementing* an intervention. The plan of work enables the client, with your help, to clarify his/her expectations and aims. These are translated into goals which must be negotiated and agreed with your client. Goals are the changes to be sought (the focus of a therapeutic intervention).

▶ Consider informal and/or direct solutions. Before going further with a formal intervention, consider whether informal and/or direct approaches are worth trying. These may include:
  – medical or physical examinations – for example, a hearing defect may result in a child being viewed as disobedient and difficult;

- changing a child's bedtime routine may make him or her more likely to stay in bed and go to sleep.
▶ Make the first priority for your clients the acquisition or strengthening of positive communications/actions within the family (see page 187).
▶ Select areas of change which are relevant to the individual and family.
▶ Select your intervention approach (and specific methods). The choice is wide and confusing. (Some of the options are listed in Chapters 8 to 10.) Whatever method you use, it is desirable to monitor your client's progress.

Implementation

This follows the planning stage and involves responding to a given problematic situation in several ways which include:

▶ involving people in implementing plans;
▶ sustaining relationships over time;
▶ maintaining motivation; and
▶ coordinating the overall plan of work.

Just as the planning of the intervention is a shared activity – one which empowers the recipients of a service and which engages them as far as possible as co-workers towards agreed goals – so the implementation of the plan should, wherever possible, engage the participants as colleagues working towards common objectives.

When you begin your intervention, keep a close watch on what happens in the early stages to ensure that the programme is being followed correctly and that any unforeseen problems are dealt with quickly. This may mean keeping in contact with the parents, by visiting or by phone, every two or three days in the first few weeks.

Monitoring and evaluation

Choose a convenient method of measuring or assessing the behaviour that reliably estimates the extent of the problem so that you can monitor your clients' progress. Not all interventions lend themselves to the measurement of behaviour change per se. The goals – particularly if the intervention involves a family therapy or counselling approach – may require an evaluation of a rather more subjective (self-report) kind. It is possible to develop methods which encompass the subtle complexities of clients' thoughts and feelings without sacrificing the requirements of rigorous monitoring of their progress (see *Figure II.1*).

If your intervention is not working, examine most carefully the behaviour and attitudes of all participants, and the programme, and change, if necessary, some features of the intervention. If you have

GOAL: *That Mrs Bray shall feel able to cope with her depression*

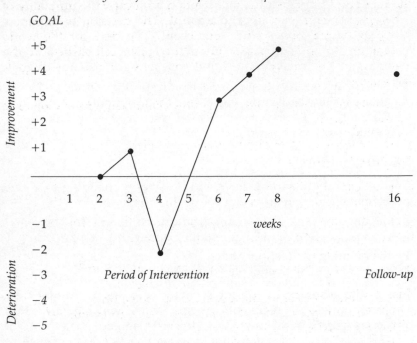

Figure II.1 An example of goal-setting and evaluation by the client

the 'story' (formulation/proposition) about the 'why's' and 'where-fores' of the case right, any difficulties are likely to be traced to the application of the approach rather than the approach per se. Ask the following questions:

▷ Are there powerful competing influences or interfering factors in the client's environment operating against the programme? Can these be modified?
▷ Are the chosen therapeutic strategies appropriate and effective?
▷ Is the family working effectively and being reinforced for its participation?
▷ Are the treatment objectives realistic? Are they within the client's repertoire (the family's tolerance level for change)?
▷ Have you proceeded too quickly? Is it necessary to go back to an earlier stage in the intervention plan?

If the treatment is working well, highlight the successes to your clients and acknowledge the contributions of other participants.

Termination

Phase out and terminate the intervention with care; the durability of any improvements may depend upon it. The decision to terminate should be made jointly with your client. The time for the work/programme to end, depends upon the goals established at the beginning of the intervention. Mind you, new (or elaborated) goals may emerge.

The questions below may be asked of the client near termination or at a follow-up interview:

- Do you think the programme worked or failed?
- Who or what made it work or fail?
- Have any of the problems recurred? (frequency)
- How badly? (intensity)
- When, where and how often?
- How does the family get on now? How is it different from before?
- How would you describe your relationship with X now?
- Do you still worry about X?
- Do you now feel more 'in control' than you did before?
- Do you spend more time playing and talking with X?
- Do you find it easier to praise X than you did before?
- Has the amount of physical contact between X and yourself changed – is there more or less contact?
- Have your relationships with other children changed?
- Have X's relationships with his/her brothers and sisters changed?
- Has X's father/mother changed in his/her attitude to X?
- Has X's behaviour towards his/her father/mother changed?

Effectiveness of Therapy

In today's climate, there is an increasing demand for cost-effectiveness and outcome-effectiveness of all professional activities. Evaluation, quality assurance, clinical audit and so on, are becoming a familiar part of the vocabulary of the helping professions. It is necessary to examine the term 'effectiveness' in the light of defined objectives. It is generally accepted that the claim of psychotherapeutic efficacy requires the demonstration of long-term effects following termination of treatment. How long is long-term, is a moot point when we are dealing with something as changeable as childhood behaviour, thoughts and feelings. In any event, the ideal follow-up studies which evaluate and compare treatment methods (controlling the many potentially confounding variables by means of large-scale, randomized, experimental designs), are extremely expensive and difficult to implement. Not surprisingly, they are rare in the area of childhood therapy.

The word effectiveness itself, is elusive. Conclusions about the relative effectiveness of different therapies may vary, depending on (1) *whether* one examines interview ratings of symptoms as opposed to direct observations; (2) *what* signifies a significant clinical change; (3) *where* – that is, the setting in which – the evaluation is made; and (4) *by whom* the evaluation is made – client or practitioner. To compound the confusion, one must ask oneself what constitutes a 'cure' or 'improvement'? How much of an improvement will suffice? Should abnormal behaviours, aversive relationships or dysfunctional emotions be improved in all situations and for ever? This would be a tall, not to say, impossible order! Should the therapist be satisfied only with the complete eradication of a problem, or with a more modest reduction in the intensity of (say) anxiety or frequency of some deviant action? If so, should it be a 50 per cent or 70 per cent decrement? There is no simple answer. It depends on the nature and definition of the problem, its implications (for example, the risk it poses), the context in which it occurs, and so on.

Developmental considerations are important in discussing the efficacy of all therapy (most people continue to change and 'grow' even as adults); child treatment in particular must be evaluated in the light of what happens to children as they grow up. I began this discussion by mentioning the criterion of stability of change as a measure of effectiveness. But there is a need for caution in applying this to children's behaviour. Depending on the age of the child, and what is being learnt, parents have to go on and on repeating themselves: rewarding their children, instructing them, sanctioning antisocial actions and rehearsing prosocial behaviours. Parents do not expect to teach their children in short 'programmatic' bursts of activity, even if they wish training could be that brief. Teaching goes on until the child has internalized certain crucial social behaviours. Time scales for learning vary, depending on the age and maturity of the child and the nature of the training task. This is why I recommend the systematic scheduling of booster sessions in work with conduct disorder – a problem of childhood where failures of socialization are an important element (Herbert, 1987b).

These difficulties do not release us from the obligation (and it is an *ethical* issue, not only a technical one) to attempt to validate all therapies – and this is a Herculean task if we are to make comparisons. There are over 250 treatments for children and adolescents according to Kazdin (1988). Reviews of different techniques bearing the superordinate title 'psychological therapy', suggest that psychotherapy is better than no treatment for a large number of childhood problems, including anxiety, hyperactivity, social withdrawal and aggression (see Kazdin, 1988; Tuma, 1989). But two decades on, we still cannot answer precisely the often-quoted question: '*What* treatment, by *whom*, is more effective for *this* individual with *that* specific problem, under *which* set of circumstances?'.

FURTHER READING

Guides

The CAF Directory of Specific Conditions and Rare Syndromes (1991) London: Contact a Family.
Dale, F. J. (1990) *The Stimulation Guide: A Sourcebook of Suggestions and Activities for Multi-sensory Impaired Children and Others with Developmental Difficulties.* New York: Woodhead-Faulkner.
Lear, R. (1990) *Play Helps: Toys and Activities for Children with Special Needs.* London: Heinemann Medical Books.

Cultural/ethnic/anti-racist issues

Several informative references on a sadly neglected theme but one which the Children Act, 1989, now raises to the level of importance it deserves.

Ahmed, S. (1986) *Social Work with Black Children and their Families.* London: Batsford.
Cheetham, J. (Ed.) (1982) *Social Work and Ethnicity.* London: Allen and Unwin.
Chevannes, M. (1989) Child rearing among Jamaican families in Britain. *Health Visitor*, February, 222–3.
Dominelli, L. (1988) *Anti-racist Social Work.* London: Macmillan.
Maxime, J. (1986) *Black Like Me.* London: Emani Publications.

8 Helping strategies

The task of helping a family can be a dauntingly broad one, encom-
passing concerns ranging from poor housing and the need for day
care, to work with couples or behaviour therapy for a depressed child.
A family may be seeking help on a voluntary basis, having been
referred by a GP, health visitor, or in some other way, to a child or
family specialist. At a more formal level, a key worker (or care
manager) may be mobilizing an 'inter-agency plan'. This is a plan
devised jointly by the agencies concerned in a child's welfare which
coordinates the services they provide. The plan should specify goals
to be achieved, resources and services to be provided, the allocation
of responsibilities, and arrangements for monitoring and review. It is
important to remember that parents have new rights under the
Children Act, the right to have a say in the plans for their child's
future. Services must be provided in partnership with parents, and
after seeking and taking account of their wishes and feelings (see
Appendix II: *Provision of support for families*).

There is no doubt that intervention is possible and useful for
children with a variety of developmental and environmental risk
factors (see Schorr, 1989). The social worker's or health worker's role
might consist of being a resource mobilizer, helper, friend, adviser,
teacher, therapist or counsellor. Such diversification calls for a
remarkably flexible response on the part of the professional. The
scope of the analysis and level of intervention can also range widely,
from the large grouping (the neighbourhood or community) through
to the small group (the family), the couple (parents as partners) or the
particular individual (say, child).

Communicating with Clients

The speech and language you will encounter in your work could
range from adult speech to teenage slang, from sophisticated
conversation to baby talk, and from well-articulated words to painful
stammering. There is a great deal of power in language, and most
parents and young people are not familiar with technical terminology; so it is important not to put clients at a disadvantage with
mystifying concepts. It is just as vital to guard against the
embarrassingly artificial tone of voice and speech styles some people

adopt with children and adolescents (and, indeed, the elderly). Living, as we do, in a multi-cultural, multi-ethnic society, we need to be alert to the difficulties some people have with English and with our value-laden conceptual language (watch out for words like 'abuse', 'neglect', 'caring').

It may be useful to collect examples and metaphors which illuminate a vivid idea or provide clients with a mental picture of an important concept. I sometimes ask my clients to imagine that their child has an L plate on his or her back, to remind them to be patient and tolerant when the child makes a mistake or forgets a lesson. They are, after all, *learners* about life. I remind them of the time they learned to ride a bike and had first managed to gain balance. They continued to have a wobble and occasionally fell off. When we believe a child has mastered a new skill (for example, not wetting his or her bed), there is still likely to be a failure or two – representing the 'wobble' at the top of the learning curve. A punitive reaction would be counter-productive.

Work with Groups

There are several advantages in working with a group of people who all manifest similar difficulties. Many adults feel that they have failed miserably as parents, and that their child is uniquely difficult to understand and manage. Sharing experiences with other parents can be comforting, indeed reassuring. However, swapping 'horror stories' is fine up to a point, but must not go on too long or it will engender a mood of pessimism.

The opportunity to express feelings of apprehension, resentment and anger (the latter aimed, not uncommonly, at helping agencies) in a group setting, can be beneficial if managed well by the group organizer. Discussion groups are a popular and economical means of providing clients with learning experiences, and an opportunity to engage in mutual problem-solving. There are several basic procedures for discussion groups. David and Frank Johnson, authors of *Joining Together* (1975), make the following suggestions:

❏ *Define terms and concepts.* A group requires a shared language in order to hold a fruitful discussion. Study new terms; try to find agreement on complex, contentious or ambiguous words (for example, words like 'discipline', 'problem child', 'punishment', 'trust', 'spoilt', 'bribery', 'reinforcement', 'time-out'). Give examples, wherever possible, to illustrate a word's or concept's meaning.

❏ *Negotiate and/or establish goals.* Clarify the goals (or objectives) for every session. Themes might include: what do you do when a child cries?; discipline; sex education; adolescent risk-taking. Handouts which prepare participants for a topic or summarize the previous meeting, are appreciated. Break down major topics into sub-topics.

Spread your time over sub-topics in order of importance so that items of significance are not lost. Allow time to review homework tasks (for example, keeping records or a diary for discussion) if they are part of the agenda.

❑ *Encourage free and fair discussion.* Encourage individuals in the free (but fair) expression of ideas, feelings, attitudes, reactions, inform-ation and analysis. Do not allow the scapegoating or 'bullying' of any one member. (A few ground rules for the group could be useful here.)

❑ *Integrate the material.* Relate current themes to past topics; make connections, where they exist, between issues. Fragmentary impres-sions from several discussion sessions are unlikely to add sig-nificantly to the parent's understanding of children or increase confidence in his or her parenting skills. With parent training groups, it is important to try out practical ideas such as time-out (see page 171) by means of role-play or homework tasks.

❑ *Encourage the application of the discussion material.* Ask group members to attempt to identify the implications of the material for their own lives, the activities they engage in, and their relationships with other people. Encourage them to apply the positive things they have learned and report back to the group the 'feedback' they received from this home-based trial.

❑ *The group climate should be warm, accepting and non-threatening.* This is vital if people are to engage in controversy, expose their vulnerability, show their ignorance, take risks with touchy subjects.

❑ *Learning should be conceived as a cooperative enterprise.* This is impossible if the participants come over as hostile, competitive, ridiculing, arrogant or judgemental.

❑ *Learning should be accepted as the primary purpose of the group.* Here is a desideratum that requires painstaking and imaginative preparation of the material and sensitive but firm management of the agenda.

❑ *Every member of the group should participate in discussions.* A skilful, facilitative group leader is important in achieving this criterion.

❑ *Leadership functions might usefully be shared out for certain themes and/or sessions.*

❑ *Group sessions don't have to be endlessly solemn or heavy-going.* They should be stimulating and thus pleasurable, and, at times, sheer fun.

❑ *Evaluation should be viewed as an integral part of the group's activities.* Group skills can be improved by constructive, critical evaluation.

❏ *Members should attend regularly and come prepared.* The importance of mutual responsibility for the well-being of the group may be underlined by drawing up contracts or verbal agreements with participants.

Work with Couples

Whatever the romantic glow surrounding the decision of two people to live together as a couple, the months and years see their relationship settling into a kind of balance, tilted (or sometimes tilting) in one direction or another, somewhere between pleasure and its opposite, cooperation and its antithesis, and ultimately between stability and instability. In many, perhaps most, marriages or cohabiting partnerships, there is a great deal of interaction which is playful, complementary and joyous, as well as much that is, to some degree, hostile. The fact that a majority of marriages (albeit a diminishing one) survive, and are judged to be reasonably happy, indicates that the adjustments individuals entering a partnership have to make, as they progress from being unattached and relatively irresponsible to taking on the awesome responsibilities of parenthood, are fairly successful overall (see *Table 8.1*).

A process of bargaining may underlie the symmetries or reciprocities in partnerships of long duration. It is one of the great platitudes – part of popular wisdom – that marriage is a matter of give and take. Social exchange theory suggests that people initiate and prolong relationships of intimacy as long as those relationships are reasonably satisfactory with regard to what are called their 'rewards' and 'costs'.

Exchange theory likens social interactions and relationships to economic bargains or the exchange of gifts. All activities carried out by one individual, to the benefit of another, are termed 'rewards', while detrimental activities – hostility and selfishness – are seen as 'costs'.

A notable feature of a partnership that is 'working', is the balance in the relationship that exists between the partners, often called 'status symmetry'. It concerns the mutual respect and lack of dominance and exploitation which characterize intimate and lasting relationships. In friendly or loving relationships, there is an overall balance in the influence of each of the participants.

It is useful to draw up a balance sheet. On the debit side, the term 'cost' is applied to deterrents that may be incurred in contacts with another person – such as criticism, neglect, violence, anxiety, embarrassment, and the like. For attraction to another individual to occur (or to be maintained), the rewards should outweigh the costs to a degree that is tolerable or satisfactory to the person.

Table 8.1 Stages in a couple's life cycle

Stage of life cycle	Developmental tasks	Adaptations required to progress developmentally
1. In between family of origin and new family. Unattached young adult.	Coming to terms with separation from parents/ independence.	Establishing adult identity/autonomy. Establishing self in work. Widening intimate peer relationships.
2. Marriage/cohabiting partnership: new couple. Joining of families through this relationship.	Making a commitment to a new dyadic system.	Adjusting to life as a couple (changes in roles, rules, routines). Realignment of relationships with extended families and friends to include spouse/ partner.
3. Becoming a family with advent of first child.	Absorsing new member into the system.	Adjusting relationships to make space for child. Accepting parental roles. Realignment of relationships with extended family to include their grandparenting roles.
4. Enlarged family with subsequent children. Adolescent/s in the family.	Widening family boundaries to youngster's growing independence and testing of limits.	Adapting parent–child relationships to accommodate young adult role. Coping with tension between protecting, nurturing adolescents and allowing them independence. Dealing with mid-life marital and career issues. Growing concern for older generation.
5. Launching children and moving on.	Accepting changes in the size and shape of family (exits and entries).	Adapting to return to dyadic system if/when children leave home. Development of adult-to-adult relationships between parents and grown-up children. Realignment of relationships to include in-laws and grandchildren.

In this model, marital discord is dealt with by redistributing prevailing rates of reinforcement (satisfaction) and punishment (dissatisfaction) within the relationship. Individuals are encouraged – following discussion, negotiation and, hopefully, compromise – to maximize satisfactions (the positives) while minimizing the dissatisfaction (mutually irritating behaviours) provoked by the couple. This is where contracts can be very useful, not only for couple work, but also for family relationships that are tense and unhappy.

Conciliation (as opposed to reconciliation) focuses on assisting parties to reach agreed decisions on specific issues arising from the established breakdown of their relationship. Research suggests that conciliation services can successfully reduce conflict. One in six cases tends to result in reconciliation.

Work with Individuals

The art of talking and listening (therapeutic conversations or communications) is highly valued in the difficult task of encouraging change in the understanding and actions of adult and young clients. Helping people to discover insights into their mental processes and behaviour, is a well-known feature of therapies.

Practitioners often call themselves 'eclectic', drawing on what they regard as best or most valid from the various systems of therapy. Many theorists assert that the claims of the different schools of therapy have never been adequately vindicated. Indeed, comparative studies tend to show little difference between the outcomes of diverse approaches, even though a particular therapy, by itself, can be shown to have significant effects when compared to the absence of treatment. The assertion that there are insignificant differences between therapeutic approaches with regard to outcome, would be hotly disputed by behaviour therapists (see Further Reading). Nevertheless, it is just such an assumption which leads Jerome Frank (1973) to argue that the effective factors in all therapies are the same, and relate to the common components of any process of influence and/or healing: warmth, respect, kindness, hope, understanding and the provision of explanations.

However, among the most frequent complaints by parents are lack of concern, care and warmth on the part of professionals: in other words, the absence of a supportive relationship. This is a particularly sad state of affairs as it is widely held that these are among the most important qualities stressed in the counselling (client-centred) literature and they can affect the client's well-being and/or self-esteem. Parents also complain of insufficient and inaccurate information; an overload of information at any one time; and information that is difficult to comprehend because of technical jargon or poor presentation.

Empowering clients

Providing information is a crucial component in the empowerment of clients; this means providing them with factual data or know-how about how to get access to information. Such knowledge should help them to make informed choices and decisions. Within therapy, the therapist may increase the client's self-knowledge and self-confidence by making interpretations; by changing clients' attitudes, behaviours and perceptions; and by altering the client's pattern of thinking and way of understanding.

Providing instruction is another path to self-empowerment – for example, teaching problem-solving and social skills. Performance skills and accomplishments are the foundation of perceived self-efficacy (client confidence). The client may not be able to act effectively without instruction, training, tracking (monitoring) and feedback. According to Albert Bandura (1986), the ability to alter the patient's self-efficacy expectations is a powerful element of therapy which can affect the client's willingness to get involved in situations which are perceived as daunting, as well as his or her persistence in such situations.

Counselling

Counselling is based on a relationship of trust and confidential conversations between the professionally trained counsellor and the client. Carl Rogers played a major part in developing the client-centred, non-directive approach to counselling and therapy. In the Rogerian 'client-centred' approach, the goal of the intervention is to increase positive self-regard and self-direction. The object is to work in such a facilitative, non-intrusive manner as to remove the incongruence the individual has developed between the 'experiencing inner self' and the self he or she presents to the outside world. The following are key elements of the counselling process:

- Verbal exchange is the means of influence.
- The basic assumptions about the nature of man and woman are not pessimistic (fatalistic?) like Sigmund Freud's. The person is essentially good, rational, realistic, social, forward-looking.
- Clients may need help in realizing their basic impulse to grow. As Rogers (1951) puts it: 'It has been my experience that persons have a basically positive direction' that is 'constructive, moving toward self-actualization, growing toward maturity, growing towards socialization'.

The therapeutic process is akin to education or socialization, and is seen as a freeing of the 'growth capacities' of the individual, which permits him or her to acquire 'more mature' ways of acting and reacting, ways which are less fraught with anxiety or conflict. Rogers is talking about a learning process, within a humanistic rather than behaviourist context. The attributes of the counsellor which facilitiate such learning are thought to be:

- *Genuineness and authenticity*: the conveying of 'realness' to clients.
- *Non-possessive warmth*: the attitude of friendly concern and caring.
- *Accurate empathy*: the capacity to see things from the clients' point of view, to 'feel with' them, so that they feel they are understood.

Counselling – within this framework – involves the painstaking exploration of problems: there is an attempt to clarify conflicting issues and to discover alternative ways of describing them and/or of dealing with them. This helping method (like the problem-solving approach, see page 188) emphasizes the 'self-help' element, the need to call on the inner resources of the person who is in difficulties. To this end, the counsellor provides a non-judgemental, supportive relationship which enables individuals to enhance their self-esteem, self-respect and self-efficacy, in part, by learning to search for their *own* answers – to rely on their own resources.

Relating this helping process more specifically to parents with chronically ill or disabled children, Hilton Davis (1993) lists the following aims:

▶ To facilitate the ways in which the parents and all other family members adapt to the child and the disease, psychologically, socially, physically and in their everyday lives, minimizing or preventing disruption as far as possible.
▶ To enable the parents and other family members as best they can to meet the needs of the child who is ill or disabled, without neglecting their own needs.
▶ To enable the child who is ill to have the best quality of life by facilitating the child's adaptation to the disease/disability psychologically, socially, and in the tasks and pursuits of everyday life.

Crisis counselling

Counselling in a crisis is a vital skill for professionals. In work with children and their parents, emergencies come along – acute crises – and the professional's task is to respond quickly to alleviate the *immediate* impact of disruptive stressful events. There are many potential crises in family life: a child diagnosed as mentally/physically handicapped; separation, divorce, death; an attempted suicide in the family; mental illness (for example, schizophrenia, depression) of a member of the family; the discovery of sexual abuse of a child/adolescent in the family (by parent or sibling).

There is no substitute in an emergency for common sense, and for our purposes we shall look at a few general, common sense responses:

☐ Remember that during a crisis, most people (because their defences are down) are receptive to the right sort of help.

☐ Do not perceive yourself in this set of circumstances as a long-term therapist or a specialist in (say) bereavement counselling – although such a role, or person, may become necessary if the client doesn't seem to be regaining his or her equilibrium.

☐ You are not there to identify or resolve all of the stresses and complications brought about by the crisis.

☐ Being aware of the stages of a crisis allows you to assess whether the client is 'stuck' at a particular point in what theoreticians call 'crisis work' – thus hindering the mastering of the emergency, and delaying its final resolution. Although active crisis states vary in duration, the actual condition of intense disequilibrium is limited usually to between four and six weeks. Stages in crises of different kinds will vary, but, typically, the course of grief following bereavement, for example, encompasses pangs of grief and pining for the lost one, and a process of searching and yearning for the departed person which may look quite irrational to the observer. Anger may flare up (or guilt) – feelings which may give way to apathy and depression.

☐ Simply identifying for a person in crisis what is happening, or, for concerned relatives, explaining the normality of such events, provides untold relief and a sense of security. The unknown, especially the apparently irrational, bizarre happenings (to oneself or others) in times of crisis, add to the burden of the trauma itself. Reassurance is one of the most potent therapeutic remedies available to the emergency counsellor.

☐ Understanding is the other remedy: providing the client with a non-judgemental, sensitive ear and voice – listening and responding to his or her anguish.

There is now available a body of knowledge on how to deal with children and families following disasters (for example, dealing with post-traumatic stress syndrome – see Yule, 1991).

Psychotherapy

The word 'psychotherapy' means literally 'the treatment of problems of the mind'. The term also implies that treatment is carried out by psychological methods rather than by the use of physical measures such as drugs. Clients do a lot of talking about their lives, their present and past, their personal relationships. Psychotherapists, to a greater or lesser extent, also talk, offering interpretations, reflecting back to the clients their feelings, providing reassurance. Some analyse the so-called transference, that is to say the client's feelings that have their origins in past experience and relationships, but are now displaced on to the person of the therapist.

It is difficult to define psychotherapy in any tidy fashion because so many different theories of personality and viewpoints about the nature of mental problems determine the approach of the particular therapist. One clinician may be a psychoanalytic psychotherapist but even then he or she could be trained in the Freudian, Jungian, Kleinian, or some other offshoot of the analytic schools. Typical problems dealt with by psychotherapies include:

- an avoidance of situations/people/objects one should not have to avoid;
- a sense of emotional turmoil (anger, fear, anxiety, dread, guilt, depression, disgust);
- a feeling of helplessness;
- a feeling of having lost control;
- feelings of unhappiness, distress, misery; vague feelings that life is not being lived as meaningfully, effectively or joyfully as it should be;
- a loss of ability to make decisions;
- a loss of the ability to make choices;
- a loss of the feeling of being real, vital, committed to or enthusiastic about life;
- a sense of conflict, apathy, aimlessness;
- a sense of alienation (with self and/or society);
- a sense of being compelled to do things against one's will.

There problems may also lend themselves to a behavioural psycho-therapy approach. It is crucial in behavioural assessment and treatment to reformulate these complaints in operational terms, that is, in overt terms of what the client says and does, and in a manner that lends itself to the kind of assessment of the problem which leads *logically* to an intervention. Such problems are also the 'bread and butter' of counsellors.

Insight therapy

The therapist using this method with older children and adolescents engages in procedures which will give clients insight into the meanings of their symptoms, and into the relationship between their motivations and their behaviour. It is assumed that this insight will allow greater control over the problem behaviour. As mentioned earlier, many of our motives are thought to be unconscious and it is impossible to come to terms with an 'invisible enemy'.

An illustration

A problem in which short-term psychotherapy utilized insight and 'ventilation' (the release/expression of suppressed emotion) is the case of Farouk who acted in an extremely rebellious, disobedient and aggressive manner. His parents could not cope with him. When his innermost thoughts and feelings were tapped by analysing projective material (his stories and paintings) and by observing his repetitive games with the 'family group' of dolls, it became apparent that he believed his parents had stopped loving him when his brother was born. He had been the only child for five years and had little understanding that love can be shared rather than monopolized. He had the idea that his mother and father got angry with him and punished him, not because he was being difficult and negativistic, but simply because their feeling toward him had changed and they no longer loved him. His intense jealousy of the baby was not apparent on the surface. His over-zealous attention to the infant – as it appeared – covered feelings of hatred and envy. Not realizing this, the parents were unable to cope with the situation. In this case, the function of the treatment, as it was seen by the therapist, was not only to release and interpret the child's feelings, and to educate him about the inclusiveness of love rather than its exclusiveness, but also to help the mother to understand and tolerate the source of her child's anxieties and aggressions.

Play therapy

If the child is very young, conventional methods of psychotherapy as used with adults are not suitable. Children are not always able to put anxieties into words, or show interest in exploring the past or their attitudes. Play is a familiar mode of expression for the child, and it is deployed by some child psychotherapists as a part-equivalent to 'talking therapy'.

Virginia Mae Axline, in her book *Play Therapy* (1947), describes the non-directive form of play therapy. Her approach is based upon the fact that play is the child's natural medium of self-expression. An opportunity is given to the child to 'play out' feelings and problems, just as in certain types of adult therapy, an individual 'talks out' his or her difficulties.

Whatever the theoretical framework of a particular clinic, it is fairly common practice for children to be made to feel at ease in a playroom in which they can paint, construct things on a sand tray with miniatures, act out dramas with dolls and puppets, and give expression to a wide range of feelings and fantasies. The skilled therapist may detect recurrent themes in the child's play, preoccupations which point to conflicts or areas of tension in the family, at school or in some other aspects of the child's life, which are blocking development.

In its simplest form, play therapy is a means of modifying or reshaping attitudes and feelings. But the therapist cannot simply sit down with the child and explain the self-defeating nature of his or her attitudes. The child needs to be in touch with feelings which have become dissociated or blocked off from the rest of self, or come to see for him/herself that 'acting out' behaviours such as destructiveness or running away, are self-defeating and unnecessary. The child's attitudes need to be analysed carefully and on a broad front, and not with a superficial, facile and 'pat' formula. The basic principles which guide non-directive play therapy are as follows. The therapist:

▷ endeavours to develop a warm friendly relationship with the child;
▷ accepts the child as he or she is;
▷ establishes a feeling of permissiveness in the relationship so that the child feels entirely free to express his or her feelings;
▷ is alert to recognize the feelings expressed by children and to reflect those feelings back to them in such a manner that they gain insight into their behaviour;
▷ maintains respect for the child's ability to solve his or her own problems if given an opportunity to do so – the responsibility for making choices and for instituting change is the child's;
▷ does not attempt to hurry therapy along; it is a gradual process;
▷ does not attempt to direct the child's actions or conversation in any manner – the child leads the way and the therapist follows;
▷ establishes only those limitations to the child's behaviour that are necessary to anchor the therapy in the world of reality and to make the child aware of his or her responsibility in the relationship.

Behaviour Therapy

Behavioural methods are known by several names: behavioural psychotherapy, behaviour modification, cognitive behaviour therapy. At the broadest level, behavioural work represents a theory (indeed a philosophy) of treatment and behaviour change, rather than a technology or cookbook of 'ad hoc' techniques. It is an empirically-based theory of normal and abnormal behaviour (see Herbert, 1993). This is not to claim that all behaviours are learned and can therefore be unlearned, relatively simply. In conditions such as the Lesch-Nyhan syndome or epilepsy, and, indeed, various other organic disorders, learning processes contribute to, but are *not* the only causes of the abnormal behaviour associated with the disorders. The fact is that behavioural therapy can work without being tied to a theory about the origins of the behaviour; it can be useful in the treatment of conditions that are, in fact, organic in origin. Indeed, it is one of the strengths of behavioural work that treatment does not depend necessarily upon the discovery and understanding of the historical causes of the problem.

The behaviour therapist places most emphasis on providing the patient with *new* learning experiences. If past experiences did contribute significantly to the manner in which (say) an individual's delinquent behaviour was evolved, in practice they are seldom still functional, that is, they no longer directly maintain current deviant behaviour. This is not to deny that the past can 'live' in the present by means of attitudes which evolved earlier but which influence present actions. This is where cognitive-behavioural techniques such as cognitive restructuring come into their own.

With regard to behavioural techniques, we have a veritable Pandora's box of potential misunderstandings. Sadly, the media has contributed to the confusion and, sometimes, deliberate obfuscation of *therapeutic* techniques with methods of *social control*. It is the implementation of an *appropriate* assessment and formulation, and the negotiation of therapeutic goals that are ethically acceptable, which constitute the authenticating hallmark of behaviour therapy.

Models of learning

There are four major processes of learning: classical conditioning; instrumental (operant) learning; observational learning (imitation); and cognitive learning.

1. *Classical conditioning* occurs when a given stimulus regularly elicits a given response. A previously neutral stimulus (say, a tone) is repeatedly paired with an 'unconditioned stimulus' (say, a puff of air to the eye) and gradually acquires its response-eliciting properties – it brings about an eye blink. The response of the individual (the eye blink) has been, in technical parlance, 'conditioned' to the tone (the 'conditioned stimulus').
2. *Instrumental or operant conditioning* occurs when behaviour is 'shaped' by positive reinforcement, that is, a positive response, such as words of encouragement and praise, whenever the child's behaviour approximates the behaviour/skill which the parent has chosen to teach him or her (see also page 122).
3. *Observational learning* is the learning/acquiring of complex and novel behaviour by observing the behaviour of exemplary models (imitation). These may be people children meet in their everyday life or they may be symbolic models that they read about or see on television.

4. *Cognitive learning* is learning by means of cognitive processing of information: the operation of rules, concepts, symbols, principles and strategies. An example could be learning the rules of grammar (see page 60) or learning to distinguish the social rules that distinguish a 'white lie' from an unacceptable untruth.

All forms of learning, generally functional in their effects (they help children to adapt to life's demands), can, under certain circumstances, contribute to maladjustment. Thus a youngster who learns usefully on the basis of classical and operant 'conditioning' processes to avoid dangerous situations, can also learn in the same way (maladaptively) to fear and avoid school or social gatherings; a parent may unwittingly reinforce temper tantrums by attending to them.

An immature child who learns by imitating an adult, that is, through observational learning, will not necessarily understand when it is undesirable, say violent behaviour, that is being modelled.

Behavioural methods

Cognitive-behavioural methods

These are based upon the assumption that cognitive processes are critical in childhood learning; thus therapists accept as primary data such experiential aspects of problems as the child's descriptions of his or her fears, perceptions about temptations to transgress rules, or thoughts about unsuccessful relationships.

There is a wide range of cognitive-behavioural procedures, but they share a common assumption: that children can be taught to eliminate maladaptive behaviours by challenging their irrational beliefs and faulty logic, by getting them to instruct themselves in certain ways, or to associate wanted behaviours with positive self-statements and unwanted ones with negative self-statements. This is the method referred to as verbal self-instruction training. The child can also be taught to rearrange contingencies that influence behaviour in such a way that he or she experiences rewarding rather than aversive consequences.

Modelling

Modelling treatments are based upon 'vicarious' conditioning principles. For example, a child who is afraid of dogs might watch a video of another child interacting with a dog without coming to harm. The therapeutic intervention may be directed towards the relationship between the antecedent conditions and the problematic behaviour and/or between the problem behaviour and its consequences. The child is encouraged to imitate the behaviour being demonstrated and is provided with feedback and reinforcement for performance that matches that of the model. Thus operant principles are used to maintain the desired behaviours once they are acquired through the modelling process.

Counter conditioning

In counter conditioning or systematic desensitization, the most common method has been to arrange anxiety-evoking stimuli in a hierarchy and to present them, one at a time, while the child is in a state of relaxation, and at a pace at which he or she is able to cope with a particular stimulus without experiencing undue distress. This is the 'desensitization' aspect of the treatment and is thought to lead to the direct inhibition of the fear response. Although studies have questioned the active therapeutic mechanisms and the necessary ingredients of systematic desensitization, it remains an effective and frequently used procedure with children and adolescents.

Operant learning

Parents need principles and practical techniques for encouraging and maintaining, not only compliant, but also other prosocial behaviours. Methods of intervention, based on operant conditioning, attempt to influence or control the outcome of certain behaviours through the use of positive reinforcement, that is, pleasurable consequences. The principle underlying this method is that voluntary actions ('operants'), followed by favourable outcomes for the individual, are likely to be repeated.

A practitioner using operant methods can analyse a family system and find out how the various members reinforce undesired behaviour in other members and intentionally or unintentionally ignore or punish desired behaviour. It is then possible to make beneficial alterations by planning with the family how best to rearrange the consequences of behaviour so that all (or certain) members of the family receive social reinforcement for desired behaviours. A specific formulation which meets the needs of a particular case might sound something like this:

'Andrew has not yet learned to control his temper. He "lets go" in a frightening tantrum – banging his head, kicking, screaming and yelling – when he cannot get his own way: as when you try to insist on him doing something, refuse his commands or attend to people other than himself at a time when he wants your undivided attention. The result (usually) is that he achieves his goal, he coerces you both into giving way – a very rewarding state of affairs seen from his point of view; a very unrewarding (and sometimes humiliating) state of affairs seen from your perspective. Occasionally you stick to your guns which means that Andrew has been getting rather inconsistent messages: the consequences of his undesirable actions are not predictable. Sometimes (but rarely) you punish his unacceptable behaviour, generally when there are visitors. Sometimes you ignore it, for example, at the

supermarket. Generally you "reward" it and thus make it more likely to recur, by giving in to him. Andrew has learned to make this outcome more likely by escalating the tantrums into very violent and therefore frightening episodes. You now have to make it quite clear to him that his bad behaviour will have consequences that are not only unrewarding, but also unpleasant enough to make him relinquish his tantrum. You have tried smacking which makes him worse and you miserable. We will use a method called "time-out". But at the same time we will make it very beneficial for him to be more obedient, to ask nicely and to control his temper. We will record his successes on this star chart and show him how he can earn treats when he has collected a certain number of stars.'

(A more detailed account of the use of positive reinforcement for specific behaviour problems is provided on page 169.)

Applications

It is an indication of the versatility of contemporary behaviour therapy, that it is possible here (and in Chapters 9 and 10) to mention only a small sample of the social, psychiatric, health-related and educational problems, to which behavioural methods have been applied with some success. Their diversity calls for planning on a case-by-case basis, treatment being decided on the basis of a broad spectrum functional analysis (see page 122) and a knowledge of child development and, of course, the research literature on the causation of particular problems.

Emotional disorders

Anxiety

A wide range of methods based on *modelling procedures, operant methods* and variations on the theme of *systematic desensitization,* have proved beneficial in the treatment of anxious and fearful children (see Ollendick and King, 1991).

The most often quoted account of counter conditioning is that of Mary Cover Jones' early treatment of Peter (Jones, 1924). She successfully treated Peter's fear of rabbits by exposing him to the feared rabbit in a systematic, but gradual manner and in the presence of food (a stimulus that produced an incompatible positive response). More recently, systematic desensitization of anxiety (as it is now referred to) has relied primarily on relaxation as the competing and, therefore, inhibiting response. Younger children, however, appear to have difficulty in acquiring muscular relaxation and in being able to conjure up clearly in visual imagery (imagination) the fear-producing stimuli as is necessary in some approaches.

As a result, *in vivo desensitization* (gradual exposure, in real life, to the fear-provoking stimulus) and emotive imagery have become increasingly popular, especially with younger children. The latter, used in work with children manifesting fears, includes using stories and images of heroic characters to build up a powerfully positive feeling into which fear-eliciting stimuli are gradually interwoven. One can use various categories of imagery which arouse feelings of self-assertion, pride, affection, mirth, and similar anxiety-inhibiting responses.

An illustration (see Ollendick and King, 1991) of the emotive imagery approach is the treatment of a five-year-old child with extreme fears of the dark, noises, and shadows. Having determined that the child was fond of the comic character, Batman, the therapists created a fear hierarchy and then asked the child to imagine that 'he and Batman had joined forces and that he was appointed as a special agent'.

Next he was asked to close his eyes and to imagine the fear-producing stimuli in a graduated fashion, while accompanied by Batman. Altogether, there were four sessions of emotive imagery. Treatment, albeit uncontrolled, was successful. In this case study, muscular relaxation had been attempted and was unsuccessful.

Other case studies have illustrated the potential efficacy of systematic desensitization and its variants in the treatment of a variety of childhood fears such as dogs, dentists, water, school, bees and loud noises.

There is also empirical support for the value of operant-based procedures (that is, using appropriate reinforcement) in the treatment of anxious and withdrawn behaviours in children, and to treat a variety of fears, such as fear of the dark, dogs, riding on school buses, and sitting on the toilet. Other methods use the technique of modelling which involves the systematic demonstration (in actuality, or symbolically, on film) of a model displaying the required behaviour: a skill, an appropriate prosocial action, or a coping strategy.

Ross *et al.*, (1971) used modelling (together with social reinforcement) to treat a six-year-old boy whose fear of interactions with peers was so extreme that he actively avoided them and even refused to watch filmed presentations featuring young children. Following treatment, the child was observed to interact positively with his peers and to display few avoidant behaviours. On follow-up, two months after termination of treatment, he was observed to 'join ongoing play groups, initiate verbal contacts, and sustain effective social interactions, all with children who were complete strangers to him'.

Probably the most frequently used cognitive approach with anxious children, is verbal self-instruction training. Kanfer *et al.*, (1975) treated children of five to six who were afraid of the dark. Three groups of children were formed. The first group rehearsed active control or competence-mediating statements (for example, 'I am a brave boy (girl) and I can handle the dark'); the second group rehearsed statements aimed at reducing the aversive quality of the stimulus situation itself (for example, 'The dark is not such a bad place to be'); and the third group rehearsed neutral statements (for example, 'Mary had a little lamb'). When later exposed to a darkness tolerance test, both the competence and stimulus groups surpassed the neutral instruction group in duration of time spent in the dark. The competence and stimulus groups did not differ significantly from each other, suggesting that adaptive behaviours were acquired under both conditions.

To summarize, the new and innovative cognitive-based procedures show considerable promise in the treatment of anxious and fearful children. Although initial findings suggest that effects produced in such programmes may be long-term and generalizable, a clear and well-controlled demonstration of such effects is not yet available (see Kendall *et al.*, 1988).

Depression

Depressive reactions in children are frequently treated as concomitants of school refusal, truancy, failure-to-thrive, substance abuse and delinquency. But depression has only recently achieved the status of a problem of childhood in its own right. The need for a broad-based intervention with depressive problems seems to be the conclusion of recent studies. Medication, behaviour therapy, counselling, psychotherapy and cognitive therapy appear to be the main options, singly or in combination.

Depression in older children (and adolescents) would, on the face of it, seem to lend itself to a cognitive-behavioural approach, as depressed patients tend to manifest a high rate of intrusive negative thoughts, including selective ruminations about past events that were unhappy.

Perhaps all we can say, at present, with regard to treatment of depression, is that cognitive-behavioural methods look promising. Given the tendency of depressed children and adolescents to externalize the location of control in their lives, it would seem sensible to combine psychological methods (which enhance individuals' self-esteem and empower them) with medication. Anti-depressant drugs prescribed by psychiatrists may well be efficacious, but used alone, they are quite likely to reinforce an already existent sense of passivity and helplessness in the client.

Developmental disorders

Enuresis

Most children achieve day and night continence (in that order) by the age of four; so it is some time after that age that day or night wetting is seen as problematic and referred to as diurnal or nocturnal enuresis. The systematic treatment of enuresis originated in the 1930s; a special training pad was devised which was placed under the child when in bed. The pad, when moistened (with urine) during the night, closed a circuit and rang a bell. It was arranged that when this happened, someone would wake the child, take him or her to the toilet, and change the bed and night clothes. This 'conditioning' technique is very effective. Diurnal enuresis can also be successfully treated with a portable pants alarm.

The evidence for the superiority of the alarm method (with rates of remission between 80 and 90 per cent over no-treatment and other-treatment control procedures) is well-documented for nocturnal enuresis (see Doleys' 1977 review of data based on 600 subjects). This revealed an average relapse rate of 40 per cent; but nearly 60 per cent of these returned to continence after booster sessions.

Despite the potential of these methods, it is common, in my experience, to meet professionals who are disillusioned because behavioural methods have not worked in their cases. Sometimes, perhaps uncharitably, one suspects a lack of special skill or experience in the complainants, or a tendency to underrate the painstaking requirements of both the assessment and treatment stages. Many things can go wrong: problems of a technical nature (sweat may trigger the alarm; batteries go flat; the child's clothing and bedding are not prepared properly); inconsistency on the part of the exhausted parents; insufficient expert monitoring of the programme; premature withdrawal of therapy and so on.

Encopresis

Most children achieve foecal continence by age three. By the age of four, three per cent still soil, by seven 1.5 per cent and by ten or eleven, only 0.8 per cent (Herbert and Iwaniec, 1981). Encopresis is the generic term applied to various forms of soiling. Soiling is a common trigger for physical abuse.

Paediatric assistance is invaluable in the physical aspects of an intervention. The approach tends to involve the use of enemas, laxatives and stool softeners, together with dietary advice – all of which are important in the case of retentive encopresis.

Doleys (1978), in his review of treatment studies, found that 93 per cent of cases were successfully treated by the use of behavioural methods. Operant conditioning techniques, in particular, a combination of positive and negative reinforcement, have been used to modify the encopresis and smearing. Mothers and/or fathers of the children might be instructed to reward them for trying, as well as for actually passing a motion in the toilet. Laxatives and stool softeners are prescribed in order to ensure regular and painless bowel movements, and to restore feeling so that the body's signals about such movements are recognized by the child. The pain of going to the toilet (for a constipated child) may be sufficiently intense and enduring, to set up a conditioned and generalized aversive reaction to the entire process of 'toileting'.

FURTHER READING

Counselling

Davis, H. (1993) *Counselling Parents of Children with Chronic Illness or Disability*. Leicester: BPS Books (The British Psychological Society). [A detailed guide for health and social services personnel who require skills for counselling parents coping with children who are chronically ill or disabled.]

Davis, H. and Fallowfield, L. (1991) *Counselling and Communication in Health Care*. Chichester: John Wiley. [Deals with a wide variety of health problems and how to provide help for families.]

Egan, G. (1986) *The Skilled Helper*. Monterey: Brooks/Cole. [A superb account of a problem-solving approach to counselling.]

Worell, J. and Remer, P. (1992) *Feminist Perspectives in Therapy: An Empowerment Model for Women*. Chichester: John Wiley. [A feminist perspective of core issues in counselling and therapy with women.]

Efficacy of child therapy

The question of effectiveness is increasingly being asked by cost-conscious managers and a 'quality of care' conscious public. Some answers are provided in the references below.

Casey, R. J. and Berman, J. S. (1985) The outcome of psychotherapy with children. *Psychological Bulletin, 98*, 388–400.

Rutter, M. (1982) Psychological therapies: Issues and prospects. *Psychological Medicine, 12*, 723–740.

Weisz, J. R., Weiss, B., Alicke, M. D. and Klotz, M. L. (1987) Effectiveness of psychotherapy with children and adolescents. A meta-analysis for clinicians. *Journal of Consulting and Clinical Psychology, 55*, 542 549.

9 Family therapy strategies

Family therapists conceptualize problems in a 'lateral' as opposed to 'historical-vertical' manner; that is to say, they view the client as one facet in a multifaceted system – a complicated, dynamic pattern of personal and family relationships.

This so-called *systems* approach to problems, embraces the concept of circular reciprocal causation: the individual is affected by the attitudes and activities of other members of the family, attitudes and activities which his or her actions or decisions, in turn, influence. Of course, people do not live only within family systems; they also 'reside' in bodily systems and within particular social and cultural milieus. Such considerations have influenced practitioners of behavioural family therapy – especially those brands that find their intellectual sustenance in social learning theory.

Systems theorists in contemporary practice – those who work within a family therapy modality – are agreed in focusing interventions not only on the *content* of what individuals say and do, but also on the *process* of what is happening in terms of repeated patterns of interaction and relationship within the family. Process is the interaction among the members of a system that implicitly defines and structures the roles, rules, and functions of those members. Process is the behaviour that elicits the response, as well as the response that confirms the behaviour (for example, 'If I am weak and you are strong, then your strength helps to keep me weak, and my weakness helps to keep you strong'). Process is a circular continuum. Given this definition, problems may be formulated (in part) in terms of unsatisfactory patterns of dominance, distorted perceptions, unclear roles and boundaries for family members, poor communication and ineffective decision-making.

Families who come to therapy may suffer from any of these problems. Family members demonstrate a difficulty in changing the habitual/fixed ways in which they relate to each other. They are encouraged, by a variety of therapeutic strategies and homework tasks, to think, feel and act differently. In order to understand the family pattern across the generations (the extended family), and the alliances, conflicts and attachments within the family unit, clients are encouraged to look at themselves from a fresh perspective and to try to find alternative solutions to their dilemmas. Salvador Minuchin (1974), an eminent family therapist, gives the example of the multi-level treatment of anorexic patients and their families: taking the child into hospital; encouraging her to eat with a behavioural programme; initiating family 'lunch' sessions; providing individual therapy for the child; and marital work for the parents. These interventions are, nevertheless, only separate moves in the direction of changing patterns of behaviour in the family system which he sees as maintaining the problem manifested by the child.

Family therapy has been described as the imposition of a narrative or story line (some call it diagnosis, proposition, formulation, case history or treatment plan) on a set of statements, problems, ideas, and behaviours that the client(s) places in front of the therapist. From the moment of meeting, therapists begin to formulate a proposition or hypothesis about what went wrong or what is going wrong. They exchange ideas with their clients, offer alternatives, suggest solutions and encourage new perceptions. Essentially, family therapy is a methodology for constructing change (see Marianne Walters, 1989).

Schools of Family Therapy

There are several schools of family therapy. There are theoretical, philosophical and ideological nuances that differentiate between them, but also areas of overlap or convergence, particularly with regard to techniques. There is, however, a paucity of hard evidence as to the finer details of their effectiveness. As in psychodynamic approaches, there are features in the process of therapy that are difficult to operationalize and, therefore, to evaluate. There are difficulties in choosing outcome criteria, and of disentangling improvements in the individual (such as a decrease in symptoms) from improvements in family relationships. All of this makes it difficult to choose between schools of thought – a matter we return to shortly.

The main approaches to family therapy, according to Gurman and Kniskern (1981), are:

❑ *Psychoanalytic and object relations perspectives* which are derived from psychoanalytic theory, but which draw upon other principles as well. A leading exponent is Skynner (1976). The primary goal of therapy here is to identify how family members are projecting individual or marital difficulties unconsciously upon, say, a child of the family.

❑ *The intergenerational perspective* looks beyond the immediate family circle and enlists the cooperation of others in resolving the family's distress. Bowen (1978) is one of the foremost theorists here.

❑ *Systems theory*, now the dominant influence, is grounded in the notion of the family as a system; approaches include the 'structural' school, associated with Minuchin (1974), the 'strategic' school, associated with Haley (1976) and the 'systemic' school, developed by Palazzoli and colleagues (1978).

❏ *Behavioural perspectives* are based upon principles of social learning theory (for example, Alexander and Parsons, 1973; Herbert, 1991b; Patterson, 1982). Behavioural therapists have a strong commitment to empirical evaluation and validation of treatment outcomes.

❏ *Brief therapy*. Steve de Shazer (1988) is a major exponent of this solution-orientated approach.

Evaluation of Family Therapy

Kniskern and Gurman in *Advances in Family Intervention: Assessment and Theory* (1981), have reviewed the available evidence reporting that, despite methodological problems, family therapies (excluding behaviourally-oriented approaches) produce beneficial outcomes in about two-thirds of cases. Their analysis showed 61 per cent of marital cases and 73 per cent of family cases improved. It is important to note that these studies were generally uncontrolled; in other words, they lacked appropriate contrast groups of families who did not receive therapy. Confounding variables such as improvement (or deterioration) resulting from circumstances other than the therapy, cannot be detected, and thus excluded, as explanations. The data tell us little of the 'fine tuning' issues of 'which approach for which problem?', or about the most effective components of the intervention, but do provide, at least, a crude empirical basis for the continued practice and teaching of marital and family therapy.

There is increasing evidence highlighting the association between treatment outcome and the therapist's relationship skills. According to Gurman and Kniskern (1981), the literature suggests that it is generally important for the marital family therapist to be active and to provide some structure, but not to confront tenuous family defences very early in treatment. Excesses in directiveness are among the main contributors to premature termination, and to negative therapy outcomes. Marital and family therapies, at times, make individual patients and their marital and/or family relationships worse. It appears that about five to ten per cent of couples and families become worse at least during, if not because of, the non-behavioural family treatment they receive. There is no empirical evidence that family therapy carried out by a therapist plus co-therapist leads to more beneficial outcomes than that practised by one therapist working alone.

There is space here to provide some detail about only two of the family therapy approaches, namely, structural and behavioural family therapy. They are arguably the ones which research evidence shows to have the best track records. At a systemic level, there is a striking similarity between aspects of the two approaches (see Herbert, 1978 and Treacher and Carpenter, 1984). Both observe and analyse, *inter alia*, the developmental tasks and problems faced by the family and its members, and also day-to-day nuances of communication and relationship within the family. Some of the strategies for change have similar features despite different terminology.

Structural Family Therapy

The structural family therapist's first step is to 'join' with the family, then participate in its transactions and observe members' roles, their communications, and the boundaries within the family and between the family system and other systems. The family 'organism', like the individual person, moves between two poles: one representing the security of the known, the other being the exploration necessary for adaptation to changing conditions. When the family comes to treatment, it is in difficulty because it is stuck, trying to maintain old ways which no longer meet the needs of a changed and changing set of circumstances. The structural approach to producing family change is associated (among others) with the name, Salvador Minuchin, and the Philadelphia Child Guidance Clinic. The focus of attention is very much on the developmental tasks faced by the family and its members at various stages of its, and their, lifespan. Day-to-day patterns of relationships – communication and interaction – between members are inferred from highly charged or repetitive sequences observed and analysed in the therapy room.

The therapist, as an energetic 'intruder', works actively to restructure family organization and channels of communication by discussion (the genogram or family tree – see *Figure 9.1* – is often a good starting point), modelling, direction and the use of 'action techniques'.

Andy Treacher (1983) describes the basic sequence through which family therapy passes, as follows:

▷ The family and the therapist are originally isolated from each other. But therapists use their skills so that they become absorbed into the family through a process of accommodation. This process creates a new system – family and therapist. It may take several sessions to create the new system.
▷ Once the new system is functioning, the major restructuring 'work' occurs. Restructuring interventions are made during sessions and consolidating homework tasks are set between sessions.
▷ The next phase involves testing the family's ability to 'fire' the

(a) *Family tree symbols*

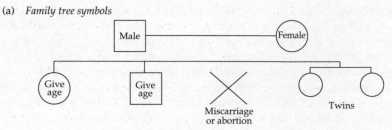

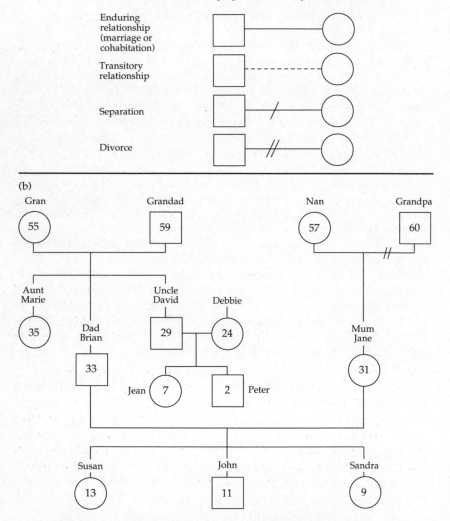

Figure 9.1 (a) How to make a genogram (b) An example

The genogram provides a helpful and visual representation of the family group. It makes a valuable interview aide if drawn on a flip-chart with the help of the child and/or parents, pausing to discuss relationships and particular persons of significance.

therapist and go it alone. The 'ghost' of the therapist is left behind by getting the family to stimulate its ability to solve new problems and to deal with old problems if they recur.

▷ A follow-up session after three months, six months or a year enables the therapist to evaluate the impact of therapy and test whether it has been successful in achieving second order change, which means enabling family rules and family functioning to change in such a way that the family generates effective solutions to problems.

In order to facilitate change during therapy, the therapist aims to create the conditions for change (a 'creative turmoil') in order to put the family onto a new and harmonious path. Techniques include (to name just a few) the following:

Enactment. This is the direct illustration by the clients (as opposed to mere description) of the problems that exist between them. Clients are encouraged, where appropriate, to talk directly to one another rather than to (or through) the therapist.

Boundary clarification. The creation or clarification of boundaries between family members is a feature of structural work. A mother who babies her teenager may hear with surprise her daughter's answer to the question, 'How old do you think your mother treats you as – three or thirteen?'.

Changing space. Asking clients in the therapy room to move about can intensify an interaction or underline an interpretation being made about a relationship. For example, if a husband and wife never confront one another directly, but always use their child as a mediator or channel of communication, the therapist blocks that manoeuvre (called triangulation) by moving the child from between the parents. He or she may comment, 'Let's move Claire from the middle so you can work it out together'.

Reframing. This is an important method in fulfilling the objective of helping clients change in a covert (less directed) manner. It is an alteration of the emotional or conceptual viewpoint in relation to which a situation is experienced. That experience is placed in another 'frame' which fits the facts of the situation as well (or more plausibly), thereby transforming its entire meaning. Giving people different 'stories' to tell themselves about themselves or about events – stories that are less self-defeating or destructive – is also a feature of behavioural work.

Behavioural Family Therapy

Some versions of family therapy have explicit roots in the application of social learning theory as developed, *inter alia*, by Albert Bandura (1986) and Gerald Patterson (1982). It is a theory that is sufficiently comprehensive and coherent to encompass the complex problems and assumptions of contemporary cognitive-behavioural methods which are major components of family-orientated behavioural work.

According to social learning theory (see page 121), learning occurs within a social nexus; rewards, punishments and other events are mediated by human agents and within attachment and social systems, and are not simply the impersonal consequences of behaviour. Children do not simply respond to stimuli; they interpret them. They are relating to, interacting with, and learning from people who have meaning and value for them. They feel antipathetic to some, attached by respect and/or affection to others, and thus may perceive (say) an encouraging word from the latter as 'rewarding' (that is, positively reinforcing), but from the former as valueless, perhaps even 'aversive'.

Not surprisingly, behavioural work is increasingly systemic. It not only deals with caregivers and nominated child 'patients' in their own right as individuals, but also analyses their relationships to each other (as dyadic attachment sub-systems) and assesses their communications, interactions, boundaries and perceptions within the holistic and dynamic family system.

Formulation of the problem within the family system

Learning, for children, is all about change, as is growth and development. Their parents and family are, like themselves, locked into a developmental life cycle with its stage-related life tasks. The nature, sources and consequences of parents' ideas about development, and the ramifications of transition and change in family life, are vitally important in the child therapist's assessment of children and their problems (Herbert, 1991a and b). This is especially so in the case of the conduct disorders; dysfunctional family life tends to be the 'norm' for children and adolescents with these problems. There is, for example, a strong association between marital disturbance in parents and antisocial behaviour in children.

Of interest to the practitioner in search of a formulation leading to an intervention, have been the studies on the interactional characteristics of these families carried out by Gerald Patterson and his team (see Patterson, 1982). Observing in great detail the behaviour of aggressive children at home, they found that their families differed from the families of normal children in a number of ways. Among other things, the parents of aggressive children showed a lack of consistency in disciplining their children. Although they use punishment very often, this is inefficient either because it is not clearly associated with transgression, or because, when the child counterattacks, the parents finally give in to his/her demands.

Another characteristic of such families is the lack of supervision or monitoring; aggressive children are more frequently left on their own. Furthermore, parents of aggressive children are described as lacking warmth, unable to involve themselves in pleasant shared activities or to clearly show the children what is right and what is wrong or what they are expected to do or not to do in any situation.

Researchers found that mothers of aggressive children are likely to identify *themselves* as victims of their child's hostile aggression. It is hypothesized that this leads to a poor self-image, resulting in a predisposition to act aggressively, particularly in threatening inter-personal situations. Children use aggressive behaviour to terminate such aversive interactions with their parents or other members of the family. This process is neatly described by Patterson as the 'coercive family process' (see Chapter 3). The theory postulates that aggressive, conduct-disordered children engage in excessive rates of behaviour which are aversive for parents who, in turn, retaliate with equally excessive rates of aversive actions, which lead on to an upwardly escalating spiral of unremitting sound and fury. Such interactions are negatively reinforcing both to the children and to the parents. Children are reinforced by their parents' eventual compliance. It is difficult in these circumstances to know what is cause and what is effect. However, in terms of the development of antisocial behaviour, these processes can be conceptualized as a series of positive feedback loops – inept parenting fosters antisocial child behaviour and deficits in the child's skills, and these are characteristics which, in turn, make child rearing more difficult for the parents, and so on.

Intervention

Given what has just been said, it is not surprising that there is much less emphasis in behaviour therapy today, compared with past practice, on the contingency management of specific childhood target problems of the kind described in Chapter 8, although they continue to loom large in clinical work. The focus is more on *broad principles* of child management, the setting of limits (boundaries), the inter-personal interactions of members of the family, the marital relation-ships, and the perceived self-efficacy of caregivers. Such an approach lends itself particularly to the growing number of cases of child abuse where disciplinary, child management, communication and attach-ment (bonding) difficulties abound. The approach is multimodel, and often rooted in work with the whole family or, in the case of 'challenging' behaviours in residential settings, with staff groups. (For an account of intervention methods in coercive family systems, see page 185: Behavioural Parent Training).

A case illustration

A return to the case of Emma and the Bray family provides us with an example of this kind of work in the family setting. Mrs Bray made the following notes soon after the beginning of treatment:

'First of all there was a feeling of relief. Something was at last being done. Something concrete. I was going to be helped. For a short while I felt euphoric . . . but I was defensive as well because I knew that I must accept a certain responsibility for the way Emma was. I did not want to do that. I had enough of failure. But I recognized I would have to face up to the truth if I went ahead with treatment. It was quite a struggle at times and my pride took quite a battering . . .'

There were problems in initiating the programme, as Emma's mother says:

'At the beginning of Dr Herbert's intervention, however, I was unable to cooperate effectively. I was desperately unhappy and depressed with no clear understanding of how I came to be so. Each day I moved through a suffocating fog of failure, frustration and guilt. Myself I saw as an unattractive and undesirable individual. I felt that my intellect had atrophied. My daily round of housework and bringing up children held no rewards, but left me bored and exhausted. Against this background, a natural shyness had developed into a real fear of going out and talking to people. The fear of rejection was greater than the fact of loneliness. My home had become a prison. Because of these feelings, Dr Herbert decided to work on two levels: with the whole family on our relationships and Emma's behaviour, and with myself.

The angry feelings from failing to cope with Emma gradually eased as my work with Emma, and our family discussions progressed, and I learned to express the resentment I felt when she misbehaved, but in a more controlled manner, by giving appropriate commands. We discussed my parents' way of bringing me up and how it had influenced my attitudes; also what I (and my husband) saw of ourselves in Emma. The hardest problem to deal with was the self-doubts and isolation. Being depressed for several years and feeling inadequate had eroded my self-confidence and produced a profound dislike for myself. It was necessary to change that before I could look up and outwards.

In one of my individual sessions, Dr Herbert asked me to role-play as a means of learning new ways of coping with my fears and suspicions of people. I started by writing a self-portrait. He took each point and changed it to some extent. Where I was serious, introverted, careful, I was to be rather more spontaneous and impulsive, even a little frivolous – without "overdoing" it. I was to think and act like an attractive woman; in fact, we created a different "persona" and role to my usual ones, but not too far out to make the task impossible. We went over it in great detail like a script.

The next step was not easy. What I had to do was to go out and live my role daily. It was certainly very difficult at first. I felt like a second rate actress with severe stage fright. But the remarkable thing was how it gradually became easier; and when the results were good I felt elated. I discovered casual conversations with local mothers, in the park or at the shops, soon unearthed common interests and I gradually developed new friendships with women in similar circumstances to myself, all with children for Emma and Stella to play with. For the first time since Emma's birth, we were making regular visits outside the immediate family. Social skills are like any other – the more practice you get, the better you become. As my confidence grew with each success, so Emma also relaxed and she began to look forward to the visits eagerly. Throughout this period, during which there were regular discussions about my own situation and problems, we also met, when we were not meeting as a family, as a couple, and worked on some marital disagreements and issues to do with the way we used Emma as an excuse for some of the arguments and bickered over her management.'

Behaviour management

With regard to the behaviour management components of the casework, treatment objectives were negotiated between the therapist and the parents. The first goal was to increase adaptive behaviours in certain specified situations, as identified by the parents, with the main aim of creating opportunities for Emma to win positive reinforcement for socially appropriate behaviour. A detailed plan was worked out with regard to the behaviours that the parents wished to encourage. A contract was designed, one which specified precisely how the parents were to behave proactively and how they were to respond to Emma. The parents and therapist spent much time going over precisely what both parents were going to say when they issued commands to her. What came through very forcibly, was that both parents tended to indulge in an internal debate when action was required. They would silently argue with themselves, 'Should I?' before they gave Emma a command. They were often reluctant to carry through a threatened (that is, promised) sanction, feeling 'sorry' for her or guilty afterwards.

Precise cues were suggested to the parents in order to avoid these agonizing dilemmas, so they could act at the right time in a decisive manner. Authoritative commands, it was hoped, would nip Emma's target behaviours in the bud and prevent their unpleasant repercussions.

We know from the research literature that parents with reasonably obedient children give more so-called 'alpha' commands. Alpha commands are characterized by being specific and direct, being given one at a time, and being followed by a wait of five seconds. Parents can be taught to use these, rather than 'beta' commands – chain commands, vague commands, question commands, 'let's' commands, and commands followed by a rationale or verbalization. Compliance can be facilitated by working with parents on the following themes: ensuring that rules are clear and reasonable; that obedience or disobedience is sanctioned consistently; and that the requests and commands that give effect to rules are precise and comprehensible. If there are difficulties with the latter, you might model how to make effective requests and commands by demonstrating, and then checking, the client's performance.

Alan Hudson (1987), an Australian psychologist, recommends the following steps which we rehearsed with Emma's parents.

▷ Use the child's name.
▷ Give a specific direction.
▷ Include a mention of time (for example, 'right now' or 'when you have finished the chapter').
▷ Say 'please'.
▷ Put all the words together in the form of a statement, not a question. Do not say: 'Sandy, will you get dressed for Mummy?' Do say: 'Sandy, I would like you to get dressed now, please'.
▷ Make the request standing close to the child; with a small child, get down close to the height of the little one.
▷ Use a pleasant, but firm, tone of voice – no pleading, cajoling, wheedling!
▷ Try to look at the child. It may be helpful to say: 'Sandy, look at me now, please', and then give the desired command.
▷ If the child obeys or disobeys (ignores/refuses) within (say) ten seconds, follow the behaviour with clear and predictable consequences:
    – obedience is followed by positive consequences (for example, praise);
    – disobedience is followed by negative consequences (for example, loss of privileges, time-out (see *Figure 9.2*).
  Discourage parents from smacking or shouting.
▷ In the case of special circumstances (shopping, visiting) or places (church, restaurants), help parents to pre-empt problems by working out a scenario:
    – explain to the child what is going to happen;
    – promise (specify) a treat/privilege if the child behaves well;
    – engage the child in prosocial behaviours that compete with the unwanted behaviours (for example, helping mum to pack the shopping box rather than taking items off the shelves at the check-out counter).
▷ Do not keep repeating the requests! Don't nag. Follow non-compliant actions with the penalty.

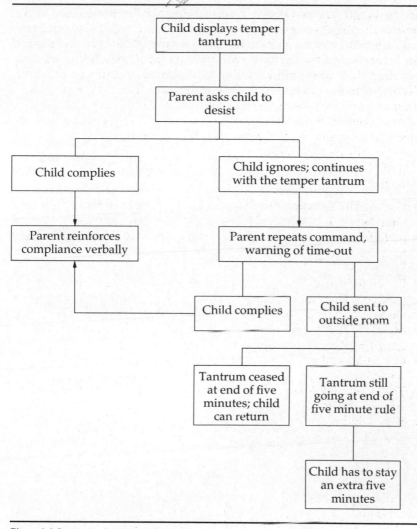

Figure 9.2 Stages in the use of time-out

It was suggested that when Emma tried her delaying strategies, say, at the point of implementing time-out, she was to be picked up, with no eye contact and no verbal communication, and placed in the hall (for five minutes), thus eliminating the attention she was gaining from her diversions. The response to this detailed plan was encouraging, and the frequency of the target behaviours decreased gradually. As Emma's positive behaviours increased, there were more opportunities for the parents to 'enjoy' her which, in turn, stimulated a high degree of mutual social reinforcement.

Emma now gave the appearance of being a far happier child to the therapist (and more important), to her parents and their relatives. Mrs Bray no longer looked the harassed woman of the not-too-distant past. The relationship between the parents which had been strained, was described toward the end of our regular meetings with both parents, as much more harmonious and supportive.

Developmental counselling

This is a common feature of behavioural family work, focusing, *inter alia*, on the discussion of disciplinary issues with parents, individually or in groups. In the Behaviour Therapy Clinic at the Child and Family Consultation Centre in Plymouth, we raise various issues for debate and clarification. We also provide guidelines for parents which are based on a reading of the child development and clinical literature. Some of the following recommendations have been made:

▶ Work out a general strategy on discipline.
▶ Have clear priorities.
▶ Work out the 'house rules'.
▶ Restrict requests and demands to those that are reasonable and fair, that is, appropriate to the child's age and ability.
▶ Set limits (boundaries) for the child.
▶ Demonstrate affection visibly, and foster the child's love and respect.
▶ Try to be around enough to encourage the child in his/her efforts to learn about and cope with life.
▶ Explain the reasons behind disciplinary actions.
▶ Listen carefully to what the child (or teenager) is saying.
▶ Prepare the child for life by encouraging good personal habits and routines.
▶ Make good behaviour worthwhile, that is to say, accentuate the positive.
▶ Judge when to ignore the child's misbehaviour.
▶ Consequences (positive or negative) should *promptly* follow the behaviour they are designed to encourage or discourage.

Agreements and contracts

Reciprocal contractual agreements are not unusual – they exist in families and other groupings, whether explicit or implicit. Many of the problems that arise are due to the arrangement not being reciprocal or explicit enough. Contracts (whether written down or agreed verbally) have the effect of structuring reciprocal exchanges. They specify who is to do what, for whom and under what circumstances. Reinforcement contingencies, to take one example, can be made explicit between individuals who wish behaviour to change (for example, parents, teachers, nurses) and those whose behaviour is to be changed (children, students, patients).

At a time of crisis, when marital partners or teenagers and their parents (or indeed brothers and sisters) are at loggerheads, contracts provide an opportunity for a family to take stock and to break through vicious circles of retribution and unreason. The cognitive processes of discussion, negotiation and compromise (which are strangers to some families) may well be as important as the content of the contract.

Contingency agreements are contracts drawn up between two or more people in which a set of mutual expectations is written down, detailing reciprocal benefits and the 'costs' or penalties for transgressions. The main assumption underlying the use of formal verbal agreements or the stronger written form of contract is that the publicly endorsed, unambiguous and specific commitment to a future course of action will prove more binding and a better guarantee of compliance, than more casual 'promises' or ephemeral statements of intention (think of those failed New Year resolutions). To obtain this result, however, the parties concerned must not feel they have been unduly coerced into their contractual arrangements.

The following elements of contracting are among those that are most important for the client:

- Be very specific in spelling out the desired action.
- Pay attention to the details of the privileges and conditions for both parties; they should be (a) important as opposed to trivial, (b) functional.
- If parents wish their youngster (or adults, their partner) to desist from certain actions and activities, encourage them to express these in terms of positive change. Rather than being negative, they should specify the change they wish to bring about by inviting X to accentuate the positive, the pleasant or praiseworthy. This would then have to be spelled out in terms of specific examples of behaviour. (Reciprocal requirements can be asked of parents or partner.)
- Get parents (or child or partner) to write down five items of behaviour (actions) they wish their son or daughter (or parents or partner) would do more often.
- Don't let the parties be vague (for example, 'I wish he'd be more helpful'). Be concrete and specific ('I wish he'd help me set and clear the table').

Ethical Imperatives

The overall principles governing the choice of treatment should be those of alleviating distress, enhancing personal and social performance and, with it, quality of life. This requires that a treatment should always carry some primary benefit for the individual client; that such benefits should endure beyond the immediacies of the treatment process; and that a specific treatment should always be used within an overall plan of management. There are also several specific ethical issues to be taken into account when using behavioural treatments with children. The Royal College of Psychiatrists' Working Party has addressed these in their *Guidelines to Good Practice* (1989) (to which the author was a contributor). Some of these issues are summarized below:

☐ The proposed method of treatment should be explained in detail and it is helpful and sensible to offer written explanatory information.

☐ Children may be limited in their understanding of a treatment or its implications and consequently unable to give full consent. It may, nevertheless, still be necessary to use that treatment. If so, it is essential that it is applied in such a way as to take the special needs of children into account, particularly those arising from their dependency, immaturity, difficulties in understanding and problems in communicating.

☐ In evaluating the acceptability of a behavioural method or goal, the current social and professional consensus as well as the legitimately held values and beliefs of the patient, should be considered in relation to the seriousness of the disturbance, and its repercussions to the patient and to society. The majority of behavioural treatments and procedures are ethically unexceptionable but some (for example, time-out) may give rise to problems and anxieties.

☐ If the only effective method available involves any distress or risk, the decision to apply it must reflect the importance of change to the patient and to others. Such treatments should be discussed with a clinical ethical committee.

☐ It is essential to consider the presenting problems as objectively as possible. Parents (or care staff) may ask for treatment to make the child conform to a regime or to values which may be at odds with the child's best interests. It is crucial that the practitioner's role here is one of advocacy for, and protection of, the child.

Reservations about Behavioural Work

Among the many criticisms of behavioural work (see Herbert, 1978), the major ones concern its alleged assault on humanistic sensitivities and sensibilities, most notably the person's freedom of choice and potential for self-actualization. It is of interest that, despite behaviour therapists' predilection for explicit and objective methods, Sloane *et al.* (1975) still found that their patients rated them at least as high on interpersonal factors such as warmth and empathy, as non-behavioural therapists. One might also suggest that the emphasis of behaviour therapy on *explicit* objectives and *self-direction*, together with the client's access to a self-empowering knowledge base of behavioural principles, makes for liberating therapeutic philosophy.

For some critics of behavioural work, the belief in the causal role of the family in childhood problems has led to a neglect of factors intrinsic to the child (for example, temperament) in the genesis of psychiatric disorder. And behaviour therapy is still viewed as very much a method of treatment aimed at the individual child, and therefore out of key with systemic thinking. For other critics, a commitment to ethical relativism – the conviction that there are no objective ethical standards for judging the rightness or wrongness of an action – is the main objection.

Among these objections is sometimes a deep distrust of science and its findings. A scientific approach to treatment is often rejected as impersonal, manipulative (that is, political) and mechanistic (that is, simplistic). It is, therefore, not surprising that a presentation of encouraging behavioural research findings may be met with indifference. Certainly, a healthy scepticism of science is appropriate, but to reject it out of hand would seem to represent a worrying retreat into subjectivism and superstition.

The point has been made that behavioural work, for all its proven track record, provides no panacea. As with other therapeutic methods, it is a case of 'horses for courses'. The trouble is that we are still not certain which horses are best for which courses – a continuing research task for the future.

What can be asserted confidently, is that family-orientated behavioural work is a useful 'craft', and one that is essentially a blend of applied science and art. There is the art of teaching children *and* adult caregivers; the art of finding and using imaginative materials to capture the interest of children and adults; the art of explaining abstract principles to, and unravelling complex problems for, clients of all ages. There is also the all-important art of increasing patients' perceived self-efficacy by means of a shared therapeutic collaboration, a role for which a demystified version of behaviour therapy is ideally suited.

FURTHER READING

Behavioural work

Dangel, R. F. and Polster, R. A. (1988) *Teaching Child Management Skills.* London: Pergamon Press. [A key reference on parent training.]

Herbert, M. (1987) *Behavioural Treatment of Children with Problems: A Practice Manual*. London: Academic Press. [A nuts-and-bolts, how to do it guide, with casework examples.]

Hudson, B. L. and MacDonald, G. M. (1986) *Behavioural Social Work: An Introduction*. [An excellent introduction to behavioural social work – a sadly neglected social work method.]

Working with families

Buchan, L., Clemerson, J. and Davis, H. (1988) Working with Families of Children with Special Needs: The Parent Adviser Scheme. *Child: Care, Health and Development, 14*, 81–91. [A multidisciplinary counselling scheme of particular promise.]

Cunningham, C. and Sloper, P. (1978) *Helping Your Handicapped Baby*. London: Souvenir Press. [Guide to parents coping with handicap.]

Pless, I. and Nolan, T. (1991) Revision, replication and neglect in research on maladjustment in chronic illness. *Journal of Child Psychology and Psychiatry, 32*, 347–365. [Review of research on effects of chronic illness.]

10 *Intervention in child abuse*

Social and health workers are likely to be faced with any of the following specific problems in families when child abuse cases are referred to them.

Deficits
- Skill deficits (poor problem-solving skills; ineffective communication skills; ineffective reinforcement skills).
- Social isolation.
- Withholding attention (ignoring, for example, annoying activities until there's a crisis).
- Failure to track minor incidents before they blow up in major confrontations.
- Failure to acknowledge/notice/reward prosocial behaviour.
- Few family recreational activities together.
- Low self-esteem/low perception of self-efficacy.
- Less positive emotional expression.

Excess/surplus problems
- Use of aversive (negative, coercive, punitive) means of influencing or changing others (criticism/physical assaults).
- Parental yelling, shouting, nagging, threats, complaints.
- Punishment of prosocial behaviour.
- High parental stress/distress (marital discord, inadequate income, poor housing, lack of emotional/social support).
- Alcohol/drug abuse.
- Acting out, antisocial conduct problems.

Inappropriate beliefs/attitudes/knowledge/behaviour
- Faulty attributions (cause-and-effect inferences).
- Reinforcement of inappropriate/deviant actions.
- Unpredictable/inconsistent parenting.
- Mutual avoidance.
- Faulty expectations due to absence of basic knowledge about child development.
- Inflexibility in child disciplinary situations.

It is common practice to identify three levels of intervention in the field of child abuse: primary, secondary and tertiary.

Primary Intervention

The focus here is on interventions to prevent child abuse; the aim is to reduce the *incidence* or the number of new cases in a population. The three main approaches are:

(1) Adapting existing services so as to enhance parental competence and promote change by means of, for example, parent education. Olds (1986) set up an intensive home visiting service by health visitors to young parents during pregnancy and the first two years of a baby's life. This primary intervention strategy had a significant effect on poor, unmarried mothers under the age of 19 years.

(2) Mobilizing community resources and offering voluntary help by means of networks and crisis services (for example, telephone helplines).

(3) Educating the public through specific projects, such as public and professional awareness and publicity campaigns.

Parents who abuse their children share a common pattern of social isolation, poor work history and few friendships outside the home. This isolation tends to mean that child abusing parents are not always willing or able to seek help from agencies that could provide assistance or from people who have the means to give advice and emotional support. Nevertheless, community-based actions have proved useful. Such work includes the involvement of 'community mothers', that is, experienced parents who offer support and help to isolated young mothers; and also the help of 'foster grandparents' who take a particular interest in young families and offer non-judgemental support. In addition, there is the development of networks of support in the form of self-help groups or visiting schemes staffed by volunteers. Other schemes include the voluntary agencies that offer help through direct contact with parents. NEWPIN, for example, runs support groups for depressed mothers in impoverished parts of London. HOMESTART, which originated in Leicester, now has a nationwide service of experienced volunteer mothers willing to befriend and assist less experienced parents.

Secondary Intervention

Secondary prevention or intervention has as its goal the reduction of the prevalence (the number of existing cases) of abuse and neglect by early detection and intervention. Families identified as being at high risk by screening may be offered treatment before any serious harm has occurred to the child, thereby (hopefully) reducing the chance of the child being taken into the care of the designated local authority

[s.31(1)(a)] at some later date. Obviously, a prerequisite of this intervention is the ability to detect reliably those families which are
vulnerable. Special attention is given to parents most in need of
help in coping with their children so that violence or other inappropriate behaviour is avoided. A corollary to these desiderata, if effective
work is to be carried out, is the need for appropriate training of staff;
access to expert advice and support; regular review and monitoring of
job content and workload; and mechanisms for supervision of case
management.

Screening families at risk

Screening techniques aimed at the early prediction and identification
of potential or actual child maltreatment provide the opportunity for
secondary preventive/intervention work. This might include counselling, home visits or family work in clinics, health centres or hospitals.
Practitioners – notably social workers, health visitors and members of
primary care teams – are in a position to screen routinely for 'risky'
characteristics in families who come in contact with their services. But
how reliable are screening instruments?

The effectiveness of one particular checklist (see *Table 3.2*, page 42)
as a screening instrument, was assessed by Browne (1988) in order to
evaluate how well the scores obtained allowed a known 'abuse' group
to be discriminated from a 'non-abuse' group (a technique known as
'discriminant function analysis').

It was found that fully completed checklists, with the relative
weighting for each factor taken into account, could correctly classify
86 per cent of cases. This is a better success rate than most studies.
However extreme caution is required before putting faith in this sort
of screening device. The instrument was sensitive to 82 per cent of the
abusing, non-accidental injury (NAI) families, and specified 88 per
cent of the control families as non-abusing. However, if the checklist
of risk factors is used in this way, it will misclassify 18 per cent of the
abusing families as non-risk cases, and incorrectly identify 12 per cent
of the non-abusing families as potential NAI cases. Research suggests
that although known risk factors significantly *predispose* families to
child abuse, they are *not sufficient* to actually precipitate violence in
the vast majority of families under stress.

The chances of situational stressors (risk factors) resulting in child
abuse and other forms of family violence are mediated by, and
depend upon, the relationships within the family. A secure
relationship between family members will 'buffer' effects of stress
and facilitate coping strategies on the part of the family. At the end of
the day, despite much research effort, it has to be acknowledged that
no amount of screening can protect vulnerable children from assault.

Tertiary Intervention

The focus here is upon intervention in families *after* abuse has occurred and has been investigated. The aim is to reduce the adverse effects resulting from abuse by means of appropriate support, care and services. The main intervention strategies are systemic family therapy and the training of maltreating parents within a social learning theory (behavioural) framework, that is, in child management skills. There is also intervention in children's behaviours which parents find particularly demoralizing, such as whining, disobedience and aggression. Rory Nicol (1988), in a review of interventions in the home setting, concludes that it does seem, from the research available at present, that some families where child abuse has occurred can be helped by home-based treatment programmes. It would seem safe, therefore, to say that in any given case *that seems suitable*, a trial of treatment could be undertaken. Intervention can be conceptualized as 'further assessment' – assessment, in practice, of whether clients are *capable of change*.

Emotional and Physical Abuse: A Case Vignette

The following note describes our first impressions (see Iwaniec, Herbert and McNeish, 1985):

'*Jimmy Grant is a chubby, rose-cheeked boisterous two-year-old. He appears to be a happy, mischievous boy, running, playing, talking and laughing. He comes to his mother for help and comfort and cuddles up to her spontaneously. He responds readily to her attention and affection. She smiles at him, picks him up, sits him on her lap, plays with him . . . On the edge of the room, like a stranger, stands Wayne – Jimmy's twin. He stands rigid, staring fixedly at us. He is a sad, lethargic-looking child, very small and extremely thin. His pale face throws into relief the dark shadows under his eyes. He remains in one spot, as if at attention; by now he is gazing unswervingly at his mother. She takes no notice of him. When asked to call Wayne over to her she looks in his direction; as she does so, her face hardens and her eyes are angry. She addresses him with a dry command; when he hesitates she shouts at him.*'

Our observations of his interactions with Wayne's mother (several visits) which gave us baseline data, indicated that her only physical contact came about when she fed, bathed or dressed him, and at such times, her handling was rough and silent. When she approached him, he appeared to be frightened and occasionally burst into tears. He would never come to her for comfort or help and she never approached him except to carry out the bare essentials of care and control. The children were both meticulously clean and well-dressed.

Home-based observations allowed us to see that when his father returned from work, Wayne brightened a little; he became somewhat more alert and lively, especially when his mother was out of sight. When she entered the room he stiffened up. Jimmy and Wayne didn't play together. Jimmy frequently pushed his brother and smacked him; Wayne's cries were largely ignored by his mother.

Looking at Wayne and Jimmy it is hard to believe that they were of about the same weight at birth. Wayne's small stature was now reflected in a height and weight that were below the third centile curve of normal growth. Wayne had been hospitalized several times because of his failure to gain weight. During the latest hospitalization Wayne's mother refused to visit him and requested his reception into care; she appeared to be very depressed and said that she could no longer cope with trying to feed him (he would refuse food, or spit it out screaming loudly). She added that she could no longer tolerate his behaviour ('defiance', whining and crying) and her hostile feelings towards him. At the stage of our entry into the case, Wayne had to be fed by a combination of the health visitor, father and a neighbour.

Failure to thrive

It was clear (after the essential, exhaustive, medical tests) that Wayne's retarded growth at this stage of his life was not due to physical (organic) disease. This was a case of non-organic failure to thrive. Studies of such children and their families have shown that the most commonly identified forerunners to these problems are emotional disturbance and environmental deprivation – with the wide range of psychological and social disorganization that these concepts imply. The deprivation often involves rejection, isolation from social contacts and neglect. Occasionally, physical abuse enters the picture. Our enquiries soon indicated that on several occasions, Wayne had shown severe bruising. The child protection case conference had him placed on the child protection register.

The Grant family – in acute crisis – received a form of assessment and a broadly-based form of behavioural family therapy. Wayne had been a difficult baby to feed from the word 'go'. He vomited frequently and seemed to cry or scream incessantly for the first few weeks of life. He took an inordinately long time to feed. The situation deteriorated when solids were introduced at the age of five months. He persistently refused to take them and gradually stopped taking liquids as well. From that time onwards, feeding time became a battle.

By the time Wayne was 14 months old, his mother finally found it almost impossible to cope with his reluctance to eat. She screamed at him, smacked him, shook him, getting angrier and more frustrated each day. When she forced him to eat, he screamed, vomited immediately and then had diarrhoea. Soon Wayne began to scream at the sight of his mother. She could not touch him or come near him. In anger and helpless despair, she would take him upstairs and leave him there for hours. Wayne took some food from his father and next door neighbour and was fed only when they were available. Because he was losing weight rapidly, he was admitted to hospital for investigation.

In hospital, Wayne cried a lot and was, at first, unresponsive to nurses and movements around him. When not crying, he looked blank and lethargic. Gradually he began to take food and became more alert and lively, doing well enough in the end to be discharged. This pattern of 'failure to thrive', improving in hospital, and deteriorating soon after going home, was to be repeated several times. In the end, Mrs Grant refused to have Wayne back home from the hospital.

Our work after some initial sessions in the hospital, was carried out in the home with both parents and children. In order to be able to institute a full programme of assessment and treatment, we had to teach Mrs Grant to relax and to structure small, manageable daily tasks to counter her tension and her inertia and apathy. A period of counselling, support-giving and relaxation-training covered several weeks. We arranged for full-time attendance for the twins at a day nursery.

Intervention programme

A variety of methods are used. Attention is paid to immediate needs (crisis intervention) of the child and family by:

► Ensuring that the child is safe, fed and stimulated.
► Arranging attendance at a day nursery (in part a safety measure). This allows for the child to be monitored for a substantial part of the day. It provides the mother with a 'break' and the space to work on her problem with the practitioner. It also gives the child some much needed social stimulation.
► Arranging for health visitors, home-start volunteers and neighbours to assist mothers with feeding and child care and to provide moral support.
► Assisting parents with problems of housing, financing, welfare rights, etc. where and when appropriate.
► Providing supervision by regular visits and phone calls (also emotional support).
► Placing children on the child protection register because of extreme rejection and/or abuse (failure to thrive).
► Beginning and supporting self-help parents group (composed of earlier clients) which parents can attend.
► Desensitizing (where necessary) the tension, anger and

resentment when in the child's company. It is almost always necessary for the mothers of these children to learn to control and resolve feelings of anger and resentment and to deal with high levels of anxiety. This was sometimes achieved (before any formal feeding programme could be initiated) by training in relaxation, stress management and self-control.

Longer term, after the attention to the immediate safety and needs of child and family, the intervention focuses on critical issues such as the mother's relationship with the infant, her ability to feed the child and the child's ability to receive (and benefit from) sustenance. Treatment also addresses parents' frequent depression and/or anxiety, their relationship, and so on.

During this phase the treatment of failure to thrive cases consists of a multi-level 'package' of psychosocial methods, ranging from developmental counselling to behavioural family casework methods (including discussion, clarification of problems, task-setting and support-giving).

Phase 1

Before we could initiate a programme dealing with the interactions between Mrs Grant and her child, we had to cope with the crisis issue of the mother's feeding her child. After all, Wayne was wasting away.

This was tackled in a highly structured (and thus, directive) manner. At first we had to make the mealtimes more relaxed. Mrs Grant agreed (albeit reluctantly and sceptically) to desist from screaming, shouting and threatening the child over his meals. The period of eating was made quiet and calm. Mrs Grant was asked to talk soothingly and pleasantly to him.

This was extremely difficult for her. (The social worker joined the family for a few meals, helping to reassure Wayne, prompting the mother to help him eat in a gentle manner when he was in difficulties.) Mrs Grant was encouraged to look at him, smile, and occasionally touch him. If Wayne refused his food, she was to leave him. We encouraged her to coax him by play or soft words. The food was arranged to look attractive.

Phase II

This phase (as with earlier stages of treatment) was discussed in detail with both parents. A contract was drawn up specifying the mutual obligations and rules for the family and ourselves. The following objectives were identified:

- To deliberately, and in planned fashion, increase positive interactions and decrease negative interactions between mother and child.

- To desensitize Wayne's anxieties with regard to mother's caregiving (and other) activities.
- To desensitize mother's tension, anger and resentment when in Wayne's company.
- To increase and make more general the interactions with other members of the family (for example, as a group, between Wayne and his brother, etc.).

Mrs Grant agreed to play exclusively with Wayne every evening after her husband returned from work, for ten minutes during the first week; 15 minutes during the second week; 20 minutes during the third week, and 25 minutes during the fourth and subsequent weeks. The father took Jimmy for a walk, or to another room, while Wayne had this period of play. Afterwards they would join in for a family play session. The mother was asked to play with Wayne on the floor – this was demonstrated and rehearsed – and she was encouraged to talk to him in a soft reassuring manner, encouraging him to participate in the play.

She was also instructed to smile at Wayne, look at him, touch him briefly, or praise him for each positive response she detected from him. (His tentative approaches toward her were 'shaped' by just such a series of successive approximations.) After a period of weeks, she was guided to seek proximity to him by hugging him briefly and then holding him on her lap for increasing intervals of time, eventually holding him close, but gently, while reading him a story. (These graduated, affection and proximity-encouraging interactions can be elaborated to encourage responsive parenting and 'bonding' in cases where they are problematic – especially during what has been called 'the window of opportunity', the first year or so of the infant's life.)

There is no doubt that Mrs Grant found these times difficult, and, at times, distasteful; but they became gradually less so as time passed and especially as Wayne shyly began to seek her out and to smile and chat to her. We had to provide a good deal of support and encouragement to both parents during frequent visits or by phone calls. (Reinforcing the reinforcer is critical in this work.) Three months were occupied by this stage of the intervention.

Phase III
The formal programme was faded out gradually (over a period of several weeks) after discussing with both parents the importance of a stimulating environment and providing much encouragement for the maintenance of the improvements they both detected in the family interactions and in the mother's feelings and attitudes (these were monitored for us by herself). Our assessment of Wayne's improved health, weight and height (and indeed his general psychological well-being) were confirmed by the assessments of the paediatrician, the

dietary consultant, and a health visitor. Mrs Grant's sense of attachment (bonding) to Wayne had returned.

Behavioural Parent Training (BPT)

Parent training has provided a promising therapeutic response to the difficult challenge of the conduct disorders which are commonly found in families that are abusive (see also Chapter 9). To meet the shortfall in professional resources, agencies have looked increasingly to training parents in group settings.

Group programmes

These programmes emphasize methods designed to reduce confrontations and antagonistic interactions among family members, to increase the effectiveness of positive interactions and moderate the intensity of parental punishment. The rationale comes from research indicating that parents of aggressive, antisocial children often lack certain basic parenting skills. They frequently indulge in coercive commands and criticisms, and make extensive use of threats, anger, nagging and negative consequences.

In these groups, parents learn (it is argued) not only a new model of behaviour but also learn to understand the consequences of their behaviour and the role it plays in the maintenance of their child's 'problem' behaviour. In effect, they learn a new language – verbal and non-verbal – for communicating with their children.

The seminal influence on parent training theory and practice, is the work of Patterson, Reid and their colleagues at the Oregon Social Learning Centre (OSLC), where they have treated over 200 families with extremely aggressive, antisocial children over a period of some two decades. Patterson (1982) summarizes encouraging evidence that changing family management styles (by means of manuals and personal therapeutic input) can produce significant changes in such antisocial behaviours as aggression, non-compliance, destructiveness, disruption and hyperactivity.

There are many unresolved problems. Among these are high drop-out rates, the difficulty of maintaining improvements and the intractability of specific delinquencies such as stealing. (A detailed account of the advantages and disadvantages of this and more recent work with antisocial children is given in Herbert, 1987a and b, 1991.)

Five family management practices form the core components of the OSLC programme:

(1) Parents are taught how to pinpoint the problematic activities of concern and how to track them at home (for example, compliance versus non-compliance).

(2) They are taught reinforcement techniques (for example, praise, point systems) and disciplinary methods.
(3) When parents see their children behaving inappropriately, they learn to apply a mild consequence such as time-out (see page 171) or a short-term deprivation of privileges (response-cost).
(4) They are taught to 'monitor' (that is, to supervise) their children even when they are away from home. This involves parents knowing where their children are at all times, what they are doing, and when they will be returning home.
(5) Finally, they are taught problem-solving and negotiation strategies and become increasingly responsible for designing their own programmes.

Twenty hours of direct contact with individual families is the typical pattern in the OSLC treatment package. The therapist must be skilled in coping with the resistance to change that characterizes the majority of the families referred for treatment. Ordinarily, this level of clinical skill requires several years of supervised clinical experience.

Another successful parent training programme for young conduct-disordered children (ages three to eight) has been developed by Carolyn Webster-Stratton (see Webster-Stratton, 1991). It includes components of other effective treatment packages as well as elements of problem-solving and communication skills. The GDVM (Group Discussion Videotape Modelling) programme is notable for its imaginative and systematic use of videotape modelling methods. The series of ten videotapes uses models of differing sexes, ages, cultures, socio-economic backgrounds and temperaments, so that parents can perceive the models as being similar to themselves and their children. In addition, the videotapes show parent models in natural situations (unrehearsed) with their children 'doing it right' and 'doing it wrong'. The video (consisting of 250 vignettes of parenting skills, each of which lasts approximately eight to 12 minutes) is shown by a therapist to groups of parents (eight to 12 parents per group). After each vignette, the therapist leads a group discussion and encourages parents to express their ideas. This can lead to problem-solving, role-play and rehearsal. The programme has also been given to over 80 parents and conduct-disordered children as a completely self-administered intervention.

Another videotape programme (ENHANCE), is based on six videotape programmes and has been developed to focus on family issues other than parenting skills, such as anger management, coping with depression, marital communication skills, problem-solving strategies, and how to teach children to problem-solve and manage their anger more effectively.

An example of a British effort, is the Scott programme which was developed for, and validated on, typical social service clientele, namely, single parent, low income or state benefit families (Scott and Stradling, 1987). The programme can be administered by social workers or assistants familiar with the Programme Manual. The programme consists of six 90-minute sessions run at weekly intervals during which a variety of behavioural techniques (for example, planned ignoring, social reinforcement, time-out, response-cost, new skills) are taught, largely through role-play, with a follow-up session a month later. The groups are made up of five to eight mothers.

All the above programmes have received high ratings from parents on acceptability and consumer satisfaction. Significant changes in parents' and children's actions, and in parental perceptions of child adjustment, have indicated encouraging short-term successes. Observations in the home setting have suggested that parents are successful in reducing children's level of aggression by 20 to 60 per cent. All of the programmes report generalization of behaviour improvements from the clinic setting to the home over follow-up periods ranging from six months to four years. (See Webster-Stratton, 1991, for a review of the evidence relating to BPT).

Individual training programmes

Group parent training programmes are not always appropriate or practical. Manuals have been published containing structured courses designed for use with individuals (Lawes, 1992). Otherwise behavioural strategies are taught on an *ad hoc* basis, depending on an individual assessment. Among those most commonly used are the following:

Differential attention

The differential use of attention and ignoring is widely advocated as the first step in behavioural interventions with families. It is particularly pertinent if the child is not receiving enough positive reinforcement (attention) and/or is receiving it at inappropriate times.

Forehand and McMahon (1981) proposed an 'attention rule': a child will work for attention from others, especially parents. The attention can either be positive (for example, praise) or negative (for example, scolding, criticism) in nature. If the child is not receiving positive attention, he or she will work to receive negative attention. It is rather like the actress who said, 'I'd rather have bad publicity than no publicity at all!'. (Mind you, some children are not very responsive – indeed, appear counter-reactive – to what adults think of as positive attention.)

A prerequisite for parent training programmes is thought, by many, to be an assurance that parents can provide meaningful, positive attention to the child, in a manner that is consistent, while ignoring inappropriate actions.

Tactics such as attending, giving verbal rewards (praise) and an extinction procedure (ignoring) are taught; the emphasis is on social rather than material reinforcers. In essence, this is a *planned praising* and *planned (judicious) ignoring* strategy. It is the first phase (often) in a further intervention to tackle specific problems such as non-compliance. For the 'praise-ignore' formula to work, certain conditions are essential:

- Parental attention must be capable of reinforcing the child's behaviour.
- The parent is capable of giving attention of the right kind at the right times.
- Attention, and not other consequences, is maintaining the inappropriate behaviour.
- Non-reinforcement alone is an effective means of eliminating unwanted behaviour.
- Ignoring is aversive or non-reinforcing.
- Continuation of the unwanted behaviour will not be harmful to the child or others.
- Parental reactions are influenced by the child's appropriate and inappropriate behaviour with reasonable consistency. That is, it appears that the parents have consistent expectations from day to day, and the child could learn the definitions of appropriate and inappropriate, from changes in parental reactions to their behaviour.

Happy adult–child relationships result from mutually reinforcing interactions, so the methods described above are well worth trying with clients. The same can be said of methods introducing change to children in a *gradual* fashion, be it settling to sleep (see Douglas and Richman, 1984), developing a better appetite (Douglas, 1989) or training children to use the toilet or potty (see Herbert 1987a for a review of various methods).

In the case of behaviours which are complex and difficult to perform, it is essential to reward the child for *trying* as well as for success.

Problem-solving strategies
In the problem-solving approach (see Spivack *et al.*, 1976), 'small' is not so much 'beautiful' as 'manageable'. Problems are not manageable when they are conceived in large global terms ('Everything is going wrong'; 'He will never change'; 'There is no hope'; 'I seem to have the world on my shoulders').

You break through this rhetoric by trying to establish and obtain the relevant facts – attempting to 'unpack' the complicated-looking dilemma. The more your clients can adopt a mental set that they *can* cope with a problem, the greater is the likelihood that, with your help, they will come up with the solution to it.

The feeling of being in control is vital to self-empowerment and the successful working through of difficult situations – be it in day-to-day or crisis circumstances. You 'relabel' the problem for the clients, defining what they once thought of as impenetrable as 'manageable' – given thought and calm application of a series of interpersonal problem-solving strategies.

The emphasis is very much (but not exclusively) on how the person thinks; the goal in therapy or training is to generate a way of thinking, a way of utilizing beliefs and values in decision-making when problems arise. The following steps are involved:

- the client is encouraged to generate different solutions to interpersonal problems (something called 'alternative solution thinking');
- he or she is helped to think through the steps needed to arrive at a solution ('means-end' thinking);
- then to identify the likely consequences that flow from each solution, if attempted;
- also to understand how one event leads to another ('causal thinking'); and
- finally, to become aware of potential difficulties with others ('sensitivity to interpersonal problems').

Self-control training

In order to strengthen self-control (see Kendall, 1984), techniques have been developed to change the individual's instructions to him/ herself. Training moves through a series of stages: first, the worker models the performance of a task, making appropriate overt self-statements. The client then practises the same behaviour, gradually moving to whispered self-instruction. Clients are encouraged to use self-statements so that they can observe, evaluate and reinforce appropriate overt behaviours in themselves.

This method can be used with children and young adults. Snyder and White (1979) made use of self-instructional training with aggressive adolescents with a history of criminal behaviour living in a residential establishment. The programme identified the delinquent's self-statements prior to an aggressive episode, then explored, with the client, the consequences of such statements and the actions which followed. In the second stage of the intervention, more appropriate, less aggressive verbalizations were modelled, rehearsed, and practised, first overtly then covertly. The new verbalizations included self-reinforcing statements for successful behaviour. In the third and final stage of the programme, homework assignments were used to develop further self-monitoring and self-reinforcement skills. The experimental evaluation of this programme compared the cognitive self-instruction group with two control groups. The treatment group showed superior performance to both controls at a point immediately following training and at an eight-week follow-up session.

Features of Child Sexual Abuse

One of the consequences of the Cleveland Child Abuse Enquiry, chaired by Lord Justice Butler-Sloss (1988), was that multidisciplinary teams had to review their response to suspicion, disclosure (some people prefer the less 'foreclosing' term *enquiry*) and treatment of child sexual abuse. The DHSS document, *Working Together* (1991), provides systematic and comprehensive guidelines for professional work across disciplines on a national basis. The subject of child sexual abuse is too vast to deal with other than briefly here. Nevertheless, there are some key issues which need summarizing. The first arises from the covert nature of the abuse.

Because of the secretive, intimidatory nature of child sexual abuse, it is most likely to be a tertiary intervention that is put into effect. For the victim of abuse, the consequences may be intense and long-lasting. The puzzle – as with other stressors that affect children as they grow up – is the considerable variation in the adult adjustment of individuals who were abused in their early years. Some experience various psychological problems of differing severity, while others appear to be relatively unscathed. *Table 10.1* lists some variables *hypothesized* to be predictive of psychological problems in later life.

Derek Jehu (1988, 1991, 1992 a and b) has attempted to address the issues of accounting for the individual differences in outcome following child sexual abuse, and of identifying some psychological processes that may provide the link between such abuse and the occurrence of psychological problems in adulthood. According to Jehu, people develop 'schemas' in response to life experiences. In particular, traumatic experiences early in life, especially those of an ongoing and cumulative nature, are alleged to be important in the establishment of maladaptive schemas which are persistent.

Schemas are cognitive structures that organize experience and behaviour. They contain certain core beliefs about oneself, other people, and the world in which one lives. These beliefs influence one's thoughts, feelings, and actions. More particularly, they interpret and attach meaning to certain relevant events. Some schemas that are commonly negative or maladaptive among victims are shown in *Table 10.2*. The very long-term nature of such schemas may result from certain cognitive, behavioural or affective processes which create self-fulfilling prophecies. Cognitively, the perception of

Table 10.1 Some circumstances of sexual abuse predictive of psychological problems in adulthood (adapted with permission from Jehu, 1981, 1988)

---

1. Sexual activities:
   (a) penetration of any body orifice by any means, including sexual intercourse;
   (b) bizarre sexual activities, such as 'black magic' or pseudo-religious rituals, or bestiality;
   (c) involvement in pornography.

2. Use of coercion, force, or violence by offenders.

3. More than one offender, including participation in sex rings or group sex.

4. Abuse over a lengthy period.

5. Abuse by father figure.

6. Age factors:
   (a) victim older when abuse ended, particularly including abuse during adolescence;
   (b) victim substantially younger than offender;
   (c) abuse by adolescent offender.

Table 10.2 Childhood experiences contributing to maladaptive self-esteem schemas (adapted from Jehu, 1991, 1992 a and b)

Typical negative schemas
- I am bad, evil or destructive.
- I am responsible for bad, evil or destructive acts, including my own traumatic experiences.
- I deserve to suffer and be punished.
- I am basically flawed, defective and damaged.
- I am not a worthy person in that I am not loveable, competent, acceptable or desirable to others, and do not deserve their attention, love and respect.

Contributory experiences in childhood
- I was made to feel responsible for the abuse.
- I must have permitted the abuse to happen.
- I made excuses for the offender's abusive behaviour.
- I thought it was wrong to get erections during the abuse.
- I was molested by so many people that I thought I must be bad.
- I was constantly blamed and punished whether or not I had done something wrong.
- I thought there must be something not nice about me because people were always angry with me and punishing me.

---

events is influenced by schemas and this may contribute to their maintenance. Input from these events is selected and interpreted in ways that are consistent with existing schemas, so that input that confirms a schema is likely to be emphasized and exaggerated, while input that is discrepant with a schema tends to be denied, minimized, or rationalized.

Individuals may engage in those forms of behaviour that confirm their existing schemas. For instance, victims who believe and expect that they will be unable to protect themselves, may fail to mobilize coping resources to deal with real threats and therefore suffer harm, which confirms their schema that they are unable to protect themselves. Furthermore, such self-defeating behaviour may evoke responses from others which confirm the victim's schemas. Thus a victim who does not trust others may act towards them with suspicion, so that in turn they respond to the victim with rejection and hostility, which serve to confirm the victim's lack of trust in people.

Affectively, schemas may be maintained because to change or relinquish well-established and familiar beliefs can be very threatening and anxiety evoking ('What will it be like to be different?', 'Will I get hurt or distressed?', 'Will my partner still love me if I'm different?'). Schemas have been likened to an old shoe, too comfortable to throw away. Furthermore, individuals often feel hopeless about changing their schemas which they perceive as being inextricably part of themselves ('This is how I have always been', 'This is who I am').

Schemas are activated when the individual is confronted by life events that are relevant to a particular schema. The activation of maladaptive schemas is usually accompanied by a high level of emotional arousal. The emotion experienced varies depending on the nature of the life event and the particular schema evoked. Therefore, certain relevant events will be accompanied by a particular psychological response pattern which may be, for example, depression (dysphoria), guilt, self-hatred, self-punishment, relentless striving for achievement, social withdrawal, anxiety, shame, anger or denial.

Jehu's research (1991) shows that child sexual abuse and its surrounding circumstances does contribute to disturbances of mood and many related problems in childhood. Given that this association is mediated by certain distorted beliefs concerning the traumatic experiences, it follows that the therapeutic correction of the beliefs is likely to be accompanied by an alleviation of the mood disturbances.

Treatment issues in sexual abuse

There are, it is suggested, at least nine 'impact and treatment' issues for victims of child sexual abuse:

- 'Damaged goods' syndrome: a mixture of self doubt, fear and anxiety.
- Guilt: many child victims feel responsible for the sexual activity.
- Fear: of being powerless; of being injured; of social responses.
- Depression.
- Low self-esteem and poor social skills.
- Repressed anger and hostility.
- Role confusion.
- Pseudomaturity, but failure to accomplish developmental tasks.
- Failure to achieve feelings of being in control.

Self-blaming beliefs

Derek Jehu's investigations indicate (as we have seen) that many victims hold beliefs that they are themselves responsible for the sexual abuse they experienced in childhood. Such distorted beliefs are likely to give rise particularly to feelings of guilt as well as to low self-esteem and depressive episodes. The results of a cognitive-behavioural approach to these problems was encouraging (Jehu, 1988). How much better if we can pre-empt some of this suffering by being aware of the consequences of child sexual abuse? Jehu's findings are highly relevant here. For example, 80 per cent of victims in his research series reacted with passive compliance when they were being abused. This connoted self-blame to many victims. The item on the research instrument (the Belief Inventory) that read, 'I must have permitted sex to happen because I wasn't forced into it' was endorsed as partly, mostly, or absolutely true by 84 per cent of victims during their initial assessment. Ninety-six per cent of the victims kept their abuse a secret for a period of time. This silence contributed to the belief that they were responsible for their own victimization (86 per cent of victims endorsed as partly, mostly, or absolutely true the item on the Belief Inventory that says, 'I must have been responsible for the sex when I was young because it went on for so long').

A total of 58 per cent of abuse victims reported that they remembered experiencing physical pleasure when they were being sexually abused, and this is often a powerful source of guilt among victims (86 per cent of victims endorsed as partly, mostly, or absolutely true the item on the Belief Inventory that reads, 'It must be unnatural to feel any pleasure during molestation').

Of the victims, 64 per cent reported that they used the abusive sexual encounters to obtain attention and/or affection from the offender. This was perceived as blameworthy by some victims. In total, 41 per cent of the victims reported that they used their sexual abuse to obtain material favours and rewards, and 18 per cent kept the abuse secret at least in part in order to retain material benefits.

Because they did so, some victims believe that they were to blame for the abuse.

Self-denigrating beliefs
Some related beliefs give rise to low self-esteem as well as to guilt and depression. Seventy-eight per cent of victims reported on the Belief Inventory that they considered the statement, 'I am worthless and bad', to be partly, mostly, or absolutely true. Eight-eight per cent of victims complained of feeling different from others (for example, 'I must be an extremely rare woman to have experienced sex with an older person when I was a child').

Victims may feel stigmatized by having been abused. For example, the Belief Inventory item that reads, 'Anyone who knows what happened to me sexually will not want anything to do with me', was endorsed as partly, mostly, or absolutely true by 82 per cent of victims, and similar endorsements of 'Only bad, worthless guys would be interested in me' were made by 58 per cent.

Several items on the Belief Inventory indicate the tendency of many victims to subordinate their own rights to those of others.

Work with sexually abused children

Afman and Smith (1992) conducted a survey of United Kingdom child protection teams to gather information about current child sexual abuse practice. Interventions fall into three categories: punitive, protective and therapeutic. When it comes to the latter, the treatment of child sexual abuse victims can be divided into three main stages (Sgroi, 1982):

Crisis intervention
During this stage, following disclosure of the abuse by the child or other person, a great many forms of intervention, medical, legal, social work and other, have to be coordinated. The family is often in a state of acute disturbance and stress, yet major decisions have to be made against this background, for example, who will be caring for the child?; will the child be remaining in the same house as an alleged perpetrator? and so on. At this stage, the research emerging from the study of crisis intervention is likely to be relevant (see page 147).

Short-term therapy (six to 12 months)
Sgroi suggests that, in general, the greater the degree of support for the child in his or her family circle or community, the more likely it will be that short-term therapy will be able to resolve the treatment issues. The perpetrator's relationship to the victim is also a key factor. If, for example, the perpetrator does not reside in the victim's home and the parents' response is supportive, short-term therapy may be

indicated. Family therapy may be an effective option (see Further Reading and Chapter 9).

Long-term therapy (two years or more)

Jehu offers detailed guidance to experienced practitioners upon how to offer intensive therapy for women suffering from prolonged distress. These methods can be used (with adaptations suited to their age) with children and adolescents. On the basis of his research into the long-term effects of treatment of child sexual abuse (CSA), Jehu notes how traumatic the experience is for most children. He is of the opinion that there are certain advantages in conceptualizing some of the problems experienced by CSA survivors within the general DSM-III-R diagnosis of post-traumatic stress disorder. To do so, makes links between them and the victims of many other forms of trauma such as rape, violence, medical and surgical procedures, road traffic accidents, terrorist incidents and other disasters.

According to Mowrer's two-factor theory of learning, any features present during the abuse are liable to become triggers for similar reactions and may lead to self-defeating assumptions or rules by means of which victims interpret their experiences and regulate their behaviour. As a result of her lack of power and control during the abuse, a victim may internalize the assumption that to be safe from pain or harm she must maintain complete control over herself and other people. For such a victim, losing control of herself by (say) sharing control with her partner during lovemaking, may elicit thoughts of danger and precipitate a stress reaction as described in the following extract (see Jehu, 1991).

Arousal is strongly contingent on my being in absolute control of the situation. If (partner) in any way takes the lead or if I sense or allow myself to think that he wants me sexually I will either get angry and push him away or click off and initiate intercourse and direct him to ejaculate as quickly as possible; anything to get it over and done with.'

Once certain stimuli (or features) have become established as triggers, then new features associated with them can also become triggers for fearful reactions. As a result, post-traumatic stress reactions may be evoked by a wide range of stimuli.

Victims also acquire ways of avoiding situations that are stressful. Although such avoidance is functional and adaptive during abuse in childhood, it is dysfunctional in non-abusive situations in adulthood. These reactions tend to be persistent and very difficult to eradicate. Not surprisingly, one example is the loss of all interest in sex, together with the refusal of advances from the partner, thereby avoiding stressful sexual encounters and alleviating the anxiety occasioned by anticipation of such events.

Cognitive-behavioural methods in abuse work

Behavioural methods have been used to manage and alleviate post-traumatic stress reactions associated with sexual abuse. There are three concurrent processes in abuse work:

(1) exposure to stressful features related to the abuse in safe therapeutic conditions;
(2) training in skills which will help the client to cope better with these stressful features; and
(3) changing the meaning of the abuse so that it is less stressful for the client.

Each of these processes may involve a number of specific procedures.

Therapeutic exposure
There is overwhelming evidence that in order to alleviate stress reactions, it is necessary for clients to be exposed to the threatening features that elicit these reactions. This must be carried out in safe circumstances where actual harm will not result, for example, by discussion of stressful features related to the abuse in the safety of treatment sessions. This helps clients to recall traumatic memories and to express the emotions associated with them. It is important that clients recall not only relevant facts, but also that they experience the accompanying feelings. Of course, discussion continues throughout therapy until the client can recall and tolerate memories and feelings associated with the abuse. Clients may also write about their experiences and reactions.

Total recall is probably not essential for recovery and clients need not be pressured to achieve this. It is important for therapists to help clients to pace themselves so that they are not overwhelmed by intense traumatic memories and feelings which are too threatening, or which they are not yet able to cope with.

Imaginal desensitization
Imaginal flooding is similar to desensitization (see page 154) except that clients are not exposed to stressful features related to the abuse. The procedure consists of:

- training clients in muscle relaxation;
- preparing with them a hierarchy or hierarchies of stressful features from the least to the most disturbing;
- relaxing them and asking them to imagine the least disturbing item in the hierarchy for short periods until they can do so without distress, at which point the procedure is repeated for the next most disturbing item, and so on up the hierarchy.

Coping skills
Skills can be taught to clients to enable them to cope better with stressful features related to the abuse. Breath control and/or deep muscular relaxation can help them to cope with stress in several ways:

- reducing bodily tension which is a common reaction to stress;
- producing a state of psychological calmness;
- distracting their attention from their stress reactions;
- enabling them to exercise some control and mastery in stress situations.

Guided self-dialogue (self-talk)
This technique is based upon the principle that thoughts can influence how clients react to and cope with stressful features related to their abuse. Suitable statements that they can say to themselves when faced with such features, are worked out (for example, 'I'm doing this, I've chosen to do it, I want to do it, and I can stop anytime'; 'Losing control for a few seconds during climax can't harm me, I'm in a safe place').

Imagery rehearsal
This technique consists of clients imagining themselves confronting and coping with situations that are stressful for them. Thus, they are able to rehearse and practise in their imagination the implementation of the coping skills they have learned, as a bridge to doing this in a graded series of *in vivo* assignments in which they confront and cope with a hierarchy of stressful situations in real life.

Cognitive restructuring
This approach tackles the abused victim's distorted beliefs – those which have adverse effects on their feelings and behaviour. The technique involves:

- helping clients to identify any beliefs that may be contributing to their problems;
- assisting them to recognize any distortions in these beliefs; and
- exploring with them more accurate and realistic beliefs as alternatives to the distorted beliefs.

It is necessary to reaffirm, as we approach the end of this text, that Derek Jehu's treatment of survivors (Jehu, 1988) can be used alongside other methods (family therapy) to alleviate the immediate effects of child sexual abuse and (hopefully) pre-empt some of the long-term consequences. The wish, of course, is that more effective means may be discovered to *prevent* the suffering inflicted on child abuse victims.

FURTHER READING

Cook, M. and Howells, K. (Eds) (1981) *Adult Sexual Interest in Children*. New York: Academic Press. [Explores, *inter alia*, the deviant sexual arousal hypothesis of child sexual abuse.]

Freund, K., McKnight, C. and Langevin, R. (1972) The female child as a surrogate object. *Archives of Sexual Behaviour*, 2, 119–133. [A discussion of the disinhibition hypothesis of child sexual abuse.]

Furniss, T. (1983) Family process in the treatment of intrafamilial child sexual abuse. *Journal of Family Therapy*, 5, 263–278. [The dysfunctional family model of child sexual abuse.]

Gordon, L. and O'Keefe, P. (1984) Incest as a form of family violence. *Journal of Marriage and the Family*, February, 27–34. [Concepts of power and control in child sexual abuse.]

Watkins, B. and Bentovim, A. (1992) The sexual abuse of male children and adolescents: A review of current research. *Journal of Child Psychology and Psychiatry*, 33, 197–248. [The male victim of abuse has tended to be overlooked.]

EPILOGUE

I am conscious at the end of this book of a paradox for the reader, be he or she a student or an experienced practitioner. These pages contain so much about families, parents, children and others . . . and, yet, so little. The subject is so vast that we have only scratched the surface. This is not simply a matter of the limited space available in one guide; it is intrinsic to the topic. We have so much to learn, so much research to initiate. Fortunately, there is no reason for an attitude of pessimism or helplessness. We know enough to be of service to those whose family life is floundering, whose children are in distress, and who, consequently, are calling for help.

REFERENCES

Afman, S. and Smith, J. (1992) Working together? A survey of current sexual abuse practice. *Newsletter of the Association for Child Psychology and Psychiatry, 14*, 11–16.

Ainsworth, M. D. (1982) Attachment: retrospective and prospect. In C. M. Parkes and J. Stevenson-Hinds (Eds) *The Place of Attachment in Human Behaviour*. New York: Basic Books.

Ainsworth, M. D., Blehar, M. S., Waters, E. and Wall, S. (1978) *Patterns of Attachment*. Hillsdale, New Jersey: Erlbaum.

Alexander, J. F. and Parsons, B. (1973) Short term behavioral intervention with delinquent families: Impact on family process and recidivism. *Journal of Abnormal Psychology, 81*, 219–225.

Anderson, E. M. and Clarke, L. (1982) *Disability in Adolescence*. London: Methuen.

Axline, V. M. (1947) *Play Therapy: The Inner Dynamics of Childhood*. Boston: Houghton Mifflin.

Babiker, G. (1992) *Psychological Measurement in Child Sexual Abuse*. Unpublished PhD Thesis, University of Bristol.

Baldwin, S. (1976) *Some Practical Consequences of Caring for Handicapped Children at Home*. York: University of York: Social Policy Research Unit.

Bandura, A. (1986) *Social Foundations of Thought and Action: A Social Cognitive Theory*. Englewood Cliffs, NJ: Prentice-Hall.

Baumrind, D. (1971) Current patterns of parental authority. *Developmental Psychology Monographs, 4*, (1), Pt 2, 1–103.

Belsky, J. and Nezworski, T. (1988) *Clinical Implications of Attachment*. Hillsdale, NJ: Lawrence Erlbaum.

Bowen, M. (1978) *Family Therapy in Clinical Practice*. NY: Jason Aronson.

Bromley, D. B. (1986) *The Case-study Method in Psychology and Related Disciplines*. Chichester: John Wiley.

Browne, K. D. (1988) The naturalistic context of family violence and child abuse. In J. Archer and K. D. Browne (Eds) *Aggression: Naturalistic Approaches*. Kent: Croom Helm.

Carter, E. C. and McGoldrick (1992) *The Changing Family Life Cycle: A Framework for Family Therapy*, 2nd edn. Boston: Allyn & Bacon. (see chapter 'Forming a remarried family' by McGoldrick and Carter)

Clarke, A. M. and Clarke, A. D. B. (1976) *Early Experience: Myth and Reality*. London: Open Books.

Clarke, M. M., Riach, J. and Cheyne, W. M. (1977) *Handicapped Children and Pre-school Education*. Glasgow: University of Strathclyde: Report to Warnock Committee on Special Education.

Davis, H. (1993) *Counselling Parents of Children with Chronic Illness or Disability*. Leicester: BPS Books (British Psychological Society).

De Myer, K. K., Kingten, J. N. and Jackson, R. K. (1981) Infantile autism reviewed: A decade of research. *Schizophrenia Bulletin, 7*, 338–351.

De Shazer, S. (1988) *Clues: Investigating Solutions in Brief Therapy*. New York: Norton.

Doleys, D. M. (1977) Behavioral treatments of nocturnal enuresis in children: A review of the recent literature. *Psychological Bulletin, 8*, 30–54.

Doleys, D. M. (1978) Assessment and treatment of enuresis and encopresis in children. In M. Hersen, R. M. Eisler and P. M. Miller (Eds) *Progress in Behavior Modification, 6*, 85–121. New York: Academic Press.

Douglas, J. (1989) *Behaviour Problems in Young Children*. London: Tavistock/ Routledge.

Douglas, J. (1993) *Psychology and Nursing Children*. Leicester: BPS Books (British Psychological Society).

Douglas, J. and Richman, N. (1984) *My Child Won't Sleep*. Harmondsworth: Penguin.

Erikson, E. (1965) *Childhood and Society*. Harmondsworth: Penguin.

Fahlberg, V. (1988) Attachment and separation. In *Fitting the Pieces Together*. London: British Association for Adoption and Fostering.

Finkelhor, D. (Ed.) (1986) *A Sourcebook on Child Sexual Abuse*. Beverly Hills, CA: Sage. (Note chapters by Araji, S. and Finkelhor, D. Abusers: A review of the research, pp.89–118; and Browne, A. and Finkelhor, D. Initial and long-term effects: A review of research, pp.143–179.)

Forehand, R. and Atkeson, B. M. (1977) Generality of treatment effects with parents as therapists. A review of assessment and implementation procedures. *Behavior Therapy*, 8, 575–593.

Forehand, R. and McMahon, R. J. (1981) *Helping the Noncompliant Child: A Clinician's Guide to Effective Parent Training*. New York: Guilford Press.

Fraiberg, S. (1980) *Clinical Studies in Infant Mental Health: The First Year of Life*. London: Tavistock.

Frank, J. (1973) *Persuasion and Healing*. Baltimore: The John Hopkins University Press.

Freud, A. (1946) *The Psychoanalytic Treatment of Children*. New York: International Universities Press.

Frodi, A. M. and Lamb, M. E. (1980) Child abusers' responses to infant smiles and cries. *Child Development*, 51, 238–241.

Frude, N. (1991) *Understanding Family Problems: A Psychological Approach*. Chichester: John Wiley.

Fryers, T. (1984) *The Epidemiology of Intellectual Impairment*. London: Academic Press.

Gelles, R. J. (1974) *The Violent Home*. Beverly Hills: Sage Publications.

Goffman, E. (1968) *Stigma: Notes on the Management of a Spoiled Identity*. New York: Prentice-Hall.

Gurman, A. S. and Kniskern, D. P. (1978) Research on marital and family therapy: Progress, perspective and prospect. In S. Garfield and A. E. Bergin (Eds) *Handbook of Psychotherapy and Behaviour Change*. Chichester: Wiley.

Gurman, A. S. and Kniskern, D. P. (1981) *Handbook of Family Therapy*. New York: Brunner/Mazel.

Haley, J. (1976) *Problem Solving Therapy*. San Francisco: Jossey-Bass.

Hall, D. M. B. (1992) Child health promotion, screening and surveillance. *Journal of Child Psychology and Psychiatry*, 33, 649–657.

Hardiker, P. (1992) Children Act: Family support services and children with disabilities. In J. Gibbons (Ed.) *Family Support and the Children Act*. London: HMSO.

Heiman, M. L. (1992) Putting the puzzle together: Validating allegations of child sexual abuse. *Journal of Child Psychology and Psychiatry*, 33, 311–329.

Herbert, M. (1987a) *Behavioural Treatment of Children with Problems: A Practice Manual*. London: Academic Press (revised edn).

Herbert, M. (1987b) *Conduct Disorders of Childhood and Adolescence: A Social-learning Perspective*. Chichester: John Wiley (revised edn) (1978: 1st edition).

Herbert, M. (1988) *Working with Children and their Families*. Leicester: BPS Books (British Psychological Society).

Herbert, M. (1991a) *Child Care and the Family: A Resource Pack*. Windsor: National Foundation of Educational Research.

Herbert, M. (1991b) *Clinical Child Psychology: Social Learning, Development and Behaviour*. Chichester: Wiley.

Herbert, M. (1993) Behavioural methods. In M. Rutter, I. Hersov and E. Taylor (Eds) *Child and Adolescent Psychiatry: Modern Approaches*, 3rd edn. Oxford: Blackwell.

Herbert, M. and Iwaniec, D. (1981) Behavioural psychotherapy in natural home settings: An empirical study applied to conduct disordered and incontinent children. *Behavioural Psychotherapy, 9*, 55–76.

Howlin, P. (1984) Parents as therapists: A critical review. In D. Muller (Ed.) *Remediating Children's Language: Behavioural and Naturalist Approaches*. London: Croom Helm.

Hudson, A. (1987) *Personal Communication*. Melbourne: Philip Institute of Technology.

Ioannou, C. (1992) *Acute Pain in Chronically Ill Children: Psychological Assessment and Intervention*. Unpublished PhD thesis, University of Leicester.

Iwaniec, D., Herbert, M. and McNeish, S. (1985) Social work with failure-to-thrive children and their families. Part I: Psychosocial factors. Part II: Behavioural casework. *British Journal of Social Work, 15*, Nos 3 (June) and 4 (August) respectively.

Jehu, D. (1988) *Beyond Sexual Abuse: Therapy with Women who were Childhood Victims*. Chichester: Wiley.

Jehu, D. (1991) Post-traumatic stress reactions among adults molested as children. *Sexual and Marital Therapy, 6*, 227–243.

Jehu, D. (1992a) Adult survivors of sexual abuse. In R. T. Ammerman and M. Hersen (Eds) *Assessment of Family Violence: A Clinical and Legal Sourcebook*. New York: Wiley.

Jehu, D. (1992b) Personality Problems Among Adults Molested as Children. *Sexual and Marital Therapy, 7* (3), 231–249.

Johnson, D. W. and Johnson, F. R. (1975) *Joining Together*. New York: Prentice Hall.

Jones, D. and McGraw, J. M. (1987) Reliable and fictitious accounts of sexual abuse to children. *Journal of Interpersonal Violence, 2*, 27–45.

Jones, D., Pickett, J., Oates, M. and Barber, P. (1987) *Understanding Child Abuse*, 2nd edn. Basingstoke: Macmillan Education.

Jones, M. C. (1924) The elimination of children's fears. *Journal of Experimental Psychology, 7*, 382–390.

Kane, B. (1979) Children's concept of death. *Journal of Genetic Psychology, 134*, 141–153.

Kanfer, F. H., Karoly, P. and Newman, A. (1975) Reduction of children's fear of the dark by competence-related and situational threat-related verbal cues. *Journal of Consulting Clinical Psychology, 43*, 251–258.

Kazdin, A. E. (1978) *History of Behavior Modification: Experimental Foundations of Contemporary Research*. Baltimore: University Park Press.

Kazdin, A. E. (1988) *Child Psychotherapy: Developing and Identifying Effective Treatments*. Oxford: Pergamon.

Kelly, G. (1955) *The Psychology of Personal Constructs*. New York: Norton.

Kendall, P. C. (1984) Cognitive-behavioural self-control therapy for children. *Journal of Child Psychology and Psychiatry, 25*, 173–179.

Kendall, P. C., Howard, B. L. and Epps, J. (1988) The anxious child: Cognitive-behavioural treatment strategies. *Behaviour Modification, 12*, 281–310.

Kniskern, D. and Gurman, A. (1981) Advances and prospects for family therapy research. In J. P. Vincent (Ed.) *Advances in Family Intervention, Assessment and Theory*, Vol. 2. Greenwich, Connecticut: Jai Press.

Kohlberg, L. (1976) *Moral Development*. New York: Holt, Rinehart & Winston.

Lawes, G. (1992) Individual parent training implemented by nursery nurses. *Behavioural Psychotherapy, 20*, 239–256.

Lee, S. G. and Herbert, M. (1970) *Freud and Psychology*. Harmondsworth: Penguin Books.

Levy, A. (1992) The Children Act 1989: Policies and prognosis. *Young Minds Newsletter*, No. 11, July, 1–4.

Lewis, V. (1987) *Development and Handicap*. Oxford: Basil Blackwell.

MacFarlene, K. and Krebs, S. (1986) Techniques for interviewing and evidence gathering. In K. MacFarlene and J. Waterman (Eds) *Sexual Abuse of Young Children*. NY: Guilford Press.

Masson, J. (1990) *The Children Act 1989: Text and Commentary*. London: Sweet & Maxwell.

Meisels, S. J. (1988) Developmental screening in early childhood: The interaction of research and social policy. In L. Breslow, J. E. Fielding, and L. B. Lane (Eds) *Annual Review of Public Health*, Vol. 9. Palo Alto, CA: Annual Review.

Millham, S., Bullock, R., Hosie, K. and Little, M. (1986) *Lost in Care*. London: Gower.

Minuchin, S. (1974) *Families and Family Therapy*. Cambridge, MA: Harvard University Press.

Nicol, R. (1988) The treatment of child abuse in the home environment. In K. Browne, C. Davies and P. Stratton (Eds) *Early Prediction and Prevention of Child Abuse*. Chichester: John Wiley.

Nissin, R. (1992) *Family Placement: A Review of the Evidence*. Unpublished paper. Oxfordshire Social Services.

Nolan, M. and Tucker, I. G. (1988) *The Hearing Impaired Child and the Family*. London: Souvenir Press.

Novaco, R. W. (1975) *Anger Control: The Development and Evaluation of an Experimental Treatment*. Lexington, MA: D. C. Heath.

Olds, D. L. (1986) *Final Report: Prenatal/early Infancy Project*. Washington, DC: Maternal Health and Child Care Research, National Institute of Health.

Ollendick, T. H. and King, N. J. (1991) Fears and phobias of childhood. In M. Herbert *Clinical Child Psychology: Social Learning, Development and Behaviour*. Chichester: John Wiley.

Palazzoli, M. S., Boscolo, L., Cecchin, G. and Prata, G. (1978) *Paradox and Counter-paradox*. New York: Jason Aronson.

Parkes, C. M. (1972) *Bereavement*. London: Tavistock Publications.

Patterson, G. R. (1982) *Coercive Family Process*. Eugene, Oregon: Castalia.

Patterson, G. R., Chamberlain, P. and Reid, J. B. (1982) A comparative evaluation of a parent training program. *Behavior Therapy, 13*, 638–650.

Philp, M. and Duckworth, D. (1982) *Children with Disabilities and their Families: A Review of Research*. Windsor: N.F.E.R.-Nelson.

Piaget, J. (1953) *Origins of Intelligence in the Child*. London: Routledge & Kegan Paul.

Richards, M. and Dyson, M. (1982) *Separation, Divorce and the Development of Children: A Review*. Cambridge: Child Care and Development Group.

Robins, L. and Rutter, M. (Eds) (1990) *Straight and Deviant Pathways from Childhood to Adulthood*. Cambridge: Cambridge University Press.

Rogers, C. R. (1951) *Client-Centred Therapy*. Boston: Houghton-Mifflin.

Ross, D., Ross, S. and Evans, T. A. (1971) The modification of extreme social withdrawal by modification with guided practice. *Journal of Behaviour Therapy and Experimental Psychiatry, 2*, 273–279.

Royal College of Psychiatrists (1989) *Report of the Working Party to Produce Guidelines to Good Practice in the Use of Behavioural Treatments*. Approved by Council, October, 1989.

Rutter, M. (1981) Stress, coping and development. *Journal of Child Psychology and Psychiatry, 22*, (4), 323–357.

Rutter, M. and Madge, N. (1976) *Cycles of Disadvantage*. London: Heinemann.

Rycroft, C. (1970) Causes and meaning. In S. G. Lee and M. Herbert (Eds) *Freud and Psychology*. Harmondsworth: Penguin.

Schaffer, H. R. (1990) *Making Decisions about Children: Psychological Questions and Answers*. Oxford: Basil Blackwell.

Schorr, L. B. (1989) *Within our Reach*. New York: Doubleday (Anchor Books).

Scott, M. J. and Stradling, S. G. (1987) Evaluation of a group programme for parents of problem children. *Behavioural Psychotherapy, 15*, 224–239.

Seligman, M. E. P. (1975) *Helplessness*. San Francisco: Freeman.

Selman, R. L. (1980) *The Growth of Interpersonal Understanding: Developmental and Clinical Analysis*. New York: Academic Press.

Sgroi, S. (Ed.) (1982) *Handbook of Clinical Intervention in Child Sexual Abuse*. Lexington, MA: Lexington Books.

Shaw, M. (1986) Substitute parenting. In W. Sluckin and M. Herbert (Eds) *Parental Behaviour*. Chichester: John Wiley.

Skynner, A. R. C. (1976) *One Flesh, Separate Persons*. London: Constable.

Sloane, R. B., Staples, F. R., Cristol, A. H., Yorkston, N. J. and Whipple, K. (1975) *Psychotherapy versus Behavior Therapy*. Cambridge, MA: Harvard University Press.

Sluckin, W. and Herbert, M. (Eds) (1986) *Parental Behaviour*. Chichester: John Wiley.

Snyder, J. J. and White, M. J. (1979) The use of cognitive self-instruction in the treatment of behaviourally disturbed adolescents. *Behavior Therapy, 10*, 227–235.

Spencer, J. R. and Flin, R. H. (1990) *The Evidence of Children: The Law and the Psychology*. London: Blackstone Press.

Spivack, G., Platt, J. J. and Shure, M. B. (1976) *The Problem-solving Approach to Adjustment*. San Francisco: Jossey-Bass.

Sutton, C. (1988) *A Handbook of Research for the Helping Professions*. London: Routledge & Kegan Paul.

Sutton, C. and Herbert, M. (1992) *Mental Health*: A Client Support Resource Pack. Windsor: N.F.E.R.-Nelson.

Svegedy-Maszak, M. (1989) Who's to judge? *New York Times Magazine*, May 21, p.28.

Thomas, A., Chess, S. and Birch, H. G. (1968) *Temperament and Behaviour Disorders in Children*. London: London University Press.

Treacher, A. (1983) Family therapy with children: The structural approach. In G. Edwards (Ed.) *Current Issues in Clinical Psychology*, Vol. 4. London: Plenum.

Treacher, A. and Carpenter, J. (Eds) (1984) *Using Family Therapy*. Oxford: Basil Blackwell.

Tuma, J. M. (1989) Traditional therapies with children. In T. H. Ollendick and M. Hersen (Eds) *Handbook of Child Psychopathology*, 2nd edn. New York: Plenum.

Von Bertalanffy, L. (1968) *General Systems Theory*. Harmondsworth: Penguin.

Walters, M. (1989) A feminist perspective in family therapy. In R. J. Perelberg and A. C. Miller (Eds) *Gender and Power in Families*. London: Tavistock/Routledge.

Warnock Committee (1978) *Special Education Needs: Report of the Committee of Enquiry into the Education of Handicapped Children and Young People*. Cmnd 7212, London: HMSO.

Webster-Stratton, C. (1991) Strategies for helping families with conduct disorders. *Journal of Child Psychology and Psychiatry, 32*, 1047–1062.

Webster-Stratton, C. and Herbert, M. (1993) *Families under Seige*. Chichester: John Wiley.

Werner, E. E. and Smith, R. S. (1982) *Vulnerable, but Invincible. A Longitudinal Study of Resilient Children and Youth*. New York: McGraw-Hill.

White, R. (1991) Examining the threshold criteria. In M. Adcock, R. White and A. Hollows (Eds) *Significant Harm: Its Management and Outcome*. Croydon: Significant Publications.

Winnicott, D. (1958) *Collected Papers*. London: Tavistock.

Wolfe, D. (1987) *Child Abuse: Implications for Child Development and Psychopathology*. London: Sage.

World Health Organization (1980) *International Classification of Impairments, Disabilities and Handicaps*. Geneva: World Health Organization.

Yule, W. (1991) Working with disasters. In M. Herbert *Clinical Child Psychology: Social Learning, Behaviour and Development*. Chichester: John Wiley.

The main messages of the Children Act, 1989

The main messages of the Children Act can be summarized as follows:

- *The child's welfare is paramount.*
  A 'welfare checklist' is included to facilitate consistency across different levels of courts and across the country.
- *Children should be brought up in their own families.*
  The Act highlights this point by creating a new category of children 'in need' (which includes disabled children). The local authority has a duty to provide adequate services to help the family maintain the child at home.
- *Parents are responsible.*
  The new concept of parental responsibility shifts the emphasis from parents' rights over a child, to their duties and responsibilities toward him or her.
- *There is a continuing role for parents and the wider family.*
  Parental responsibility cannot be taken away (except by adoption) and is, therefore, shared with everyone else who acquires it (for example, the local authority).
- *Child protection is crucial but open to challenge.*
  The Act addresses the difficult task of protecting children from harm, families from unwarranted intervention and the right of families to challenge decisions.
- *The child's voice should be heard; the child should be informed about what is happening.*
  The first item on the 'welfare checklist' considers the ascertainable wishes and feelings of the child.
- *The child's background is taken into account in making decisions.*
  The local authority, when providing services (for example, day care or accommodation), and when cancelling registration under Part X, must give due consideration to the 'child's religious persuasion, racial origin, cultural and linguistic background'. A specific duty is required so that arrangements are made to ensure that issues of race, religious persuasion and cultural background are taken into account when recruiting foster parents.
- *Standards of child care are monitored.*
  There are greater powers to monitor child minders, residential homes and other providers of child care, and their standards.
- *The new court system* enshrines several new principles, including:
  – *No delay.* Courts must draw up a timetable for the disposal of an

application without delay. They should give priority to children's cases.

– *No order*. No order will be made 'unless it is considered better for the child than making no order at all'.

Structure of the Children Act, 1989

The Children Act reforms and brings together the public and private law relating to children, and will now apply in all three levels of court permitted to deal with family proceedings: the High Court, the County Court and the new Magistrates Family Proceedings Court. It has 108 sections and 15 schedules and has generated numerous sets of rules and regulations.

Briefly, *public law* deals with those areas where society intervenes in the action of individuals (such as care proceedings), and *private law* addresses the behaviour of individuals towards each other (such as with whom the children should live following divorce). The Lord Chancellor, Lord Mackay, described the Children Act as 'the most comprehensive and far reaching reform of child law which has come before Parliament in living memory' (Hansard, H. L., Vol. 502, col.488). The Act is divided into 12 parts, each one relating to a different aspect of child law. It must, however, be read as a whole; every part of the Act is interrelated and no part stands alone. The schedules contain important details of the private law of child support; local authorities' duties to children in the community and to children they are looking after; and the duties of other people and organizations caring for children.

Basic principles underlying the Act

The Act attempts to align the balance of power between families and the State so as: to protect families from unwarranted State interference; to emphasize that local authorities have an important role in supporting families in difficulty; and to indicate that there is a continuing role for parents when their children are looked after by a local authority. The new concept of *parental responsibility* seeks to balance the rights and duties of parents with the welfare of the child. 'Parental responsibility' is defined in Section 3(1): '(It) means any of the rights, duties, powers, responsibilities and authority which by law a parent of a child has in relation to the child and his property'. According to Alan Levy (1992), nobody quite knows what this actually means and the use of the word 'rights' lies ill with the supposed child-orientated Act. From a human point of view, the conferring of parental responsibility will not necessarily make the person a responsible parent!

Section 2 (7) of the Act could lead to confusion: 'Where more than one person has parental responsibility for a child, each of them may act alone and without the other (or others) in meeting that responsibility; but nothing in this part of the Act shall be taken to affect the operation of any enactment which requires the consent of more than one person in a matter affecting the child'. (See Masson, 1990, for an excellent commentary and annotations on the Act.)

A crucial principle of the Act is that the welfare of the child should come before and above any other consideration in deciding whether to make any order. It is a matter of policy that the court should not make an order unless it considers that to do so would be better for the child than making no order at all [s.1(5)]. This has important implications for practitioners in that, at the very outset, one must consider whether the court is likely to make any order at all.

The arrangement for the first five parts of the Act are given below:

PART I
INTRODUCTORY

SECTION

1. Welfare of the child.
2. Parental responsibility for children.
3. Meaning of 'parental responsibility'.
4. Acquisition of parental responsibility by father.
5. Appointment of guardians.
6. Guardians: revocation and disclaimer.
7. Welfare reports.

PART II
ORDERS WITH RESPECT TO CHILDREN IN FAMILY PROCEEDINGS
General

8. Residence, contact and other orders with respect to children.
9. Restrictions on making section 8 orders.
10. Power of court to make section 8 orders.
11. General principles and supplementary provisions.
12. Residence orders and parental responsibility.
13. Change of child's name or removal from jurisdiction.
14. Enforcement of residence orders.

Financial relief

15. Orders for financial relief with respect to children.

Family assistance orders

16. Family assistance orders.

PART III
LOCAL AUTHORITY SUPPORT FOR CHILDREN AND FAMILIES
Provision of services for children and their families

17. Provision of services for children in need, their families and others.
18. Day care for pre-school and other children.
19. Review of provision for day care, child minding etc.

45. Duration of emergency protection orders and other supplemental provisions.
46. Removal and accommodation of children by police in cases of emergency.
47. Local authority's duty to investigate.
48. Powers to assist in discovery of children who may be in need of emergency protection.
49. Abduction of children in care etc.
50. Recovery of abducted children etc.
51. Refuges for children at risk.
52. Rules and regulations.

FURTHER READING

The law now has an enormous impact on the work of health, education and social services. The references below will provide you with a strong knowledge base in understanding relevant legislation.

Black, D. and Wolkind, S. (1991) *Child Psychiatry and the Law*, 2nd edn. London: Gaskell (for the Royal College of Psychiatrists).

H.M.S.O. (1989) *An Introduction to the Children Act, 1989: A New Framework for the Care and Upbringing of Children*. London: Her Majesty's Stationery Office.

H.M.S.O. (1991) *Patterns and Outcomes in Child Placement – Messages from Current Research and their Implications*. London: Her Majesty's Stationery Office.

Macdonald, S. (1990) *All Equal Under the Act*. London: Race Equality Unit, NISW.

APPENDIX II

Provision of support for families

Local Authority Duties Towards Children in Need

The local authority is under a general duty:

(a) to safeguard and promote the welfare of children within its area who are in need;

(b) so far as is consistent with that duty, to promote the upbringing of such children by their families, by providing a range and level of services appropriate to those children's needs [s.17(1)].

A child is in need if:
'he is unlikely to achieve or maintain, or to have the opportunity of achieving or maintaining, a reasonable standard of health and development without the provision for him of services by a local authority under this Part; his health or development is likely to be significantly impaired, or further impaired, without the provision for him of such services; or he is disabled.' [s.17(10)].

The Act also outlines a number of *specific duties* for the local authority:

(1) to identify the extent to which there are children in need within its area and publish information about services available to them [Sched 2, para 1];

(2) to provide day care for children in need aged five and under as is appropriate [s.18(1)];

(3) to have regard to the different racial groups to which children within its area who are in need belong in making any arrangements for the provision of day care or in making arrangements designed to encourage persons to act as local authority foster parents [Sched 2, para 11];

(4) to open and maintain a register of disabled children within its area and provide services designed to allow them to live as normal a life as possible [Sched 2, paras 2 and 6];

(5) to secure that the accommodation that it provides for disabled children whom it is looking after is not unsuitable to their particular needs [s.23(8)];

(6) to provide accommodation for children in need where they have no parent, are lost or abandoned or where their parents cannot care for them [s.23(1)];

(7) to provide accommodation for any child aged between 16 and 18 whose welfare would otherwise be seriously impaired [s.20(3)].

The local authority is not always the sole provider of services. It will facilitate the provision of services for children by others, including voluntary organizations [s.17(5)]; and, where children in need are living with their families, provide, as appropriate: occupational, social, cultural and recreational activities; home help; facilities so that they can make use of services provided under this Act; also assistance to enable the child and family to have a holiday [Sched 2, para 8]. Where children in need (not looked after by the local authority) are living away from home, the Social Services Department is required to take steps to enable them to live with their families, or to promote contact between children and their families if this is necessary in order to promote and safeguard their welfare [Sched 2, para 10].

The *range of services* which the local authority might provide includes:

• day care, out of school care, toy libraries, drop-in centres;
• services such as family centres or family aides;
• advice, guidance and counselling.

APPENDIX III

Protection, care and supervision

Protection of children:
The child protection orders include:

- a child assessment order [s.43] (see below);
- an emergency protection order [s.44] (see page 215);
- removal and accommodation of children by police in cases of emergency [s.46];
- recovery of abducted children etc. [s.50].

Care and supervision
Care and supervision are the two main public law orders (see page 216):

- a care order places the child into the care of a local authority [s.31];
- a supervision order puts a child under the supervision of a Social Services Department (SSD) or a probation officer [s.35].

The grounds for obtaining care or supervision orders are new. Section 31(2) provides that a court may only make a care order or supervision order if it is satisfied (a) that the child concerned is suffering, or is likely to suffer, significant harm; and (b) that harm, or likelihood of harm, is attributable to (i) that care given to the child, or likely to be given to him/her if the order were not made, not being what it would be reasonable to expect a parent to give to him/her; or (ii) the child's being beyond parental control.
Note: Parental responsibility is shared with the SSD who have the power to decide how much the parents may exercise their parental responsibility, but may only do so if it is necessary to safeguard or promote the child's welfare. The SSD *must* allow parents reasonable contact with children who are the subject of a care order and try to promote such contact, unless this will put the child's welfare at risk. The SSD will have to produce a plan for the future of each child in its care, and the progress of each child will be subject to periodic review to ensure that the child is being provided with the right kind of care.

'Looked after' (by the local authority) is the generic term to describe a child's situation when in the care of (on a care order), or provided with accommodation by, the local authority.

Child Assessment Orders [s.43]

One of the options open to the local authority is the child assessment order. It is one of a number of new measures regarding the protection of children which include emergency protection orders and police powers of protection. One important power outside the Children Act, is Section 17(1)(e) of the Police and Criminal Evidence Act 1984 which permits a police officer without a warrant to enter and search any premises for the purpose of saving life or limb.

The child assessment order was introduced at a late stage during the Bill's progress through Parliament in response to a call for the power to be able to see, examine and assess a child where there is concern as to his or her welfare in the face of lack of cooperation from those responsible for the child. There was some uncertainty at first as to whether an order was needed, but the legislators eventually felt that there are circumstances in which there might be serious cause for concern about the child's welfare. There may be a repeated failure to produce a child, but perhaps it cannot be asserted that the matter is quite so urgent that there is an *immediate* need to intervene to take the child away (see page 12).

Powers and duties:

The order requires any person who is in a position to produce the child:
(a) to produce him or her to such person as may be named in the order; and
(b) to comply with such directions relating to the assessment of the child as the court thinks fit to specify in the order [s.43(6)].

The child can only be kept away from home in accordance with directions and for a period or periods specified in the order if it is necessary for the purposes of the assessment [s.43(9)].

The order authorizes any person carrying out the assessment to do so in accordance with the terms of the order, but the mature minor can refuse to submit to such assessment [s.43(7) and (8)].

Criteria

- A local authority or an 'authorised person' can apply for an order [s.43(1)].

- The court can make a child assessment order if it is satisfied that:
  (1) the applicant has reasonable cause to suspect that the child is suffering, or is likely to suffer, significant harm; *and*
  (2) an assessment is required to enable the applicant to determine whether this is so; *and*
  (3) it is unlikely that such an assessment will be made, or be satisfactory, in the absence of an order [s.43(1)(a)–(c)].

- The child's welfare is the court's paramount consideration [s.1(1)]. There is a presumption of no order unless the court considers that to make an order would be better for the child [s.1(5)].

- The order lasts for a maximum of seven days from a date specified in the order [s.43(5)]. There can be no further application for a child assessment order within six months without the leave of the court [s.91(15)].

The court may treat an application under Section 43 as an application for an emergency protection order [s.43(2)] and, if so, make one, if the criteria are satisfied.

Emergency Protection Orders [s.44 and 45]

Powers and duties

The order requires any person who is in a position to produce the child to do so if required [s.44(4)(a)]. It authorizes:

(1) Removal of the child to accommodation provided by the applicant where necessary in order to safeguard the welfare of the child [s.44(4)(b) and (5)(a)].
(2) Prevention of the removal of the child from a hospital or other places in which s/he was being accommodated immediately before the making of the order [s.44(4)(b)(ii)].
(3) The applicant to have parental responsibility for the child [s.44(4)(c)].

The court has the power to give directions with respect to:
(1) the contact which is or is not to be allowed between the child and any named person;
(2) medical or psychiatric examination or other assessment of the child [s.44(6)], but the mature minor can refuse to submit to such examination etc. [s.44(7)].

Criteria

- 'Any person', a local authority or an 'authorised person' can apply for an order [s.44(1)].

- The court may make an emergency protection order if it is satisfied that:
  (1) where the applicant is *any person*, there is reasonable cause to believe that the child is likely to suffer significant harm if s/he is not removed, or does not remain where s/he is [s.44(1)(a)];
  (2) where the applicant is a *local authority*, enquiries are being made with respect to the child under s.47(1)(b) (that a child who lives, or is found in their area is suffering or is likely to suffer significant harm) *and* those enquiries are being frustrated by access being unreasonably refused and access is required urgently [s.44(1)(b)];

   (3) where the applicant is an *authorized person*, the applicant has reasonable cause to suspect that a child is suffering, or is likely to suffer, significant harm; the applicant is making enquiries and those enquiries are being frustrated by access being unreasonably refused and access is required urgently [s.44(1)(c)].

- The child's welfare is the court's paramount consideration [s.1(1)]. There is a presumption of no order unless the court considers that to make an order would be better for the child [s.1(5)].

- The order lasts a maximum of eight days. There can be an application for an extension which lasts for a maximum of a further seven days if 'the court has reasonable cause to believe that the child concerned is likely to suffer significant harm if the order is not extended' [s.45(1) to (6)]. Irrespective of these limits, the child must be returned as soon as it is safe to do so [s.44(10)].

Care Orders [s.31]

Powers and duties

The local authority is under a duty to receive the child into its care and to keep him/her in care while the order remains in force. This includes providing accommodation for and maintaining the child [s.33(1) and 23(1)].

The local authority acquires parental responsibility for the child which it shares with the parents. However, it can determine the extent to which a parent or guardian may meet his/her parental responsibility for the child in order to safeguard the child's welfare [s.33(3)(b) and (4); s.2(7)].

Specific duties are specified in Section 23(6) to (9) and Schedule 2, part II. Specific restrictions on the local authority powers under a care order are detailed in Section 33(5) to (9). Before making a care order, the court must consider the arrangements that the local authority has made, or proposes to make, for affording any person contact with the child and invite the parties to the proceedings to comment on those arrangements [s.34(11)]. There is a presumption of reasonable contact between the child and:

- a parent;
- a guardian;
- any person who held a residence order in respect of the child;
- any person who had care of the child under the inherent jurisdiction of the High Court before the care order was made.

Where the presumption operates or there is an order under Section 34, decisions about contact, its frequency, duration and possible termination can only be made by the court. Exceptions are provided for in the regulations where the local authority and the person in relation to whom the order is made agree, or in presumption cases, where the local authority and person concerned agree. A local authority can refuse to allow contact where the presumption operates or where there is an order under Section 34 to safeguard or promote the child's welfare, if the matter is urgent; such refusal cannot last more than seven days [s.34(6)].

Criteria

- A local authority or an 'authorised person' can apply for an order [s.31(1)].

- 'A court may only make a care order . . . if it is satisfied:
  - (a) that the child concerned is suffering, or is likely to suffer, significant harm; and
  - (b) that the harm, or likelihood of harm, is attributable to:
    - (1) the care given to the child, or likely to be given to him if the order were not made, not being what it would be reasonable to expect a parent to give him; or
    - (2) the child's being beyond parental control' [s.31(2)].

- The child's welfare is the court's paramount consideration [s.1(1)]. There is a presumption of no order unless the court considers that to make an order would be better for the child [s.1(5)]. The welfare checklist applies [s.1(3)].

- A care order lasts until the child's eighteenth birthday unless it is brought to an end earlier [s.91(12)].

- A care order is discharged by:
  - (1) adoption [Sched 10, para 3);
  - (2) the making of a residence order [s.91(1)];
  - (3) the making of a supervision order [Sched 3, para 10];
  - (4) either the child, the local authority or any person with parental responsibility for the child applying for discharge of the care order. On such an application the court can substitute a supervision order for the care order [s.39].

The Role of the Courts

The provisions for Part I inform the interpretation of the Act generally by stating the principle which the courts must apply in considering certain cases concerning children – the welfare principle (see page 4) – and defining the rights of parents and guardians.

New court orders

The Act introduces a number of new orders which are available to the courts (for detailed guidance see Volume 1: Court Orders in the Children Act series).

Public law orders:
- Investigation and assessment [Sections 43 and 47]: The local authority's responsibilities in investigating cases where a child may be harmed, are clarified.
- Emergency protection orders [Sections 44 and 45]: 'Place of safety orders' are replaced with more restrictive 'emergency protection orders'.
- Supervision orders [Sections 31, 35 and Schedule 3].
- Care orders [Sections 31–34]: There used to be 20 or so routes into care. Now there is only one – the one defined in the Act.

Note: Health professionals may be called upon to give an expert opinion in either private or public law cases.

Court structure, jurisdiction and legal aid

The 'Domestic Court' is renamed the 'Family Proceedings Court' and is able to handle most cases. Care cases will usually start in that court, but the rules contain a power to transfer cases to specified County Courts or the High Court [s.92 and Sched 11, Pt I].

Most public law cases will thus be heard by magistrates drawn from new Family Panels and will be specially trained to deal with cases under the Children Act. If cases are particularly complex or urgent, they will be heard by judges who have been specially trained, and who sit in courts designated as care centres or family hearing centres. The procedure in the courts will be made to feel less threatening and more informal, especially for children.

Appeals in care cases will be heard in the High Court. Care proceedings are brought within the civil legal aid scheme [s.99].

Family Placement

The 1990 HMSO publication, *The Care of Children: Principle and Practice in Regulations and Guidance*, lists the following principles as a guide to family placement decisions:

- ☐ The development of a working partnership with parents is usually the most effective route to providing supplementary or substitute care.
- ☐ If young people cannot remain at home, placement with relatives or friends should be explored before other forms of placement are considered.

- [ ] If young people have to live apart from their family of origin, they and their parents should be helped to consider alternatives and contribute to the making of an informed choice about what is most appropriate.
- [ ] When out of home care is necessary, active steps should be taken to ensure speedy return home.
- [ ] Parents should be expected and enabled to retain their responsibilities . . . even if the child cannot live at home either temporarily or permanently.
- [ ] Siblings should not be separated . . . unless this is part of a well thought out plan based on the child's needs.
- [ ] Family links should be actively maintained through visits and other forms of contact. Fathers should not be overlooked.
- [ ] Wider families matter as well, especially siblings and grandparents.
- [ ] Continuity of relationships is important.
- [ ] Changes (whether of home, caregiver, social worker or school) almost always carry some risk to the child's development and welfare.
- [ ] Time is a crucial element . . . and should be reckoned in days and months rather than years.
- [ ] Corporate parenting is not 'good enough' on its own.
- [ ] Children's welfare must be protected by attention to their health and education, both in short-term and long-term care.
- [ ] The young person's wishes must be elicited and taken seriously.

Breakdown of placement

Ruth Nissin (1982) cautions that if long spells of care are to be avoided (*short* spells can be useful), every effort should be made to engage the family of origin and promote change there, if change is feasible. Young people who remain in care for more than six weeks are destined for a lengthy or very lengthy stay in care. Are there other lessons to be learned from the evidence concerning the success or failure (breakdown) of placements?

Some of the factors most strongly associated with placement breakdown include:

- age (breakdowns increase with the child's age, from below five per cent for children under three, to nearly 45 per cent at fourteen);
- little or no contact with original family, siblings and relatives (this includes being placed alone);
- longer periods in care;
- long periods on placement waiting lists;
- previous placement breakdown (whether attempting rehabilitation at home or alternative family placement);

- presence of other children in the household close in age to the placed child (this does not apply to siblings placed together);
- if the young person is ambivalent or opposed to the placement;
- if the parents or carers have unrealistic expectations;
- if the young person has severe behavioural or emotional problems;
- changes of school, neighbourhood and friends;
- other risk factors including being of mixed race, having a history of abuse or neglect, or having special needs in addition to those already listed.

The measurement of success of family placements is a complex issue and can involve several criteria (see Shaw, 1986). Bearing that caveat in mind, *adoption* success rates average around 75 per cent (Shaw, 1986) while *fostering* ends in a depressingly high percentage of breakdowns – the long-term placement failures reaching around the 50 per cent region within five years. The figure also rises as the child's age increases. It is vital to 'unpack' these generalizations by looking at *particular circumstances* when making specific, individual decisions.

The worrying issue, according to Nissin's review of the evidence, is the cavalier attitude of many professionals to the findings about family breakdown when it comes to their planning for the care of children. She gives, as an example, the study by Bebbington and Miles (1989) of 2,500 children in care. They identified several features in common:

- seventy-five per cent of the children came from single-parent families;
- seventy-five per cent of the children's families were on income support;
- eighty per cent of the families did not have their own homes;
- fifty per cent of the families lived in 'poor neighbourhoods'.

Other factors which precipitated receptions into care included:
- overcrowding (more than one person to a room);
- large family size (four or more children);
- the age of the mother (youth);
- if the child was of mixed race;
- lack of social/community support networks.

Studies suggest that social workers seldom mention any of the above factors when asked what they think has led to family breakdown. Explanations are more likely to describe relationship problems without setting them in the context of disadvantage. Nissin states that the corollary of this is that their attempted solutions will tend to be focused at the relationship level within families, rather than taking account of the implications of issues such as those mentioned above. This can result in an insuperable mismatch between family of origin and foster home.

APPENDIX IV

Assessing children in need

Each child should be assessed in terms of:

- *Physical well-being and physical care* (see Chapters 2 and 4 and refer to checklist on the child's physical care – *Table 2.1* – and health and development questionnaire in this Appendix)
- *Mental health* (see Chapters 4, 6 and 7)
- *Social and intellectual development* (see Chapters 4 and 5)
- *Emotional development* (see Chapters 2, 4, 6 and 7 and checklists on the quality of parental care – *Tables 2.2* and *4.1*)
- *Behaviour* (see Chapters 4 and 6 and checklists in this Appendix).

Each professional should refer to their own practice tools and guidance.

Criteria for assessing health and development

All criteria relate to a child similar in age, gender and from a similar cultural, racial and religious background.

- *Reasonable standard:* A child is determined as *not* achieving or maintaining a 'reasonable standard' of health or development when their conduct, presentation or care detrimentally sets them apart (see Chapter 4).
- *Significant impairment:* The health and development of a child is to be regarded as 'significantly impaired' where there is objective evidence (developmental assessments, child protection events, etc.) that the child's development is being adversely and avoidably impaired through lack of parenting skills/resources (see Chapters 2, 3 and 4).
- *Disability:* Is there visual impairment, hearing impairment, serious communication difficulties, substantial handicap stemming from illness, injury or congenital conditions? (see Chapter 5)
- *Significant risk:* Whether a child is 'significantly at risk' needs to be determined by a child protection case conference (see Part II). Some children may be at risk and in turn 'in need' although there is no evidence that they are not achieving or maintaining a 'reasonable standard of health and development' (see also Chapters 3 and 7).
- *Significant harm:* A child's health and/or development is being 'significantly harmed' through acts of omission or commission on the part of the parent(s)/carer(s) or because the child is beyond parental control (see Chapters 1, 2, 3 and 4).

Service requirements

- *Direct help for the child:* This help specifically focuses on the child and may include help through speech/language aides, special toys, special diet and recreational activities (see Chapter 4).
- *Parenting skills:* This may include help in developing basic child care, home-making or domestic skills, but may also entail specialist help in responding to a child's specific/special needs (see Chapters 5, 6, 8, 9 and 10).
- *Parenting resources:* This includes practical equipment and financial resources as well as support networks such as extended family and friends who help share the demands of child care (see Part II).

HEALTH AND DEVELOPMENT QUESTIONNAIRE

Ask caregiver/s:

1. Has . . . had any serious illnesses other than normal childhood illness?
2. Has he/she ever been in hospital? If so when? For what? For how long?
3. Does . . . have any current illness or disability? Is he/she attending a hospital, clinic or seeing a GP for this?
4. Does . . . currently (or in the past) have a problem with hearing or sight?
5. How would you describe . . .'s developmental progress and growth so far?
6. (a) What did . . . weigh at birth?
   (b) Did he/she gain weight quickly or slowly?
   (c) When did/he she double their birth weight?
7. At what age did . . . sit unaided?
8. At what age did . . . walk?
9. At what age did . . . talk? (Single words/sentences)
10. At what ages did . . . become clean and dry respectively
    (a) by day?
    (b) by night?
11. Does . . . have any problem at school either in relation to school work, general behaviour, attendance, or with friends?
    If so, describe it.
12. Does he/she seem to be different at school than at home?
13. What are the interests, hobbies, activities . . . most enjoys?
14. Does . . . make friends easily? Is he/she socially isolated?

Ask yourself:

15. Is the child's behaviour appropriate to his/her age, intelligence and social situation?
16. Is the environment making reasonable demands of the child?
17. Is the environment satisfying the crucial needs of the child, that is, the needs that are vital at his/her particular stage of development?

Note: You may need to seek the assistance of medical and health visitor colleagues to ensure that information about the child's growth and development is collated and properly interpreted. Health authorities have arrangements for children to have a developmental surveillance by a doctor or health visitor at specified intervals. Paediatricians stress the importance of monitoring children's growth by the regular use of weight and height charts and it is generally agreed that such charts should be kept for all young children.

BEHAVIOURAL PROBLEM CHECKLIST

Does your child do any of the following?
Tick one of the boxes to indicate how often any of the following happen, if at all.
Also indicate whether the behaviour is a worry to you.

	NEVER	SOMETIMES	OFTEN	MOST OF THE TIME	WORRY	NOT A WORRY
PART 1						
Have temper tantrums?						
Make threats?						
Physically assault others (hit, push, pinch, pull hair, throw things)?						
Quarrel with others (brothers, sisters, friends, etc)?						
Damage property (own/others)?						
Disrupt, that is, interfere with others' activities (interrupting, distracting, etc)?						
Bully other children?						
Inconvenience others (e.g. playing record player too loud, being late for meals)?						
Tease others in a hurtful manner?						
Abuse others with name-calling, obscenities, etc?						
Engage in unwanted, inappropriate physical contact (clinging, squeezing)?						
Lie about him or herself?						
Lie about others?						
React inappropriately, sulking, withdrawing, angry if he or she cannot get own way?						
Steal money, shop goods, etc?						
Have problems attending school?						
Disobey you?						
Make unreasonable, excessive demands?						
Run away?						
Seem overactive?						
Have poor concentration (e.g. short attention span)?						
PART 2						
Seem tense, agitated, nervy, restless?						
Appear apathetic, lacking in energy?						
Seem shy?						
Seem depressed, miserable?						
Appear fearful, anxious?						
Seem socially withdrawn?						
Wander away?						
Behave in a babyish manner (e.g. whining, 'baby talking')?						
Appear secretive, furtive, mysterious?						
Seek attention excessively (clingy, showing off, asking for help unnecessarily)?						
PART 3						
Have bedtime problems (e.g. getting to bed, staying there)?						
Wet the bed?						
Soil him or herself, or pass motions in the wrong place?						
Show inappropriate or precocious sexual behaviour (e.g. masturbating, exposing in public)						
Have problems communicating with others? (e.g. expressing him/herself)?						

SITUATIONAL PROBLEM CHECKLIST

Do you have difficulty with your child at the following places or in the following circumstances? Circle the number that best sums up your opinion.

PLACE/CIRCUMSTANCE	Never	Sometimes	Often	Do you see it as a worrying problem?
Visiting friends	1	2	3	Yes/No
Shopping (e.g. supermarket)	1	2	3	Yes/No
Going on a bus	1	2	3	Yes/No
People visiting your home	1	2	3	Yes/No
Taking the child to school	1	2	3	Yes/No
or nursery	1	2	3	Yes/No
Leaving the child at playgroup	1	2	3	Yes/No
Getting the child dressed	1	2	3	Yes/No
Mealtimes	1	2	3	Yes/No
Getting the child to bed	1	2	3	Yes/No
Getting the child to stay in bed	1	2	3	Yes/No
Quarrelling with brothers/	1	2	3	Yes/No
sisters/	1	2	3	Yes/No
friends	1	2	3	Yes/No
Getting the child to go to parties (friends' homes)	1	2	3	Yes/No
Getting the child to speak to people	1	2	3	Yes/No
Taking other children's toys	1	2	3	Yes/No
Getting the child to share toys	1	2	3	Yes/No
Getting the child to be polite	1	2	3	Yes/No

Index

Note: There is no entry under 'children' as most entries refer to children unless stated otherwise; the reader is advised to seek more specific references, for example, 'abuse', 'development', etc.